Landing on my Feet

Teaching and Learning During a Career in Education

JAMES KLEINER

Foreword by Dr. Peter Loel Boonshaft, Professor Emeritus, Hofstra University

Copyright © 2024 by James Kleiner

ISBN: 978-1-77883-439-4 (Paperback)

All rights reserved. No part of this publication may be reproduced, distributed, or transmitted in any form or by any means, including photocopying, recording, or other electronic or mechanical methods, without the prior written permission of the publisher, except in the case brief quotations embodied in critical reviews and other noncommercial uses permitted by copyright law.

The views expressed in this book are solely those of the author and do not necessarily reflect the views of the publisher, and the publisher hereby disclaims any responsibility for them.

BookSide Press
877-741-8091
www.booksidepress.com
orders@booksidepress.com

CONTENTS

Foreword viii
Prologue x

1 - A Fateful Visit To My Musical Mentor 1
2 - The Journey Begins 5
3 - Recollection I – The Beginnings (1948-58) 9
4 - It's All Downhill From Here 12
5 - Recollection II – Off and Running (1958-61) 28
6 - Vernon, Year Two 31
7 - Recollection III – Total Immersion (1960-63) 35
8 - Don't Get Comfortable 40
9 - Back To My Old Stomping Grounds 43
10 - Recollection IV – Exciting And Fun Times (1964, 1965) 47
11 - The Report Card Incident 51
12 - A Time To Reflect 55
13 - Recollection V – The Saxophone And The Class Of 1966 58
14 - Scenes From The Podium 65
15 - The First Of April 68
16 - The Show Must Go On 71
17 - Recollection VI – Suny Fredonia, 1966–70 74
18 - Box Score Bombed 80
19 - The Troubled Ones 82
20 - Memories And Mementos 87
21 - Recollection VII – The Willett Connection 90
22 - A "No-Brainer" 95
23 - A Reality Check 99
24 - Assignment: Marching Band 102
25 - Stepping High 106
26 - The Winter Concert 111
27 - Exciting Plans Take Shape 114
28 - A Parallel Universe 116

Chapter	Title	Page
29	Pondering The Future	119
30	The Trip, Before And After	123
31	Tough Day	126
32	A Smooth Landing	128
33	The Joke Of The Day	130
34	Teach And Learn	132
35	Marching Into The Elements	135
36	Another Roller - Coaster Ride	137
37	Grad School Decisions	141
38	Ellington And A Fork In The Road	144
39	The Hartford, A New World	153
40	A Senseless Tragedy	158
41	A Transition	161
42	*Mr. Holland's Opus* – The Movie	164
43	Parish Hill – A Rockin' School	167
44	Small School – Not A Problem	171
45	A Stable Situation, Until It Wasn't	174
46	My "Mr. Holland" Moment	179
47	A Shorter Drive	184
48	Two For The Price Of One	187
49	A Disappointing Reunion	189
50	A Full-Time Teacher Once Again	194
51	Learning From My Students	196
52	Staying Put	200
53	An Odd Decision	202
54	Another Leap Of Faith	204
55	Standing My Ground	207
56	Sticking Our Necks Out	211
57	Twice As Much In Half The Time	215
58	The Evolution At Bms	218
59	Scenes From The Third Floor	223
60	Marching Down Main Street	236
61	Time For Changes	239

62 - **Holding It Together**	243
63 - **Two Drummers**	249
64 - **A Day Like None Other**	251
65 - **Goodbye To Cheney**	254
66 - **It Doesn't Get Any Better**	257
67 - **Packing Up**	259
68 - **The Bridge Years At The Elementary Schools**	263
69 - **The Academy Beckons**	276
70 - **The New Bennet Academy**	278
71 - **Getting The Kinks Out**	281
72 - **The Numbers Game**	285
73 - **A Tough Crowd**	289
74 - **An Educator's Learning Never Ends**	293
75 - **The Unthinkable**	298
76 - **The Light At The End Of The Tunnel**	300
77 - **A New Plan Emerges**	302
78 - **The Final Concert**	305
79 - **Reflections**	308

Acknowledgements	312
Bibliography	313

> *"Teaching is probably the noblest profession in the World . . . the most unselfish, difficult, and honorable profession, but it is the most unappreciated, underrated, underpaid, and under-praised profession in the world."*
>
> LEONARD BERNSTEIN, "A TRIBUTE TO TEACHERS," 1963

Dedication

To Nicholas and Irene, my parents, who enabled me follow my dreams with love and encouragement.

To Joann, who gave me sisterly advice that was always level-headed and loving.

To Cheryll, my wife and educational inspiration, who has filled me with love and advice on a daily basis.

To Janet, who gave her dad an important reason to go on when things were tough, and eventually followed her parents into the educational profession.

FOREWORD

AS I LOOK BACK ON my career, I truly consider myself the luckiest person on earth. I have had the most wonderful experiences as a teacher and conductor. And when my mind floods with those memories, one experience always emerges as a source of incredible joy: my days as a student teacher under Mr. Jim Kleiner at Rockville High School in 1979. I remember it as if it was yesterday. From the first day I walked into his office full of excitement, to the bittersweet day I left just before graduating to begin my teaching career. That excitement was born out of the knowledge that I was going to be working with a dedicated and talented teacher in an extraordinary school district. The bittersweet came from the knowledge that I was leaving a special place, never to return; a place that taught me so much, brought me endless happiness, and gave me a true sense of belonging. That time in my life offered me opportunities and experiences that defy description. Truly, those days were some of the best of my life. Days I would do anything to be able to savor once again.

At the heart of that was working with Jim Kleiner as my cooperating teacher. Long before walking into the halls of RHS, I had heard about Mr. Kleiner. He was well known as a wonderful musician and teacher. What I didn't know until I had the chance to be under his wing was that he was also a remarkable human being.

When Jim asked me to write the foreword to his memoir, I was incredibly humbled and truly honored. I immediately jumped at the chance. I received a draft of the book just as I was headed to California to speak at a conference. I planned to take it with me to read on the cross-country flight. When I took off from New York City, I had planned to read a bit of it, and then work on the material I was to do for that event. But I could not stop reading it. I just couldn't. The next thing I knew, I was landing in San Francisco having read, no, devoured, no, delighted in the entire book. It was revealing, heartfelt, and captivating. Jim beautifully documents and describes his career in vivid detail, sharing how each facet of his life unfolded. With each page, the reader is captivated by the peaks and valleys – the ups and downs – of the journey that was his path. After reading about his life's work, one can't help but be amazed at what life brought him, but far more importantly, what Jim brought to those times in his life. How he responded to each of the events portrayed in the book is the essence of Jim Kleiner. One can't help but be inspired by how Jim rose to each challenge, embraced each change, and pursued excellence at every turn. We, the reader, like the leagues of students Jim has taught over all the years, are the beneficiaries of the spirit with which Jim lived his career and the lessons of his persistence, resilience, and dedication.

Cullen Hightower declared, "A true measure of your worth includes all the benefits others have gained from your success." No words could be more true when describing Jim Kleiner. This book reveals as much about Jim as a teacher, as it does about Jim as a wonderful, kind, caring, thoughtful, and sincere person. A person who at every juncture of his life truly "landed on his feet." Thank you, Jim!

    Dr. Peter Loel Boonshaft
    Professor Emeritus, Hofstra University
    Director of Education, KHS America/
    Jupiter Band Instruments

PROLOGUE

I JUST WALKED OUT OF Bennet Academy, a sixth-grade school in Manchester, Connecticut, at 3:35 pm on June 22, 2015, forty-four years and ten months after I walked into Vernon (Connecticut) Middle School for the first of countless career teachers' meetings in September 1971. My teaching career was officially over. I taught for thirty-three of those years in several public schools in Connecticut. I felt numb and found it hard to comprehend that my career was coming to an end.

Many thoughts swirled through my head. I remembered the nervous feeling in my stomach on that very first day so long ago, as well as not sleeping well the night before. There were many people to meet that day and I was definitely running on adrenaline. In contrast, this past June found me very calm and at peace with my decision to retire. The plan had originally been for me to teach one more year, but a series of events took place this past spring which caused me to adjust my timetable.

I walked out of the building to my already loaded car containing all my personal belongings and mementos. I had essentially wiped clean the large ensemble room of any trace of myself. I felt I needed to do that to make it easier for the new teacher. The rehearsal room, my home since 2008, definitely had my touch in and around it. I needed to leave a room that my successor could make their own. There would be no remembrance of me by my students in that room, since they all were going into a different building next September. I liked this situation, since during my career I had left students behind in more than one school and a few times before the school year ended. I was leaving with little fanfare and drama. I was very glad about that.

I felt a sadness at leaving the profession for many reasons, which will be explained later in this book. But I also felt a sense of satisfaction that I had done my best. I believe in my heart I did make a difference in the lives of countless youngsters along the way. I think teachers always have that feeling. I felt it during my first year and every year in between.

I wrote this book for two reasons: the first being to help teachers in the profession, and people with interest in becoming educators—I hope I can give them some advice on how to deal with the ups and downs of the profession—and secondly, to perhaps give an insight to anyone who wonders what it has been like to teach during the evolution of the profession over the past four and a half decades. The dynamics of teacher, administrator and parent relationships are at the center of my story.

I have had many of the worst things happen to me in my career that could ever happen to a teacher. But I always managed to learn from my experiences, land on my feet, and go on. There were also some wonderful episodes happening at the time that seemed to balance out the bad times and serve as an inspiration for me to keep going. I got to help kids from grades 4 to 12 experience music in ways which would enhance their lives forever. I was inspired during my school years by so many great teachers. Teaching was what I wanted to do with my life for as long as I can remember.

"My life was saved by teachers"
—STEPHEN SONDHEIM

1 -
A FATEFUL VISIT TO MY MUSICAL MENTOR

MY MASTER'S DEGREE PROGRAM AT the Hartt School of Music, University of Hartford, Connecticut, was winding down in mid-July 1971. It was a lovely day and I had been checking the Hartt School Music Education job-opening postings. Because of the lack of internet in those days, finding a job was often down through the school bulletin board. One needed to be on top of that every day, it seemed.

That week had already been an eventful one. During a hallway discussion with the well-known saxophone virtuoso and Hartt faculty member Don Sinta, I had found out that there had been a reopening of a job that had been filled earlier that year by another Hartt graduate. Don related to me that this student that had been hired for a high school music job down in New Jersey had just died in an auto accident. As Don said, "I don't want to sound like a ghoul, but that job is now open again." He gave me the phone number of the school system down there, and I set up an interview for early the following week.

Within a couple of days another piece of information came my way. I found out that a Hicksville, Long Island, New York, elementary school had a one-year opening for an instrumental teacher, since their current teacher was out on maternity leave. I grew up in Hicksville and was a proud graduate of the Hicksville schools.

I called the Hicksville Schools main administrative office and spoke to Bill Gollecke, one of the town's music administrators. After a discussion, he offered me the position. However, he could not guarantee the position would last beyond the one year.

As fate would have it, within a few days I had two possible employment opportunities. And this after wondering if I was going to get a job before the fall! And as I usually did when I needed advice, I sought out Dr. William Willett, my musical mentor. Dr. Willett was the chair of the Music Education Department at Hartt and was the reason I was at Hartt to begin with. He suggested I meet with him the following day during the late morning, about 11.

I strolled into his office to find him there, doing some paperwork. After the usual warm greeting I always received from him, we took some time to chat about these employment opportunities that had presented themselves over the past week.

As we were about fifteen minutes into our discussion, a distinguished gentleman poked his head in through the door and Dr. Willett invited him in. He introduced me to Sam Goldfarb, who was the music supervisor for the town of Vernon. Vernon was a suburban town east of the Connecticut River, a couple of towns over from where I lived in East Hartford.

Sam shook both our hands and related to Dr. Willett about how one of his instrumental music teachers had just left Vernon for another job opportunity. Vernon had an opening. It included fifth-grade elementary beginning lessons at two schools and also the ninth-grade school's band and sectional lessons.

I sat up and tried to make myself as "presentable" as possible and I noticed a wry smile from Dr. Willett. My mentor then uttered the words that would change my life. He said to Sam, "Why don't you talk to this young man right here, since Jim is actively searching for a teaching position and is one of our most outstanding candidates here at Hartt?" Sam smiled, and as he sat down, Dr. Willett left the room for a "cup of coffee." Sam then proceeded to ask me a few questions. I answered as best I could, realizing that I was now taking part in an unplanned interview.

Sam went into more detail about the job. I would be travelling between the three schools each day during the week and it would be fifth to ninth grades, and sometimes back again. I had already determined in my mind for the past few years that I would love to teach beginners how to play all the winds, brass, and percussion. I felt I was well prepared to do that. And, it also would give me the opportunity to teach and conduct high school freshmen as well.

After about ten minutes, Sam met with Dr. Willett out in the hallway. Out of earshot, they chatted for a couple of minutes, and then Sam came to me and asked if I would like to have an interview with the Vernon Assistant Superintendent of Schools the following day. Of course, I agreed!

Sam shook my hand and left the office as Dr. Willett walked back in. He had a huge smile on his face. He then related to me that the Vernon Schools music program was one of the top instrumental music programs in the state. The Rockville High School Wind Ensemble under Sam's direction had a long history of excellence, including many performances at Connecticut Music Educators Association (CMEA) and Music Educators National Conference (MENC) in the past. He could not contain his excitement in talking about this program and told me this was a prime job opportunity. I was incredibly excited by this point and thanked him profusely for his "on the spot" recommendation. Of course, I still had to impress the superintendent the next day, but I had such a good feeling about this opportunity.

Talk about good karma! Three job opportunities had presented themselves within a week. But there was something about this Vernon job that put it to the top of my list. My wife, Cheryll, and I, really did not plan on staying in Connecticut, but now it looked like that might change.

The next day I drove out to Vernon. I found the school administration building without a problem. There I met Dr. Robert Linstone, and we proceeded to have an interview. He asked me about my goals and educational philosophy, among others. And yet I had a strange feeling that this hiring was a done deal. And it was. He offered me the position and I accepted instantly. He handed me an agreement to commit to the position, which I signed, and I would be presented with a contract in a few days. We shook hands. I remember him saying, "Welcome aboard."

I walked out of the office and was feeling my whole body tingle with excitement. I was now an employed public school music teacher! It was hard to believe that after all the training and hard work I had finally arrived in the profession. I thought at that moment about my Hicksville music teachers and could not wait to tell them all that had transpired with my job search.

I returned to the Vernon Public Schools building a few days later and signed a contract, which included my salary. I would be making $ 7,900 with a master's degree, which was step one of the salary scale. It seemed like a fair salary for 1971. Later in my career, I was to discover the disparity in teachers' salaries in relation to other professions. I had always heard about how teachers were not paid adequately for what they did on the job. I would be finding that out in the future.

My wife and I decided to upgrade our living arrangements and procured an apartment in Manchester. After receiving lots of information from Vernon ahead of the beginning of the school year, the thought really "kicked in" that I was about to enter the teaching profession. This was all I wanted to do since junior high. It was about to become reality.

"In a completely rational society the best of us would be teachers and the rest of us would have to settle for something else."

—LEE IACOCCA

2 - THE JOURNEY BEGINS

IT WAS A HOT, SUNNY September day. I exited my car after carefully parking in the faculty parking lot at Vernon Center Middle School and proceeded through the front door. Everything felt so deliberate that day. It was like I was living in slow motion.

As I entered the main doors I first heard and then observed an enthusiastic crowd of professionals shaking hands, giving hugs, and genuinely sounding like they would not have wanted to be anywhere else. That first impression of a group of teachers being together after a summer break gave me great encouragement. Here was a group of people not complaining about the end of their summer break but instead looking forward to the start of the new school year. *Gee*, I thought, *they must really like what they are doing!* That was a good sign.

I spotted Sam in the crowd of teachers standing outside the auditorium and he saw me and motioned me over. I sensed I was about to meet the other music staff. He introduced me to Ed DeGroat, the middle school band director, followed by my elementary instrumental colleague, Bill Belden. Both Ed and Bill were six-foot-plus, but since at 5 feet 8 inches I was actually taller than Sam, I didn't feel too out of place. Introductions were made and we proceeded into the auditorium and found seats for the morning's program.

On stage was the superintendent of schools, and seated with him I assumed were the other schoolwide administrators. After a group rendition of the "Pledge of Allegiance," a group of welcoming speeches began. Each school principal introduced the new staff that would be working in their buildings.

Ed Masker, the principal of Sykes Memorial School, introduced me amongst the new staff working in his building. All of the new teachers received polite applause, which gave a welcoming feeling to all of us newbies.

I couldn't help but gaze around the auditorium during all of the speeches. I wondered how I was going to fit in as a teaching professional in the Vernon Schools. My mind flashed back to all the music education courses I had experienced during the past several years as well as my collegiate student teaching. Was I ready to join with all these experienced staff members?

After lunch, prepared by the school cafeteria staff, Sam convened a music department meeting in the band room. I was impressed with the music wing at VCMS, which included a tiered rehearsal room for the band, another tiered room for the chorus, a few practice rooms, and a music office for the teachers. And the auditorium was spacious and modern with a large stage.

Sam introduced Bill and me to the music faculty. I was the one that was actually totally new, since Bill had completed his student teaching in Vernon the previous spring. We all spent about an hour together receiving Sam's "pep talk." Then the meeting concluded with time to go visit our home school prior to tomorrow's individual school staff meetings.

I ventured into the city of Rockville, where Sykes Memorial School was located. Sykes housed the ninth grade students. The rest of Rockville High School was in the complex up on Loveland Hill Road, about a mile and a half away. Sykes had been the original RHS back in the '30s and '40s. The new building went up in 1963. Sykes was an old but well-maintained building. I walked in the front entrance and found the auditorium. I already knew that the music rehearsals and lessons would be held on the stage. So there went my dreams of a band room, music office, practices rooms, etc.

I was to find out in the coming months that the students did not care about the facility, despite having come from VCMS. They were just interested in making music. It was my job to make this area a musically exciting one for my students. And it was my first teaching space, so I had to take ownership. In retrospect, I taught in a wide variety of teaching spaces over my career and some of my best teaching outcomes came in challenging facilities.

Tired and a bit overwhelmed, I left the Sykes building that first day with a sense of anticipation and excitement. My journey had begun and I felt ready.

2

After another day of home school meetings, I had the opportunity to travel to the two elementary schools where I was going to be teaching fifth grade beginning instrumental lessons. While at the schools I discovered my classroom in both instances would be the cafeteria. This was somewhat disappointing, but at the same time I realized that a smaller room anywhere near the classrooms would not be possible. Too many distracting sounds from my students, at least at first, might be quite disruptive. The cafeteria it was! Lots of room to spread out and explore the sonic beginnings of music making. The large space certainly would be a help to my hearing capabilities as well.

I was given a large canvas sack full of wire music stands that I would be using at these schools. I learned from each school principal that I had certain blocks of time to use for scheduling the lessons, before and after the lunch waves. And clean-up time for the custodians after lunch was important as well, although we would often begin afternoon lessons during the late stages of that activity. I learned throughout my career that it was certainly a benefit to get to know the school custodians and lunch ladies! Hanging around the school cafeterias was cool!

I was assigned to Center Road and Skinner Road schools—two days at Center and one day at Skinner. That would give me two full days at Sykes for lessons and what turned out to be a fifty-eight-member freshman band. The band met every day, so I would be travelling back and forth to Sykes on my three elementary days to conduct the rehearsal during the late morning. Later in my career I would look back fondly at those Vernon days when I had lots of rehearsal time. As the years progressed in music education, the luxury of this rehearsal schedule would be a thing of the past.

As far as the elementary program was concerned, Bill and I were told we would be combining our fifth graders from all the schools in April for rehearsals culminating in a May fifth grade band concert. Our task was in front of us. We had to recruit our young students and get them scheduled for weekly group lessons. It was daunting but exciting.

I had received a list and quite a bit of input from Ed about my incoming ninth grade students. I really appreciated that. There were several times later in my career when I would get little to no input about incoming students. Those times often were very challenging as I will relate later in this book.

My teaching journey was about to begin. I felt excited but a bit nervous. Was I ready? I was about to find out.

3 -
RECOLLECTION I – THE BEGINNINGS (1948-58)

MY EARLIEST REMEMBRANCE OF MUSIC has a surprising tie-in with baseball. What could it have been about those Ballantine Beer commercials during the televised Yankee games? I am not sure, but hearing the rhythmic jingle so many times would eventually cause this attentive two-year-old to sing-speak "doo-dat, doo-dat, doo-dat" whenever the commercials appeared on the screen. My dad thought it was funny and would encourage me to sing along. He would sing with me. I would flail my arms like I were conducting the jingle. This was an amazing sneak preview of things I would be doing later in life.

I have been told I used to love to sing during those early years and had a good ear for matching pitch. Another musical influence for me was when I would get to sit on the organ bench while my grandfather played the instrument during mass at the St. Stephen of Hungary Church in Manhattan, NYC. The sound was amazing to a young, impressionable kid. Watching his fingers and feet manipulate the keys and pedals filled my brain with sounds that must have shaped my brain's neural net. My destiny was in motion.

I guess it was logical that by the time I was in third grade I received the highest score on the music aptitude test given to my classmates at the Fork Lane Elementary School, Hicksville, New York. It was the spring of 1956. I remember my mom receiving a phone call from the school music teacher telling her that because of my top grade on that test the school was offering me the use of a school instrument during my fourth grade.

I was going to play an instrument! I was thrilled and chose the trumpet as my first choice. It turned out they did not have any trumpets available, but they could offer me the use of a clarinet. The clarinet had been my second choice. Not a problem.

The fourth grade had turned out to be a significant year in my life. I remember being issued the metal clarinet by my first instrumental music teacher, Mr. Val Lagueux. I carried it home proudly and could not wait for my first lesson the next week. Out of eagerness, I assembled the mouthpiece and reed on the clarinet and tried to make a sound. I took a breath and blew, following the picture in the book. The squeak that came out startled me and I immediately put things away. Better to wait!

Once that first lesson got under way, my placement of the mouthpiece in my mouth with the reed touching my top lip got a chuckle out of Mr. Lagueux. Once I had all the proper positioning of the mouth and fingers, real musical notes came out. I loved the sound! Over the first several lessons the notes on the music staff came to life as I covered the various combinations of holes and pressed the keys. The notes became melodies. I made quick progress over the first few months and Mr. L eventually told me that I would be joining the Fork Lane School Band.

January rolled around and there I was sitting in the back row of the clarinet section, all of whose members were fifth and sixth graders. I was the only fourth grader and was naturally quite nervous. I was getting weird looks from some of the band members. They were probably thinking, *Who is this fourth grader with the metal clarinet?* I tried to look inconspicuous. I was doing a pretty good job of that until the rehearsal began and Mr. Lagueux said to the group, "Ladies and gentlemen, I would like to introduce our newest band member, Swingin' Jim Kleiner. Stand up, Jim." All eyes turned in my direction. If I could have dug a hole and jumped in, I would have done so on the spot!

Some of the other kids snickered and I received a few faint catcalls but also some applause. I managed a timid smile, sat down, and "jumped into my imaginary hole." But I did receive a sincere smile from the young lady sitting next to me. That made me feel better.

The next few moments changed my life forever. The music was a simple march from the Harold Bennet band book I had on my stand. As Mr. L gave the down beat, I played my notes along with the group. I immediately could hear how my notes were blending in with the harmony. That revelation affected me like a drug. I began to get hooked. I was hearing the parts being played by the second and first clarinets as well as all the other instruments. My brain was firing on all cylinders! I was in the middle of the sound. I was surrounded by music!

I was so excited after that first rehearsal I literally floated back to class. I could not wait to get home to tell my parents how much fun I had in band.

I can honestly say that each time I play in an ensemble rehearsal, I still get that musical rush of the senses. The seeds had been planted in my psyche during that first year of band. They were inevitably going to blossom years later into the realization that someday I wanted to share that feeling with others. I did not realize it at the time, but I was on my way to becoming a music educator.

> *"If you were successful, somebody along the line gave you some help. There was a great teacher somewhere in your life."*
>
> —BARACK OBAMA

4 -
IT'S ALL DOWNHILL FROM HERE

THE RECRUITMENT AND SCHEDULING OF the fifth grade beginners were the initial tasks at the elementary schools. Working with Bill proved to be easy and fun. We were both laid-back guys, and that trait helped us during the many frustrations we would run across during those first weeks. We visited all of the fifth grades in our respective schools. Meeting the fifth grade teachers proved to be an important first step. We needed to introduce ourselves as well as schedule a time to have their students take the Selmer Music Guidance Survey. This was a pitch and rhythmic recognition test to determine who had a good musical ear. We scheduled times in each school to get these fifth graders together for this aural test. Since we only had one tape recorder and reel-to-reel tape, we each administered the test together at all the schools.

The general feeling amongst the students during these tests was one of excitement and anticipation. It was the reputation of the Vernon music program that was fueling this interest. I knew that some of these kids had older siblings who already played instruments. How exciting for them to have had the opportunity to do the same.

It was only a matter of time before the reel-to-reel tape recorder exacted some revenge on Bill and me for dragging it around to each school. During one of the school tests, the recorder jammed and caused the tape to unspool all over the floor, much to the delight of the young audience. But the newbie teachers, with calm and coolness, gathered the runaway tape off the floor and respooled it all. No harm, no foul!

Eventually we had a large number of fifth graders signed up to begin lessons. We had supplied parents with instrument rental information from the local music stores. They had a couple of weeks to rent instruments. The town music program had several trombones to give out to those kids interested in playing them. This was a good incentive to have more beginning low brass players. The percussion students had to show up with a pair of drumsticks and a drum pad.

I set up my classes with like instruments and some classes were larger than others. The flute and clarinet classes were larger than I would have liked, so I was going to have to hustle during the half hour per week I had with them. The other instruments classes were more manageable in size, although I did have to reserve a cafeteria table each week for the drum pads.

I discovered early on that teaching beginning instruments was a challenging and at times exhausting experience. I had not factored in the 3-plus-mile trip from Center Road and Skinner Road schools back and forth from Sykes. Eating lunch in my car was often necessary because of the tight time window I had for travel. But I was young and full of energy, so who cared, right? The fact that I found myself falling asleep on my couch at home in the early evening while reading the paper or watching TV proved to me that teaching was hard and exhausting, even for a guy in his mid-twenties. I was finding out what being an educator was like in real life!

I was loving the challenge of working with these beginning students. As I mentioned, some of the classes were larger than I would have liked, but I just "sucked it up" and faced those classes of six to eight flutes or clarinets with gusto! I remember one day early on, Sam came to visit me at Center Road and walked in on one of my large clarinet classes. Things were going great until he stepped up and moved the hands of one of the students. The kid had been playing with his hands reversed with the right hand on the top joint. That was embarrassing, to say the least, that the teacher, in this case an experienced clarinetist, hadn't noticed the situation. But Sam spotted it right away.

Sam watched the class for a bit more and as he left waved goodbye with a sly smile on his face. My thought was *at least the other seven players' hands were in the correct position, right?*

I was pleased with the progress of my students, although the ones that practiced regularly soon distanced themselves from the others. That creates more challenges for you as different levels of accomplishment start to populate some classes. I eventually spoke to the teachers and they let me shuffle the classes, when possible, to combine kids at different levels. Although this was a challenge, I began to appreciate what the classroom teachers went through on a regular basis. I had a maximum of only eight kids in my largest classes, while there were twenty-plus kids in their classes every day. Yikes!

2

Sykes, on the other hand, presented different kinds of challenges. I liked the fact this was a totally different environment and a different age level. During the first week there I ventured around the school visiting the classrooms where I met the teachers and staff as well as the students. I already had my band list in hand with notations concerning who needed school instruments. Mostly these were the low woodwind and brass instruments. I had a decent set of instruments to distribute and also borrowed from Rockville High School, as well as VCMS.

My instrumentation in the band was good, although I did have a few too many flutes. With the exception of double reeds, all members of the brass and woodwind families were represented. I even had a tympanist, a young lady named Dawn. She proved to be the "rock" of the percussion section all year! Although the school instruments were not in the greatest shape, I soon found out the players were!

The day of the first band rehearsal finally arrived. During my opening remarks I heard a few chuckles from some of the kids. Was it my New York accent? Anyway, we played through the Eb warmup chorale that was used in Vernon at every level. It was a beautifully written chorale that included the bass line playing a simple Eb scale in whole notes. These kids could play this chorale by memory in most cases, since they had been playing it all through VCMS. As I heard them play this music the first time, I felt chills through my body. I knew at that instant I had something very special to work with. They already had a sense of pitch and phrasing that I knew was special. My respect for their previous instrumental teachers was solidified on the spot.

Next was an arrangement of Mozart's overture to his opera *The Impresario*. I threw this piece at them right off the bat, again curious to see what would happen. Their sight-reading skills were better than I had expected. What a benefit this would have, looking forward. After that rehearsal I was feeling pretty good. I had a group that I believed could handle more challenging music, perhaps even among the list of grade-4 from the New York State School Music Association (NYSSMA) manual. How exciting for a first-year teacher!

My optimism about the potential of the Sykes program was huge during those first months. But the inevitable reality check came when I had a few malcontents who felt I was a bit too intense during rehearsals. Those kids perhaps did not like the fact that I insisted on their complete attention. I found I was getting upset at times because of their misbehavior and that would stay with me for hours. I was not dealing with my distress very well. Oftentimes the next class would find me in a sour mood. This really bothered me. I did not like the previous class affecting how I was dealing with the next one. I had to do something to remedy this before I lost my love of working with kids.

One day, as if a beam of light came down and shined on me from above, I learned a profound new strategy. I was having lunch in the Sykes faculty room and overheard a colleague mention that they felt they were "on a stage" from the moment they walked in the front school door until the moment they left the building at the end of the day. There was something about that comment that really resonated with me. Perhaps I should approach a band rehearsal with an actor's mentality. If I acted the part of the conductor, I could leave my own emotions out of the equation.

I tried that and it worked amazingly well! When a rehearsal was done, I was back "off stage," and no matter what had transpired during the previous forty-five minutes, I was able to let go of any lingering tensions. I could go back to being myself. My students never knew I was doing this in all the subsequent years of conducting rehearsals. It was one of the most powerful techniques I had learned. So, whoever was in the Sykes faculty lounge that day and uttered those words, I humbly thank you! I realized that a teacher never stops being a learner as well.

Other experiences at Sykes during those first few months were awakening me to the realities of teaching. The first was a phone call from a parent I received at school within the first couple of weeks. I don't remember the reason for the call, but the gentleman that called me eventually got around to the subject about the school "not being able to do anything right." I did not feel as though he was speaking specifically about me, but he was definitely venting. I was taken aback by his sudden bitter tone and his opinion that Sykes was an inferior school from top to bottom.

I felt awkward trying to converse with this man in the midst of a busy school office. When I got off the phone I was shaken, and the secretary looked at me and asked if anything was wrong. I guess I looked like I felt. It had been my first experience with a member of the public who had a negative opinion about the schools. I decided from that day on to try to persuade people with negative feelings about the public schools to change their minds by educating them with the truth. If I was straightforward and kept parents "in the loop" about what was going on in my classes, I might be able to give them more confidence in what I was trying to do. I found if I lent a sympathetic ear to an upset parent, they would eventually listen to what I had to say. This was a good lesson to learn during year one of my career.

The second incident really caught me off guard. One day I was sitting in the Sykes auditorium making some notes about an upcoming rehearsal. It was quiet—one of those rare times that would ever happen during a school day. The auditorium was used as a study hall venue during some of the periods when music classes were not being held. I was enjoying the silence.

The auditorium reflected the age of the building with all the chairs being made of wood. They had been varnished many times over the years. As I sat in my seat, I glanced up at the seat back in front of me. Carved into the wood were the words "Kleiner is a F**k Head." My pulse suddenly increased as a sense of shock settled into my psyche. Those were harsh words for an idealistic first year teacher to read. *Well*, I thought, *at least they spelled my name correctly.*

These two incidents I believe happened for a reason, as I would come to realize all throughout my career. Things happen and we learn from them. We gain experience and we move on. In the first instance, I learned about parents. They do not always have the same outlook on education that I do. Either through their own upbringing or life experiences, or some other prejudice, they will not support you and your profession.

A good example of this is an experience with a parent of a private student of mine. Over the course of my years in Vernon, I built up a private studio teaching clarinet. I started teaching those kids out of one of the local music stores in town. I was charging $20 for a half-hour lesson, fifteen of which I would receive and $5 to the store per lesson. I had been hearing from colleagues that they were charging $25 or $30 per half hour, so I decided at the beginning of the next school year to raise my rates to $25.

I called the parent of each student to inform them of the change in my lesson fee and with only one exception did I receive a negative response. This one mother asked me, "So what further music degree did you receive to justify the raising of your rates?" I explained that my lesson fee needed to be raised since the music store took out a room rental fee for each lesson. I guess she did not understand that lesson rates do go up from time to time. The next week I learned I had lost her daughter as a student. I was not surprised.

I tried not to let the interactions with these kinds of parents affect me. For the most part, parents in those days were very supportive. They trusted your judgement as professionals. And for the most part they were "hands off" in terms of what you were doing. They trusted your educational expertise. Later in my career I was to experience the "helicopter parent" with more frequency. More about them later in this book.

With the "my name inscribed on the back of the chair" incident, I came to realize that every student will not like you. Sure, every teacher in the profession wants their students to like them. I was finding out during my very first few months of teaching that whether or not a student liked you was not so much what you were doing as a professional but was instead the student's background at home. Was learning encouraged there? Did their parents impress upon them the value of hard work? Were they taught to respect adults as people whom they could look up to and emulate? These ideas had much more to do with how much a student might or might not like you.

This did not mean that a teacher could not develop a relationship with those kids over time. This idea turned out to be one of the most challenging and satisfying motivations that I would experience in the profession. In later years I would find myself in a few situations in which I would be hired into a school music program that was on the decline or was in chaos. I believed that students inherently want to be challenged, and once they experience success they will come over to your side, to your way of thinking.

But I do appreciate the fact that I was fortunate enough to begin my career with those Sykes students in year one. They were almost unanimously with me from the very beginning. I credit their families who were so strongly supportive of their kids' music activities. The fact that about 50 percent of my band were taking private lessons on their instruments was a prime example of that. I credit the Town of Vernon Public Schools for supporting their music program. Of course, the faculty and administration of the Sykes Ninth Grade

School has to be recognized for their flexibility and support as well. And the instrumental music staff in Vernon deserves so much credit for preparing the students I was presented with during my first year.

In many ways I had been set up for success in my first job. I was a bit naïve at the time as I thought this was going to be the way things would be forever. I had come from a top-notch music program in the Hicksville Public Schools. I had a solid learning experience at both SUNY Fredonia and The Hartt School. And I had fallen into what I would later realize was nine years of music education heaven in Vernon. Or let's say eight and a half years, as I was to later discover.

3

The Vernon Friends of Music was a parent group that supported the instrumental program in the town's schools. They met monthly, and at those meetings the staff would keep them informed of the program's activities and needs. This parent group was always ready to help. Most of the members either had kids in the music program at the time or had themselves been a member of a school band during their younger days. Most would readily volunteer their support.

During my first few months on the Vernon staff the Vernon Middle School band, under Ed DeGroat, had been planning a trip to the University of New Hampshire Music Festival. This was an honor for that group to represent Vernon and Connecticut. Funds for the trip came from fundraisers as well as the Board of Education. One of the annual fundraisers for the Friends of Music was a grinder (sub sandwich) sale at Vernon's Tri-City Plaza. Parents and students would donate the grinder food stuff, make the grinders, and sell them during the weekend. Their booth added to the many booths that were manned by other organizations supporting various other activities in Vernon and the city of Rockville.

This event also provided an opportunity for the VCMS and RHS music departments to have student ensembles perform. It was a golden opportunity to get out in the community and show the public what was going on musically in the schools. The average town resident sometimes did not know or appreciate the fact that music education was having a positive effect on the lives of so many young people. With these kinds of public performances, the public would take notice.

4

As the fall months unfolded, the Sykes Band progressed even beyond what I could have hoped for. The Christmas concert was an amazing success. Starting the concert with an arrangement of the overture to Handel's *Messiah* and including *A Christmas Festival* by Leroy Anderson, it was a night I will never forget.

The acoustics in a full Sykes Auditorium sounded amazing. What a way to begin what was to be over a hundred school concerts I would conduct over my career. The Sykes Chorus under my colleague Eileen Sullivan sounded great as well. We collaborated for a series of Christmas carols at the end of the night.

After the success of that performance, I began to think about what we could do in the spring that would be special for my band. Why not an exchange concert? My wife was from the Niagara Falls, New York area, and she was involved in a very strong music program there during her youth. What a great place to go on an exchange concert trip to perform and also get to tour Niagara Falls!

After giving this idea more thought, it was evident that the amount of money we would have to raise was substantial. The Niagara-Wheatfield music department had fundraisers in the past which involved selling oranges and grapefruits freshly picked and shipped by a company in Texas. The fruit was ordered by the box, picked, and sent by truck within a short time period, usually no more than a week. It arrived as fresh as it could be and had a reputation of being of very high quality. I learned that this was a standard money raiser all throughout the Mid-West and South. So why not in New England too!

I contacted the Langdon Barber Groves in Texas to get some information on how to conduct a fruit sale. They were quite excited to be hearing from a Connecticut group as they had not yet had a fruit sale in our state. I also reached out to the Niagara-Wheatfield Junior High School band director Jack Lis. He was all for the event and agreed to host us.

During the January Vernon Friends of Music meeting, I brought up the subject of raising money for this trip by selling fruit. They agreed to support us in our fundraiser, so the wheels were set in motion. We scheduled the fruit sale for a couple of weeks in late February and each student was encouraged to include family and friends as their customers. We would be profiting 40 percent on each box. And we found out that the fruit would be coming from groves in Vero Beach, Florida.

The Langdon Barber Company told me that if, in their words, "we really gunned it," they could see my group of 58 students raising about $1,500 or $1,600. That amount would be enough for the trip, including the two buses. So away we went! The fruit proved to be an easy sale. Everyone enjoys fruit, so why not order some from our needy band students.

The fruit was scheduled to arrive on a Wednesday in the afternoon, so we organized an unloading crew. One of our band parents volunteered their garage to store the boxes of fruit on their driveway and eventually their garage. Customer pickup would be over the next two days, on Thursday and Friday after school hours. Plans were rolling along well and the excitement was building.

The truck arrived on schedule on that Wednesday afternoon. The truck had a bit of trouble backing up on to the Somervilles' driveway, but once the driver avoided sitting on the lawn and possibly caving in their septic tank, the truck unloading crew began to do their thing. I had followed some tips from my family in Niagara Falls who had done this sort of thing before.

We organized the boxes by fruit type and box size. The company also sent an extra percentage of the order to cover spoilage. After sneaking a few samples, we realized the fruit was delicious. For myself, I had always loved fresh oranges but was not a grapefruit fan.

Now I was!

Selling freshly picked fruit from Florida had turned out to be a great way to raise funds. And lo and behold, when all was said and done, our profit totaled $3,000! The Vernon Friends of Music took notice.

5

About a week after the delivery of the fruit, my principal called me into his office. He told me that we had not formally asked the Vernon School Board for permission to take the trip. OOPS! It never dawned on me I needed to do that. And no one had mentioned it either. The Board of Education had a meeting the following Monday and our trip was on the agenda. Of course, it made perfect sense that the board would have to approve any kind of overnight field trip. I had learned an important lesson. But the worry was there. What if they didn't give us approval to go? We had already raised a lot of money. But that was the point. Never fundraise without an approved activity as a reason.

At the board meeting, I was nervous but was more confident for the fact that my principal was going to be there to support us. My turn came and they asked me about the planned trip. Or course I emphasized the music educational benefits of such an experience for my students. I also spoke about the experience of visiting Niagara Falls. Principal Ed Masker echoed the same to the board as well.

Then a member of the board spoke. He said that this was not the normal procedure for a school group, that is, to plan and raise money for an overnight trip without first getting the approval of the Board of Ed. A lump started to form in my throat. And then the chairwoman of the board took over. *Uh-oh, here it comes*, I thought. She spoke clearly and deliberately, saying how impressed she was with the fundraising effort. And she spoke about how much of a great educational experience this trip would be. She ended with a statement that she recommended that the trip be approved, and it was—by a unanimous vote!

What a great feeling! I was so happy for the fact that with

everyone's efforts, our trip was a "go." Needless to say, I slept better that night.

6

The great fundraising experiment had now come and gone. We had twice as much money as originally planned. We made an addition to our trip as a result. We scheduled a concert at the nearby North Tonawanda Junior High the night before Niagara-Wheatfield. The NTJH band was directed by another former student at State University College at Fredonia, NY, where I went to undergrad school. I liked the idea of having an opportunity to get a concert under our belt before the big night.

The day of the trip arrived in mid-April and the buses left early. From my own personal experience, I knew this trip would last eight or nine hours. When we arrived during that evening, we checked into the motel we had reserved, and the kids settled in for a good rest. I was so happy to have a great group of chaperones along on the trip, including Ed Masker, Ed DeGroat, and my brother-in-law and his wife.

The next morning, we visited the Falls. It was a cool but sunny April day. As the buses parked, you could see in the distance the spray and hear the sounds of the millions of gallons of water plunging over both the American and Canadian Falls. My colleague Ed DeGroat served also as our trip's official photographer, being that photography was a passion of his. Upon his first glance at the Horseshoe Falls, he blurted out, "Holy S**t!" as he started taking many pictures. And on top of the normal beauty of the Canadian Falls, there was a huge rainbow over them. My students were amazed at the sight before their eyes, as were the rest of us. I had been to the Falls several times and had never seen a rainbow hovering over all of that cascading water.

After a prolonged time of gawking and picture taking, we all took advantage of exploring the Scenic Tunnels. We all had to put on the provided rain slickers. You proceeded through a tunnel underneath the Falls so you would get a view from the inside out. The kids could not stop laughing at each other in those outfits, which I admit were quite amusing. And, of course, they loved getting soaked as well.

Next up was lunch and then a tour of the nearby New York State Power Plant. We learned about how the Falls help supply power to a large part of upstate New York and nearby Canada.

It was then on to North Tonawanda. The Sykes band played well that evening and it did serve as a good warmup performance for the next night. The North Tonawanda band was a good group and played well. But one moment prior to the concert was a bit disconcerting for me. I had left my band in our warmup room for a moment to check with the NT band director about a few things. When I walked in his office, I found him with two of his female students. He was sitting at his desk and was getting a neck and back massage from the girls. I am sure it must have felt great judging by the look of relaxation on his face, but I was taken aback by the very fact these students were doing this to him. My better instincts told me that this was not normal physical contact between a teacher and a student.

After I entered, the young ladies quickly stopped what they were doing and seemed a bit flustered that I had seen what was going on. The band director seemed to laugh it off. But I could tell he was embarrassed. I made a mental note that evening. That kind of interaction between a teacher and students should never occur.

The next evening's concert at Niagara-Wheatfield was a huge success. Both bands played with enthusiasm and musical expertise for groups of that age. Sykes played with confidence and poise. I was so proud of them. As I was conducting, many thoughts were going through my head. My students had worked hard and the result was a performance of high quality. I was gratified that my rehearsal philosophy of being strict but fair was working. And I was not forgetting that so many of my students' private study situations had given us the opportunity to play a higher difficulty of music.

7

The Exchange Concert trip was a great success. We had worked hard on our music and had an extremely successful fundraiser, and all this with great support from both the administration and parents. I was totally satisfied with the experience. Being a teacher was so rewarding!

We gave our Spring Concert in mid-May. With some of the extra funds we had left over from our fruit sale, we were able to have the concert professionally recorded by a recording studio who would then provide us with an LP record. I still have this vinyl today and it always brings back such incredible memories. The Sykes ninth grade band program for that night is still to this day an example of the level of performance that few freshmen bands in this day and age would achieve. The program read:

Die Meistersinger (excerpts from the opera)	Wagner–Osterling
"Soliloquy for Trumpet"	Morrissey
"Trumpet Soloist"	Bruce Taylor
Overture to *The Impresario*	Mozart–Barnes
First Suite in Eb for Military Band	Holst

1. *Chaconne*
2. *Intermezzo*
3. *March*

Chorale and Alleluia	Howard Hanson
"Flutes, Flutes, Flutes"	Madden
An American in Paris	Gershwin–Krance

At the concert, I had a wonderful surprise; it was a gift from the band. At the beginning of the school year, I had inherited a conductor podium that was wobbly and literally falling apart. It was a running joke during rehearsals about when I was finally going to fall off. But I somehow managed to survive.

That evening, as I walked out on stage, I noticed a brand-new podium sitting in front of the band. It looked super solid! I found out later that it had been made by some of my students as a project in their woodworking class. They had even covered the podium with carpeting. I was floored that they would think enough of me to do that.

After we finished our last selection, I gave out some awards to students who had distinguished themselves during the year. The top award, "The Most Sykes Band Member," went to my solo chair flute and band president Margie. She was so surprised, and I can honestly say I totally enjoyed giving her that award, which was so well deserved.

The concert ended, and as the rest of the students were going to meet their parents in the lobby, I remembered I had left my scores backstage. As I went back to get them, I heard someone sobbing. It was Margie. I asked her if she was okay, and I realized that they were tears of joy. What happened next was such a special moment for me. She thanked me profusely for giving her the award and I gave her a big hug. But then she took my face in her hands and kissed me on the cheek. My first thought was one of surprise and my second thought was *Did anyone see that?*

In the next instance, I took that gesture as a wonderful compliment, one that I have not forgotten to this day. I grabbed my handkerchief and helped Margie wipe away her tears. She composed herself and smiled as she proceeded out to the lobby to meet her family. This was the first but not the last time a student would express their appreciation to me this way. There were many hugs coming in the future.

The next morning, I found an envelope on my desk. I opened it and found this letter inside:

Mr. Kleiner,
How many times can I say how much that beautiful gift meant to me. I was so very touched. I enjoyed working for you and with you this year, but if you need my help, I'll always be here in the years to come.
Mr. Kleiner, I hope I don't embarrass you but I've got to say this. You've been like a father to me all year. You've helped me grow

up and you made me a better musician. But last night I realized how much this year has meant to me. When I was crying over the award and you comforted me, I realized, even more, what a fantastic man you are.

Thank-you again for remembering me in such a beautiful way. Good luck and God Bless You always.
Margie

I sat at my desk with a warm glow filling me up. What a blessing it was for me to have a young lady like Margie as a student during my first year as an educator. She was among so many who gave me the inspiration to do lead them on this musical journey. I had hit the lottery with this group of kids. Fate had smiled on my career, without a doubt. And don't I know it.

RECOLLECTION II – OFF AND RUNNING (1958-61)

I had officially become a "Band Geek" in the fourth grade, and the rest is history. The music program in the Hicksville Public Schools in the late '50s and throughout the '60s, I would later realize, was about as top notch as one could imagine. Of course, as you are going through it as a student you just take for granted those musical experiences and opportunities.

A weekly lesson with band rehearsals scheduled multiple times a week worked well. Technology had not intruded into daily life. The arts were not affected by social media obsession. There were no technological distractions other than running home from school to catch Dick Clark's TV show *American Bandstand*. How exciting it was to grow up during the flowering of rock and roll!

In my house, my half-hour practice session on my clarinet was a definite priority. It was my mother's rule that I could not go outside to play with my friends until I had put in my practice time. As I look back on that edict over the years, my thought has always been *Thanks, Mom*.

I started private lessons during my fifth grade year with Mr. Gerald Pellerin, who was an accomplished clarinetist and also happened to be the band director at Hicksville High School. It proved to be a nice benefit for us to get to know each other years before I would be a member of his band at HHS. Pellerin gave me a great start. He emphasized all the basic skills of clarinet playing. He was a meticulous teacher as well as conductor. He certainly got me on the right path.

2

Meanwhile down the block at the Fork Lane Elementary School, there were some great things happening. The instrumental music teacher was now Mr. J. David Abt. Val Lagueux had moved up to the Junior High School. The Fork Lane series of concerts, recitals, and marching band kept us all busy. Those marching rehearsals through the neighborhood streets, including past my house on Meeting Lane, were always fun. My mom would always be out there standing on our front lawn cheering us on, along with other moms from the block. We were rehearsing for the town's Memorial Day parade. There were eight elementary school bands besides the junior high and senior high bands in that parade. It was always a marathon event, but the people of Hicksville always came out in droves to see it.

The young fellow who lived across the street from me would walk with the rest of us to Fork Lane School, all of us carrying our instruments. I felt a bit sorry for this kid since he was trying to lug a French horn. He wasn't the biggest kid either. Some of us took turns carrying his horn to give him a break. For me it always felt "cool" to be carrying that big case.

This kid played piano as well, but this was his chance to be in an ensemble. He eventually started tinkering with the guitar, and by the time we were in junior high, he had formed a rock band which often rehearsed in his backyard. We could hear them all over the neighborhood and that was always fun. My dad would tell me in later years that Billy would sometimes lie on his roof and listen to the sounds coming out of my bedroom window of me practicing my clarinet.

My biggest regret is not going over to his backyard and crashing his rehearsal with my clarinet, or later in my high school years with my saxophone. But sadly, I was too much into Mozart and Beethoven during those years to have time for rock and roll.

But this kid, Billy, who is now a member of the Rock and Roll Hall of Fame, was smart enough to dump the French horn for his musical passion. He recently told me one of the big problems he had with the horn was finding the band tuning note. Oh, did I forget to mention this kid's name? It is Billy William Martin Joel.

3

By the sixth grade I was playing first chair clarinet. Mr. Abt was a no-nonsense sort of conductor and I really liked that. He had a "secret weapon" he used to keep us all in line during rehearsals. If we were being continuously disruptive, he would tell us to "pack up" our instruments and sit and only listen for the rest of the rehearsal. That was a fate worse than death! Once it happened to me during a rehearsal when I was too chatty with my stand mate Kathy. I never let that happen again. Good rehearsal habits are formed early, right?

During this time Mr. Pellerin had to cut back on his private teaching load due to his increasing responsibilities at HHS. As fate would have it, a young teacher had started teaching music at one of the elementary schools and inherited some of Mr. Pellerin's private students. I was one of those.

Gerry Burakoff started teaching me during that year and proved to be a fount of knowledge when it came to the clarinet, music, and life in general. He was a patient and perceptive teacher. He seemed to always know what to say and how to say it. This man essentially laid the groundwork for my own private teaching style. He was one of the most influential people in steering me towards the teaching profession. Lagueux, Pellerin, Abt, and Burakoff. All names that shaped my future.

> *"Not all superheroes wear capes. Some have teaching degrees."*
>
> —UNKNOWN

6 -
VERNON, YEAR TWO

THE INITIAL MONTHS OF MY second year of teaching played out in a similar way to year one. Intensive recruiting at all the town elementary schools for the new fifth grade beginners was the priority. Bill and I used what we had learned during our first year. We made sure we had better tape recorders to use (no more runaway spools of tape!). And we streamlined our approach to administering the Selmer Music Guidance Survey. The fifth grade teachers helped smooth out some of the scheduling issues for the testing that we had a year before. The fifth grade survey implementation was more efficient, which helped me devote more time to the Sykes band during those hectic September weeks.

I felt more confident at faculty meetings, which now were held at Rockville High School. There were less nerves on my part, partially because of seeing familiar colleagues. I felt more comfortable. What a difference a year makes!

And speaking of colleagues, I began to realize that how you treated people who worked in the school, no matter what their jobs were, made a big difference in how effectively you could do your job. I had developed a rapport with the school custodians and cafeteria workers at each of my schools. Although teaching class lessons in school cafeterias had proved not to be the optimal place for lessons, the situation actually came with some unknown benefits.

It became evident that staff members were looking after me and my program. Simple things like moving equipment such as chairs and stands, clearing stages, fixing and aiming lights on stage, and best of all, providing me with an occasional snack fresh from the cafeteria. You could always smell things cooking, and if you "played your cards right," you could charm your way into getting a treat.

Other distractions you learned to live with, like having the school speech and hearing specialist work with his students at the other end of the cafeteria. I liked the speech specialist for his sense of humor. He called his own subject "Heech and Spearing." I laughed so hard when I first heard him say that. That was my kind of humor!

2

During my music teacher collegiate training, it was never emphasized how much time would be spent lugging around and setting up chairs and stands. If I had a nickel for every chair and stand I moved and set up over the years, I would have been able to retire early and purchase a Florida vacation home! I was becoming an equipment-mover expert!

The Sykes band quickly looked as though it was shaping up to be a fine group once again. It was a different group of kids entirely, but that proved to be the beginning of my training in how to handle that reality. The camaraderie of this year's group was obvious. Although there were not as many strong players, it really did not seem to make too much of a difference.

Our holiday concert went well, and performing in the Sykes Auditorium was still a treat.

It was hard to keep up with the musical activities of all the schools. Ed's middle school band performed at the MENC (Music Educators National Conference) Eastern Division Convention in Philadelphia, as did Sam's Rockville High School Wind Ensemble. What an honor for both groups! In March the RHS Jazz Band performed at the Berklee Jazz Festival in Boston. I loved the opportunity to serve as a chaperone for all these trips.

My Sykes band got to perform at the dedication of the new firehouse in Rockville. And we also played a June performance on the Phoenix Insurance Company stage in Hartford as part of the Greater Hartford Arts Festival. And all of us had small chamber groups perform at the Vernon Tri-Town Fair at the Tri-City Plaza shopping center. So much was happening musically. I could not believe I was part of such an exciting music department.

The Sykes Spring Concert was memorable not only for the quality of the program the band performed but also for an amazing incident on stage. The concert concluded with the band and chorus performing together an arrangement of patriotic tunes. The rehearsals had gone well for this piece, and both my colleague Eileen and I were excited to be able to have the groups perform together.

The selection began with an eight-measure introduction by the band at which point Eileen Sullivan, standing in the orchestra pit in front of the stage, would cue in the chorus. The band played the intro, and before the chorus entrance I turned quickly to catch Eileen's eye. But she was looking off to the side of the pit area and did not cue in the chorus. The band was now on its own for a moment, proceeding ahead in our music. This was a scenario that a band conductor might have in a bad dream and I was now living it in real time.

We played on and then it was good news and bad news. The good news was that the chorus finally made their entrance. The bad news was that they were four measures behind the band. I could see that many of the band members were watching me carefully, sensing that something was not right. The harmonies of the band were not lining up with the chorus. I looked at the score to try to calculate where the chorus and band might regroup. I picked a rehearsal measure number that was coming up and started to say that number to the band. "Band, back to measure twenty-five on my cue," I blurted out a few times.

It was one of those magical instances where it seemed like everyone in the band was totally paying attention! We arrived at measure 24 and my words were "Band, watch. Measure twenty-five . . . NOW!" And as if we had rehearsed it, the band backtracked four measures. We were now together with the chorus. The band had pulled it off! I doubt if too many audience members knew what had happened musically, although some already knew what had caused some commotion.

Eileen told me after the performance that due to the heat in the auditorium a chorus member in the front row had begun to faint.

An audience member noticed this and got out of their seat in time to catch the young lady before she hit the floor. And Eileen had also moved over to help and thus the chorus was not brought in. I told her I was glad she brought the chorus in when she did because it made it easier for us to adjust. If there was anything that could have happened to prove to me how much my band was "on the ball" all year, this incident was it.

    A couple of weeks later, the mighty fifth grade combined elementary band concluded another great first year with their concert. This year's sixth graders had done the same thing last year as fifth graders. I knew that I would again have the opportunity to conduct those kids in a few years. Not many in the teaching profession get to have the same students at different times during their careers. I was feeling so fortunate to have a career in music education.

7 -
RECOLLECTION III – TOTAL IMMERSION (1960-63)

IT WAS NOW THE ADVENT of my junior high school experience in September of 1960. It was my first time taking a school bus to school due to the mile and a half distance. It became a daily experience of having books and an instrument in tow being squished on a bus seat with the other kids. What I was about to experience at the new school would far outweigh any uncomfortable bus rides.

With a student population of between 2,500 and 3,000, it was a reality check. I did not live in a small town. But the size of the school population, although somewhat intimidating, was a benefit for those of us in the instrumental program. The HJHS music program was comprehensive. Three concert bands, an orchestra, chamber groups, four choruses, and piano classes gave the place a conservatory feel.

Getting used to a school of this size and scope was daunting for a seventh grader. Three floors, "up only" and "down only" staircases, and three minutes between classes were problematic. But despite all of this tension, the music program for me was a lifesaver. It provided me with my "happy space." So much so, in fact, that it was during these years that the thoughts about becoming a music educator started to enter my consciousness.

My old buddy Mr. Lagueux, of my "Swingin' Jim" days at Fork Lane, was a familiar face and the conductor of the advanced, or "A," band. The "B" band and Marching Band director was Henry Gates, whom I would have an important interaction with later during my early teaching years. And Don Sitterly, a fine clarinetist in his own right, directed the "C" band and the clarinet choir. Of course, young Jim Kleiner, the hotshot clarinet player from Fork Lane, got placed in the "A" band right off the bat in grade 7.

I was excited to be there. I knew the expectations for this group were high. Playing in the third clarinet section was a good place to get my feet wet. The band performed music of grade 4, 5, and 6 difficulty, as listed in the NYSSMA (New York State School Music Association) manual. The manual was used for the numerous adjudication festivals around Long Island and the rest of New York State. And the pressure was on knowing that the "A" band had received 6A ratings for the past three years. There were no higher levels than grade 6.

I had to increase my practice time at home just to survive. And Mr. Lagueux was a taskmaster as a conductor. His standards were high for musicianship and I loved it. My ears could tell me we sounded amazing! I didn't mind the times when he lost it with us. His heart was in the right place and we all knew it. He balanced those times with a great sense of humor. I loved the way how on occasion he had us yell in unison the following words several times before a rehearsal: "WATCH THE CONDUCTOR!"

2

One day the band went to play at one of the elementary schools. I had a bad cold and did not go to school that day. I had a stuffed nose and a frequent cough. So for me it was a no go.

That afternoon after school hours, I got a phone call at home. It was from Linda, my stand partner in the clarinet section. She was in tears. She told me that the elementary school performance did not go well. After the concert, when the audience left the gym, Mr. Lagueux was so upset he threw over his music stand.

Poor Linda. I think she took things personally and I tried to calm her down. I assured her that things would be fine and most likely Mr. L felt bad about what had happened. And sure enough, at the next rehearsal he apologized to the band. I learned a good lesson from that. Here was a passionate teacher and conductor who did not hesitate to apologize to his students. I made a mental note for the future.

One of the things I loved the most about the Advanced band

was that the literature was challenging and inspiring. We were playing music listed in the NYSSMA manual as grades 4, 5, and 6! And I had not even started with the Hicksville High School band yet! The word was that the high school band did not even go to the NYSSMA Adjudication Festival since the Junior High band already was receiving the highest rating you could get—a 6A!

I moved up the ranks to the first clarinet section by the ninth grade and achieved the first chair position. I loved the challenge! I also remember taking great pride in being a member of the marching band. I loved those Memorial Day Parades, especially now with this group wearing our neat blue and white uniforms.

In 1963 the band marched in the St. Patrick's Day parade in New York City. A long-distance march in chilly but sunny weather. Having to wait to line up in the parade on a frigid, windy side street was quite uncomfortable. But once we got out on the parade route and began moving, we all felt much better. We even appeared on live TV. Too bad there was no recording of TV shows in those days. Henry Gates, our director, had done a great job preparing our group. One of the highlights of that parade was marching right next to Mr. Lagueux! I was in the last row on the far-left column and he was marching right next to me as a co-leader of the band that day. He heard every note I played. I was playing for him and I loved that!

3

There were two amazing highlights for me at HJHS. That first one was a result of Fine Arts Week at the school which was held each spring. Imagine a full week of evening concerts featuring all the students involved in the music program. The proceeds from ticket sales would go towards scholarships for the University of Vermont Summer Music Camp. I was one of the fortunate ones to receive a scholarship during the summer of 1963. The UVM summer program was four weeks of music making, field trips, and camp fun. And to make it even more special, there were eight other HJHS students attending with me.

This was the first time I had been away from home for that length of time. My dad, who was an air traffic controller, arranged to fly in the jump seat on a commercial plane flight up to Burlington, Vermont. It was my first plane flight. At one point during the flight, my dad came back the aisle and took me up to the cockpit. It really blew my mind to meet the pilots and look out the front window of the plane.

The sightseeing, the softball games, and swimming were among my other favorite things to do there. Unfortunately, I developed ear issues. The camp doctor advised me not to go swimming as a result, but of course I went and did so anyway. And the inevitable ear infection resulted. I should have listened to the doctor.

My family drove up to UVM for the concert. It was not enjoyable for me due to the fact that my left ear was partially plugged. The concert was outdoors, and as the band and chorus performed, the clouds gathered overhead. And wouldn't you know it, the orchestra performance was cut short by a rain shower, right in the middle of Tchaikovsky's *Swan Lake*.

The ride home, which included a stop at the Baseball Hall of Fame in Cooperstown, New York, was very uncomfortable for me. I was in quite a bit of pain in my ear. The doctor at home gave us the diagnosis. I had blown a hole in the eardrum. I was advised not to play my clarinet for a couple of months while the eardrum healed.

4

The other great event of my ninth grade year was when I found out I was the co-recipient of the Hicksville JHS Honor Society's "Outstanding Classmate Award." It was at a school assembly one afternoon. The clarinet choir was playing at the assembly, so I was there in the capacity of providing music for the event. I loved that idea. I thought something was strange when I saw my parents in the audience. *Why are they here?* I wondered. Well, I found out soon enough.

This particular award honored the student who made a significant contribution to the school but was not a member of the honor society. Our principal announced that this year there had been a tie vote for the first time ever. He said, "The Outstanding Classmate Award pairs two young men who have achieved exemplary exploits, one in the band room and one on the football field. They are Jim Kleiner and Bill Fyfe!" I was honored and surprised! My parents were so proud. And I felt a certain sense of accomplishment.

The thought of leaving HJHS and all my teachers made me sad. But I knew I was entering something special at HHS. And no more school bus rides. HHS was only a mile away and under the bus-ride distance. I could walk!

8 -
DON'T GET COMFORTABLE

AT THIS POINT IN MY teaching career, although it had just begun, I felt confident and settled in my environment. But I found that you'd better expect that at some point things would inevitably change. Having a "curve ball" thrown at you is more the norm rather than the exception.

My first career surprise was that after two great years at Sykes, the ninth grade and I were being moved to Rockville High School. I was to become the conductor of the ninth–tenth grade band. RHS was going on double sessions due to space issues. My students would be in session from 12:30 until 5:00 pm. While the eleventh and twelfth grade kids would be on the 7:00 to 11:30 am shift.

They called the period in between the sessions the "interim" period. That would be my band rehearsal time. As a result, I would be traveling to RHS from my elementary schools in the midday for the rehearsal, and then back again. The Sykes school would now house all the sixth graders, and Bill would be handling that program, including the band. I was assigned to a couple of additional elementary schools as well as Center Road and Skinner Road.

The good news was that I would continue to have a daily rehearsal with about one hundred students in the band. I liked the idea that I would now have my students for two years. Could I handle such a large group? We shall see.

About a week or two before the beginning of the school year, I was at a meeting at RHS with Sam and the school principal Marty Fagan. Marty was a veteran administrator who ran a fair but disciplined building, from what I could gather. Reality set in when I saw where I was going to have my band rehearsals.

The RHS auditorium was basically constructed of cement cinder blocks with a compact stage, obviously not large enough for my band. But it did have a large area in front of the stage, a "pit" area so to speak. The first four rows of the auditorium seats had been removed to give us more floor space. As I looked at the area, it still did not look like there might not be enough room. The compromise was to have the percussion stand on the stage. I could live with that although that might cause balance problems during rehearsals. But, whatever.

The next bit of news was more concerning. The band's stands and chairs would have to be set up and then taken down every day. What I thought was going to be a daily rehearsal of forty-five minutes suddenly went up in smoke. I found myself standing on the stage where my percussion would be set up. I clapped my hands to test the acoustics of the hall. After the first clap it took a few seconds for the echo to fade away. I had never experienced an echo like that! The realization that I was going to have to live with that echo was jolting.

The logistics of this situation were daunting. I did not want this setup and breakdown of equipment to get in the way of our musical goals. I simply had to have a master plan to attack this reality. I spoke to the custodians and they suggested I stack the chairs and stands off to each side of the pit area. They explained to me that it was against the fire code to leave the chairs and stands in place. I understood.

And I now understood why the RHS band frequently would play their concerts in the Middle School auditorium. There was no problem with acoustics there for sure.

The master plan began to take shape in my mind. My approach to the band had to be a strategy of "no-nonsense" rehearsals. And the year started with that in mind. My tenth graders were somewhat taken aback by that strict approach since they had just come off the Sykes Band with me last year in which they got used to a more relaxed "Mr. K." But I trusted that they would understand what I was doing, namely, that I would be establishing a proper rehearsal etiquette early on and then relaxing my approach later.

Not surprisingly, my students got used to this setup routine quickly. My initial fears about losing rehearsal time were somewhat abated. Student stagehands were appointed and they evolved into a very efficient group. And most of them were volunteers, which made me quite happy.

But there was an aspect of my daily teaching schedule with which I was having a hard time. Each day I would be expending a significant amount of energy in the mornings teaching enthusiastic fifth graders, after which I would hurriedly drive to RHS to prepare for a massive setup and then rehearsal, followed by breaking everything down. I would usually not have a break all morning. And then I had to face one hundred or so fifteen-and sixteen-year-olds who had just "exploded" into the building with maximum energy. It was their morning but not mine. It took me quite a while to get used to that dynamic. No wonder I was falling asleep on the couch after the evening TV news! Was this normal for a twenty-six-year-old? Maybe not. But after all, I was an educator. So maybe not so unusual after all. As the year went on, I adapted just like the kids. They were a good example for me. They seemed to be so resilient, and so I followed their lead.

9 -
BACK TO MY OLD STOMPING GROUNDS

I MUST ADMIT I WAS really enjoying being a part of the environment of a high school again. Teaching students of different ages and ability levels every day. I was loving that challenge.

The music library at RHS was extensive and provided some great literature from which to choose. I was also on the lookout for the latest band arrangements as well. I had a decent budget to work with. Life was good!

I was really appreciating the preparation I had received in high school and college. I felt prepared musically, there was no doubt about that. The rest of my challenges in education were an ongoing learning experience. I tried to observe the other Vernon music teachers whenever I could. I also made it a point to watch rehearsals at the state and regional music conferences. I saw several incredible conductors conduct their rehearsals.

Hicksville was definitely on my mind. I was wondering how things were going there. I began to kick around the idea in my head that perhaps an exchange concert would be a valuable educational activity for my freshman–sophomore band. I thought of the Hicksville Junior High Band as a possible group with whom to do an exchange concert. Henry Gates was the conductor of the "A" band, and I certainly would love to work with him on a project like this. I called Henry and broached the idea to him.

After a brief chat in which I gave him an update on how things were going for me as a newbie teacher, I explained to him that we were looking for a school with which to have an exchange concert. And to my delight he countered with "How about us?" I was all smiles!

We both took the next couple of weeks to approach our respective school administrations and ultimately the school boards with the idea. We had come up with a plan to stay one or two nights in the guest town, rehearse together, and play a joint concert. I knew I had the Vernon Friends of Music to support us. They agreed to fund our transportation and also assist us in organizing the band parents to house the kids from Hicksville. By December all had been arranged and it was a "done deal."

1974 arrived and in January we had our Winter Concert. And as it turned out, with a full audience the auditorium at RHS actually was not too bad from an acoustical standpoint. The human bodies in the audience were negating a lot of the echo. At the concert we made the formal announcement about the Hicksville exchange concert in April. We would be leaving on a Thursday after school and returning on Saturday after the Friday joint concert. Then Hicksville Junior High would come up from Long Island the following Friday and return on Sunday after a Saturday evening concert in Vernon.

During the early spring we were busy with preparations for the trip. The Vernon Friends of Music's help was invaluable. I was using the experience of the Niagara Falls trip from a couple of years before to guide me. One of the things I expected was that this kind of activity would promote enthusiasm and pride amongst my students. I was not disappointed that this was happening. I loved the concept of an exchange concert. So many benefits to this kind of an experience both musically and socially. Many schools I knew were involved in this kind of activity. Fortunately, in this day and time parents actually trusted other adults to house and look after their kids for a night or two. What a concept!

The concert in Hicksville was going to be at the high school auditorium. I was excited about that to no end. I was going to conduct on the stage where I had spent my high school years making music. How cool was that! The thought of performing with a music program I had grown up with was intriguing. How would we measure up to what I knew was a superior music program?

April 18th finally arrived and we boarded buses for our trip. After a normal traffic-filled trip down to Long Island, we arrived at the high school, met Henry and his students, and had a supper at the school provided by the school cafeteria. That was a great time for the students to get to know each other over some food and drink. After supper the HJHS parents showed up and my students departed for home with their guest hosts. The chaperones and I adjourned to a local hotel for the evening.

While at the hotel, I discovered a copy of the *Mid-Island Herald*, a local area newspaper I had been familiar with since I was a kid. The *Herald* on this day had an article about me! It was entitled "Former School Student With a 95 Piece Band." The article gave my background as a student at HHS as well as the honors I had received in high school and college. And, it publicized the exchange concert on Friday night in the HHS auditorium. Wow, I was a celebrity in Hicksville, even if for one weekend!

2

At this point I would be remiss if I did not talk about the town of Hicksville. During the post–World War II years, the town went through a housing boom due to the developer William Levitt, the founder of what would be called Levittown. Hicksville was the adjacent town in which affordable cookie-cutter homes were built during the years 1949 through 1952. They were mainly bought by returning War vets, which included my father. I was born in the Bronx, NY. Our family lived there for a couple of years, in an apartment a few blocks from Yankee Stadium. In 1950 my parents purchased a home in Hicksville. Meeting Lane was a great place to grow up, with nice neighbors, frequent block parties, and many kids my age with whom to grow up.

Hicksville was not a small town. There were eight elementary schools K-6 as well as large junior and senior high schools. It was a progressive school system with highly skilled teachers and great opportunities for us students to pursue our interests, no matter what they were. What a place to discover what I wanted to do as a career!

Having been involved in the instrumental program beginning in the fourth grade, I benefitted from my teachers' experience and expertise. I was inspired by all of them. To this day I am thankful that my parents moved out to this area of former potato farms. In fact, for a few years after we moved to Meeting Lane, we would consistently find potatoes coming up through the soil of our properties. All of us kids discovered that raw potatoes covered in dirt were not very appetizing. Of course, being kids, we discovered that the hard way.

3

The concerts both in Hicksville and back in Vernon were both a great success. And yes, it was a thrill to stand on the podium at HHS. My kids measured up well with HJHS. It was a good match. We were a bit older than the HJHS kids, but that did not seem to matter at all.

Both Henry and I were gratified by the support both communities had shown for this endeavor. And our students comported themselves quite admirably. The parents in both towns had nothing but good things to say about how the kids got along and behaved at the host homes. Just a couple of kids did not feel well, but the host parents took care of them without a problem. Good going, parents!

My first year with the Rockville High School Freshman–Sophomore Band came and went after a solid Spring Concert in May. Summer break was a welcome time to "recharge the batteries" for both my wife and me. I will admit to going into RHS from time to time over the summer months. Teachers had the freedom in those days to wander in and out of the school when they had work to do, even on a Saturday. No alarms, key cards, or weird looks from security guards. Twenty years later, all bets would be off on that front.

10 - RECOLLECTION IV – EXCITING AND FUN TIMES (1964, 1965)

THE 1964 WORLD'S FAIR TOOK place in Flushing Meadows, Queens, New York. Of course, the Hicksville Schools' music program took advantage of that great event. The High School Summer Band performed during that summer at the Tiparillo band shell. The fair was vast in scope and always full of visitors.

The band attracted a good audience that afternoon in July, played well, and afterwards had several hours to experience the fair on our own. Having been there already with my family a month earlier, I made a beeline towards those displays I had not seen. My friends and I discovered other international venues that featured much ethnic music. That was an eye-opening experience for a bunch of high school musicians. The icing on the cake was being able to walk over to the newly built Shea Stadium nearby to see a New York Mets baseball game. That was the first of many memorable times I spent as a kid in that stadium.

I had been so fortunate to be introduced to the saxophone during my sophomore year. Mr. Abt, who was now teaching at Hicksville High, had given me a brand-new tenor sax and asked me to learn how to play it so I could become a member of the Jazz Band. It did not take me very long to fall in love with that instrument. I loved its expressiveness and I found playing in the Jazz Band was a thrill. I was able to assimilate the fingerings and my sound improved in a short amount of time. My biggest regret is not going around the block at home to talk with a professional saxophonist who lived in the neighborhood. I often could hear him practicing his improvisations. I could have used some pointers and he would have, I am sure, helped me a lot. By my junior year I was ready for my first experience at playing in the pit orchestra for a musical. HHS was doing *Bye Bye Birdie*, and I was enlisted to play the clarinet / tenor sax book. Tom Buttice and Chuck Arnold did the orchestra and choral duties for the show. This was my first experience of being part of a multi, month-long rehearsal schedule to prepare a show's music. Progress was steady and we ultimately reached the final stages of the rehearsals now including the cast.

One rehearsal incident does stand out in my mind. There was a scene where Conrad Birdie was coming down the stairs with his "breakfast," which was a can of beer. The beer can prop was full of water. The scene called for Birdie to toss the can of beer to Harry, the father of the household in which Birdie was a guest. Harry, played by my good friend Pete, was to catch the can as Birdie said to him, "Hi-ya Fats!" This routine went fine during the rehearsals with the can always landing in Pete's sure hands. Pete never missed. It must have been due to his experience as our resident hockey goalie.

I guess some of the cast thought it would be funny if Conrad, during this particular rehearsal, tossed to Pete a real can of real beer. I guess they wanted to see Pete's reaction.

Of course, as fate would have it, the toss of the real beer can went awry. Pete missed it and the can landed in the orchestra pit, proceeding to explode on impact.

I was smack in the middle of the pungent liquid which was raining down on us and our music. Fortunately, the strings lucked out but the winds and brass took the brunt of the shower. We immediately smelled of beer and some of it had soaked our music.

Needless to say, the adults in the room were not happy campers. The rehearsal was put on pause for an impromptu cast meeting back in the band room. We orchestra members were not included, I guess because we ended up being the victims of this disaster. I had never seen Mr. Arnold so angry. He usually had the patience of a saint. Not in this case. When the cast returned after the meeting, they looked like they had seen a ghost!

The student-led prank had backfired on us all. It would not be the last student prank I would experience. However, the next time I would be on the receiving end as a teacher, not as a student participant.

2

The end of my junior year was an eventful one. I again prepared a solo to perform at the NYSSMA Adjudication Festival. The solo was a work by Max D'Ollone entitled "Fantasie Orientale." It was a typical French contest solo with beautiful melodies and technical challenges. Gerry Burakoff had picked that solo for me and guided me through the work over several months. I really grew to love this music and I guess it showed in my performance.

I had a late audition time that Friday evening in May 1965 and ended up playing after 10:00 pm. It was to be the judge's final audition of the day. The judge was cordial, but I could tell he was exhausted. By that time, I myself was running low on adrenaline. I summoned my spare gas tank of energy and got through it. I was satisfied it had gone well.

I arrived home at about 11:00 pm and soon afterwards our home phone rang. *Who could be calling this late?* wondered my parents and me. My mom answered and called me to come down the stairs from my room. She said that Mr. Pellerin was on the phone and wanted to speak to me. I did not know what to think. Did I get in trouble? Did I blow the audition?

The first thing he said to me was "Jim, are you sitting down?" I was not but immediately did. He continued, "I just spoke with your adjudication judge, who called me to tell me how much he enjoyed listening to you play your audition this evening. I just had to call you to tell you that he has recommended you for the All-State Band and that you will be solo chair first clarinet!" I was stunned. All-State Band?

Very few of us musicians at HHS were aware of All-State. All-County was what we were all striving for. Our teachers did not mention All-State very much, if at all. I did not remember anyone from HHS being selected for All-State in the past (there might have been, but I was not aware of them). Perhaps it was due to the size of the state as a whole. After all, Nassau County, of which Hicksville is a part, was a very populous area. The competition for those slots in the All-State groups was huge.

As it turned out, my music department colleague Janet, who was selected for the orchestra, and I were going to be part of the four-day All-State Festival during the following November. The event would be held at the Concord Hotel in Kiamesha Lake, NY. The enormity of this honor really sunk in when I saw articles in the HHS newspaper, *The Comet*, and in our local Long Island newspaper. They were about us and our selections to All-State Band and Orchestra.

The All-State band music arrived in late spring, and at first glance knew what I was going to be practicing over the summer. There would be ample time before November rolls around.

The summer was musically eventful in Hicksville as usual. Summer band played at the Jones Beach band shell. I continued my private lessons with Gerry Burakoff. With my high school senior year on the horizon, I began to realize with increasing certainty that music was to be my life's path. Being around such inspirational teachers continued to make me desire to someday walk in their shoes. I thought of inspiring others to love music as I did. The die was cast. There was no turning back.

"Most of us end up with no more than five or six people who remember us. Teachers have thousands of people who remember them for the rest of their lives."

—ANDY ROONEY

11 -
THE REPORT CARD INCIDENT

JUNE ARRIVED, AND AS WAS the custom all of us educators had visions of summer on our minds. The school year was coming to its inevitable end. Grades had been done for the band members and the day arrived to transfer the grades to the student report cards. Of course, in the mid '70s there were no computers or internet. Keep in mind this was still the era of the rotary phone.

I was faced with hand-entering grades and checking an "effort" box on about one hundred report cards. This was a physical impossibility in forty-five minutes, so I arranged for Ed to come up to the high school and assist me in completing this task. In the back of my mind, I was worried about the occasional surprise fire drill, which sometimes happened during the band period.

We had decided that Ed would record the freshman grades and I would do the sophomores. Once each class had brought up their report cards from their seats in the auditorium, Ed and I each had two large stacks of the two-sheeted pressure copy documents in front of us on a large table. I hated those two-ply documents, knowing how much my hand ached back in January on the previous report card day. But we were determined to get this done in the allotted time. We could do it!

The band members were unusually quiet while we began. Unexpected but welcome! If anything, I noticed a certain nervous chatter going on amongst the kids. About twenty minutes into the task, I suddenly felt a steady stream of liquid begin hitting the right side of my body and head. I turned my body that way to see what was happening. There was a steady stream of water emanating from a crack in the side exit doors to the auditorium. I was getting soaked. It lasted for about fifteen seconds or so. Then the soaking water ceased. At that point I could see the nozzle of a fire extinguisher, which was then yanked back into the darkness and I heard a big "clank." My first thoughts were *You have to be kidding!*

The adrenaline was rushing through my body, and as I was dripping water on the floor and the table, I stood up and "lost it." I picked up the folding chair I had been sitting in, turned around, and flung it against the cement wall behind me. The chair shattered into pieces. It was one of those occurrences in my life when I instantly regretted what I just had done.

Ed had stood up at the same time. I glanced out at the students for a split second. There was a mixture of facial expressions. Most had a look of surprise and horror. I yelled to Ed, "You go that way." We ran in opposite directions, each of us out of a different exit door. We had to find out who the culprit was.

I ran down the hallway wide-eyed, trying to spot the guilty party, never thinking that we had just left ninety-six students alone, unsupervised. That thought did not cross my mind for several seconds. Then, when I did not see anyone running, I went back into the auditorium to find a few students actually crying. One of them was the band president, Nancy. She was crying hysterically. A couple of her friends had gone over to try to calm her down. As I stood there, my heart pounding and my hair and clothes dripping, I noticed the tables. The report cards were soaked and ruined. The auditorium, aside from the tears, was silent.

I asked one of the kids to go get an administrator since we were close to the main office. After a minute or so, Assistant Principal Murphy came in and could not believe the scene he was looking at. "Any idea who did this?" he said after I explained to him what had happened.

"No, not at this point," I replied.

"Okay, why don't you go to the office and dry off and I will watch the students." I did what he suggested, and when I arrived at the office, there was Ed with Tom, the band vice president. Ed had caught him running down the other hallway. The bell rang and I stood there in shock. Tom? Of all the kids to be involved in something like this.

Tom was crying and literally shaking at that point, and it didn't make matters any better when Mr. Murphy walked in. John Murphy had a reputation of being a no-nonsense guy when it came to student discipline. He obviously had experience with things like this because he handed Tom a piece of paper and said, "I want you to write down the names of anyone else who was involved in this." Murphy knew that this kind of a stunt could not be a solo effort.

What further shocked me was that Tom proceeded through his tears to write down about ten names. I glanced at the list and I could not believe the names I was seeing. Kids who I thought were in my corner all the way. And Tom was certainly one of those kids. He then admitted that these kids paid him to do this.

Principal Marty Fagan came out of his office at that point and we filled him in on what had happened. When he saw me dripping wet, his expression change from one of "was this possible?" to "I don't believe it." One of the secretaries handed me a paper towel and I dried my dripping hair. I went into Marty's office and brought him up to speed on everything. John walked in with a stack of wet, ruined report cards. I agreed to take a stack of blank report cards.

Marty gave me the use of a conference room for the next day and said he would make arrangements with the elementary school I was to teach in so that I could finish the report cards in the morning. He would provide the coffee. That sounded like a good plan to me. I would have plenty of fuel to get them all filled out!

Finally, the afternoon progressed and it was time for me to go back to the elementary school of the day. I went back to retrieve my papers and roll book. The custodian was putting away the tables and asked me what had happened to the chair that was now broken into pieces. I said something like "you don't want to know." He picked up the pieces and smiled at me as if he understood. I ambled towards my car in the teachers' parking lot in a kind of fog. This had been, without a doubt, the worst incident of my teaching career.

> *"Life has occasional speed bumps. You just have to get over them."*
>
> —ANONYMOUS

12 -
A TIME TO REFLECT

IT TURNED OUT TO BE a stroke of good fortune that I had scheduled a golf date that afternoon for a quick nine holes. My colleague Bill joined me, and as we went up to the first tee I said, "This afternoon I had the shock of the year in the RHS auditorium." As we progressed around the course, I related to him what had happened and the back story concerning my student Tom.

I had always found that the golf course was a good place to clear the mind about any number of subjects. In this case I gave some serious thought to what my next step would be with those students involved in the incident. Walking the course that afternoon gave me time to come up with a strategy and to reflect.

The next day was a half day of school, and I was not scheduled to see any of the band kids. I did my hall and cafeteria duties and hung out in the band office. I had decided not to approach any of the students on Tom's list. I felt that if they had anything to say to me, they would say it in due time. I did not hear from any students that day. And I knew I had the summer to reflect on a year that was so enjoyable and yet had a disappointing conclusion.

A few days later the word came to me that Tom's parents had been called into school. Tom had not received his report card with the other kids. He received it with his parents in attendance in Marty's office. Someone had suggested that I might consider filing assault charges with the Vernon police, but I didn't hesitate in not going down that road. Tom had made a mistake. In my mind he had suffered enough embarrassment with the reaction of school administrators and fellow students. I was fine with letting it go.

As it turned out, I never spoke to Tom or any of the listed

students about the incident. Although I was disappointed, a few years later I did see a copy of that class's yearbook. He included in his comments that he had "got Klink." * Well, at least I was famous for something.

Tragically, I heard years later, Tom had died in a motorcycle accident in Texas. A life cut short.

Did my belief in "tough love" backfire after all? Did the musical goals we had achieved on so many levels not matter to certain students? I fell back on the realization that I had come to understand during my first teaching year. No matter how hard I tried to relate to my students, some of them did not like me. I could not take that fact personally. My belief was then and still is that all teachers have to deal with that reality. A few years down the road I will have discovered that there will be students who you are sure don't like you and then you will be astonished when you learn otherwise. The report card incident was a huge lesson for me. I learned from it.

2

A few weeks after school was over, I received a phone call from Sam. He asked me if I could come into RHS tomorrow for a meeting with the rest of the instrumental staff. We did have a meeting scheduled for the last few weeks of the summer break, but this seemed like it was the same thing but moved up several weeks. My spirits were raised a bit at this because I liked getting together with my colleagues to "talk shop."

We met in the music office at the middle school. Starting with this office space, VCMS had the most modern facilities for any music department in the Vernon schools. Two spacious rehearsal rooms, one for band and one for chorus, practice rooms, bathroom facilities for both adults and kids, and finally a very functional music office with exits to both rehearsal rooms. And on top of all of that, there was a good-size instrument storage closet and library.

Everyone was at the meeting except Ed. We all soon found out why he was not in attendance. Sam said, "Ed is leaving us to take a job in West Hartford. Since the high school additions are done, Jim, you are being assigned to Vernon Middle School." My immediate thought was *I am going to get to use this office as well as that awesome band room. But, teaching seventh and eighth graders?*

I was taken aback by all of this until Sam said to me, "Jim, you are going to love it here. Dave Parker (the principal) runs a tight ship. You will like working under him."

Three weeks after a career-confidence-busting event, I had another landing. And again, on my feet!

"Leap, and the net will appear."
—JOHN BURROUGHS

*Colonel Klink was a character in the popular TV show of the time *Hogan's Heroes*. He was the commandant of the German prison camp. He was portrayed as a bumbling, pseudo tough guy, often the subject of scorn and jokes by the American war prisoners.

13 -
RECOLLECTION V –
THE SAXOPHONE AND
THE CLASS OF 1966

J. DAVID ABT HAD BEEN appointed to the music faculty at Hicksville High School prior to my sophomore year. I was happy to hear this since most of us summer band members had enjoyed his direction of that group during the past few years. I owe much to those experiences for the simple reason that Mr. Abt saw something in me. He suggested at one point that I become a student conductor of the group.

As a result, he became the first of several conducting teachers I would have over the years. My first task was to conduct an arrangement of *An American in Paris*. Wow, George Gershwin! That was to be the first of several amazing experiences with Gershwin's music over the years.

2

Early on during my sophomore year, after I had gotten clearance to start playing clarinet again after my punctured eardrum had healed, Abt called me into the music office and said he had a "project" for me for the upcoming weekend. He asked me to take home the brand-new tenor saxophone the school had just purchased and whether I could begin to learn how to play it. It had never dawned on me that a clarinetist could play the saxophone. And, of course, Abt and Pellerin had an ulterior motive for this—they needed another sax for the Jazz band, so why not me? And what the heck, it was nice and shiny and brand new!

Once I started to play this instrument there was no going back. I found the tenor sax challenging and fun. I loved the way it could be so expressive, especially when using vibrato. After a month or so I made my way into the Jazz band.

The Jazz band performed at the annual HHS Variety Show as well as other venues throughout the year. I also became a member of the high school sax quartet. It was a surprise to discover so much great literature for that combination of soprano, alto, tenor, and baritone saxes.

So here was another experience which would impact my future on many levels. Little did I know it would also give me another financial bonus later in life. During all of my musical experiences at HHS, I never once thought that someday in my future there would be others who would actually pay me money to play music.

3

It was an unexpected consequence also that I was enjoying playing in the marching band more than ever since I started playing the tenor. I know it was the way that sax fits into a band arrangement, often playing with the lower sounding instruments. I felt as though my sound was projecting outdoors in a strong way. But there was one time during a halftime show where I wished my sound, and myself, could somehow disappear on the spot.

One day during the marching band football halftime show, I was marching on the far left column of the band block. At one point I took a left turn while the rest of the band pivoted on a right turn. Of course, I had my head buried in the music right in front of my eyes. Flip folders were great, but they could also take your focus away from your marching. What I was doing at that moment was a big no-no.

My brain started to register that the band's sound was fading away. My sound began to exhibit an ominous isolation. When I realized what had happened, it was too late. I picked my eyes up and realized that the other team's stands and fans were getting closer. I noticed them smiling and cheering me on. At that point I was looking for a hole on the field to hide in. Panic ensued and I stopped playing, did an about-face, and ran to catch up to the rest of the band marching in the opposite direction. It seemed like the band was 100 yards away and that it took minutes to catch up to them. Panic was affecting my sense of time and distance. I finally blended back into the "Black and Orange" once again. And behind me in the distance I heard a mock cheer emanating from the visitors' stands. I can't tell you how many times I have relived those moments in my dreams over the years.

Despite this event, I give thanks to J. David Abt for introducing me to the saxophone, and Gerald Pellerin for his guidance. I absolutely love the saxophone to this day.

4

During the first few weeks of my senior year, I was frequently in touch with my guidance counselor. We had been exploring potential schools to attend for music education. The State University of New York had two well-known schools for Music Ed., Fredonia and Potsdam. We set up auditions for both schools, both of which took place in New York City. I also chose Hofstra University on Long Island as my third school of choice. The audition there was the first one I took in October.

The SUNY schools followed within a couple of weeks. Having played so many adjudications over the years, I felt prepared to deal with any nerves that would occur during these auditions. I felt that I played well at all three and so the wait began to see if I was accepted.

My school schedule that year was something out of a dream. My mornings consisted of band rehearsal and Music Theory and Music History classes. It was after lunch break that I had World Problems, Advanced Algebra, and Literature. Even with the academics I was blessed with superior teachers who understood where I was going in my career and gave me a certain leeway when it came to being pulled out of class for music sectional lessons.

I was usually nervous about asking my Advanced Algebra teacher, Mrs. Clogher, if I could be excused from her class. She would inevitably say "Oh, go play your horn!" I didn't blame her for being upset, since I was struggling to pass her class most of the year. But I did ultimately pass with a 68 on the Advanced Algebra Regents Exam. I passed by the skin of my teeth!

My music theory teacher was Tom Buttice, who was the HHS strings teacher and orchestra conductor. His approach to teaching music theory was sprinkled with humor and encouragement. He had amazing patience. I never forgot his approach to teaching us. I made a mental note. His class was challenging for me, especially getting used to sight-singing using solfeggio syllables. We drilled hard, and as the year went along, I got the hang of it. Having a good ear didn't hurt. I could actually read a choral score and sing my part. And I know that task was made much easier by sight-singing with Mr. Buttice. Many thanks to him for not losing faith in all of us in class.

Music History was taught by Charles "Chuck" Arnold. I found his course to be fascinating. Starting with studying music of the Middle Ages and right up to the present day.

I was fortunate to have been a serious classical music listener ever since junior high. Many of the works we studied from Mozart's era and beyond I had already heard. I oftentimes thought I was a music history expert.

And that certainly included the day Mr. Arnold played a recording of a Baroque orchestra. Almost immediately I began to hear some snippets of melodies that were ringing bells in my brain. I was hearing fragments of tunes written by the Beatles! After a few minutes of hearing this, I had a revelation. The Beatles had stolen some of their melodies from Baroque composers! I wondered if anyone else in the class was struck with this thought.

Of course, my music historical awakening was blown away when Mr. Arnold held up the record jacket, which said *The Baroque Beatles*. I felt like an idiot and my ego took a huge hit. But I did go out the next week and buy the album. I thought it was so cool!

And while I am on the subject of Chuck Arnold, another incident involving him and me had a profound effect on my musical career.

One day I was walking by the choral room and all of a sudden an arm reached out of the door and grabbed me by my arm. I somehow instantly knew it was his hand, since I had spent a significant amount of time watching in awe those hands play the piano.

His words at that moment were "Jim, if you are serious about going into music education, you had better start to sing. Consider joining the summer chorus."

"Okay, Mister A, I will do that," I answered with a startled voice. The more I thought about his suggestion, the more I was glad I had committed to do that.

That summer I became a member of the Summer Mixed Chorus. A few of my music buddies, including Rich and Ralph, joined me in the group. At the first rehearsal I looked around and was pleasantly surprised. Nothing against the ladies in band, but my immediate thought was *Wow, so many lovely ladies in this group*. That was a typical high school male reaction, right? But seriously, I would come to realize that the experience in this chorus would be a huge help during my next level of music education.

5

In New York, All-State Music Festival came around in December. My violinist friend Janet and I rode up to the Kiamesha Lake Resort in the Catskill Mountain area of upstate. Upon arrival we were greeted by members of NYYSMA, who helped us get checked in and settled. Rehearsals began at 9:00 am the next day and would continue all through Thursday and Friday.

I had received the band music over the summer, so I felt prepared. The first order of business was an 8:30 audition between myself and another student from another Long Island high school. We were being auditioned to see who would play solo chair in the first clarinet section. We had to play the opening clarinet solo from the Shostakovich *Festive Overture*. It was close between the two of us, but when the other guy was chosen, I breathed a sigh of relief knowing I did not have to play that opening solo. I could relax.

The band program consisted of the aforementioned Shostakovich piece, "The Fairest of the Fair" march by Sousa, and the majestic "Songs of the Gael" by Walton O'Donnell. The Gael was a twenty-minute piece that began with a lovely English horn solo and consisted of several Scottish folk songs, arranged in a virtuosic way for a large symphonic band. It was one of the most difficult band arrangements I have ever played, even to this day.

Our conductor was James Matthews from the University of Houston. He was demanding but encouraging, and we grew to love and respect him. We loved his Texas accent too. He kept our rehearsals on the light side by allowing us to trade Texas and New York jokes back and forth. We got him pretty good and he handed it right back to us. The general consensus was that it was a "draw."

I loved this whole experience of playing music at yet another level with superb musicians. Although the HHS band was a great group, this all-state band was on another level. I will never forget the opening fanfare of the *Festive Overture* at that first rehearsal. Talk about goosebumps!

My family drove up to the Concord for the concert. I cherish the recording I have on LP to this day. Since that time, LP records and turntables have gone the way of the dinosaur, but wait . . . what do I see now in bookstores and novelty shops? Long playing records on the rack! And a brand-new turntable in my living room. Miracles do happen!

After all-state, I eagerly came back to HHS for the beginning of rehearsals for our spring musical "Finian's Rainbow." I was playing the clarinet and tenor sax book. I did not realize at the time that I would be playing musical productions as a pit musician up to the present day.

The Jazz band played at the school Variety show that spring. I was also a member of the "blackout" crew that performed short comedic skits about various issues at the school. We got to write these skits, and that was so much fun. They would parody such things as "up and down staircases," cafeteria food, and the school seal. The seal was a metallic insert into the auditorium lobby floor. The tradition at HHS was that you do not dare step on the seal, or something bad would happen to you. The blackout crew had a covered platform set up about 8 feet in the air. One by one kids would come along and inadvertently step on the seal, at which point they would fall through a trap door and disappear. They would have a soft landing on a mattress, but the audience did not see that and imagined the worst. It worked like a charm and the audience loved it. The word got around. Don't step on the school seal!

14 -
SCENES FROM THE PODIUM

WOW, A REAL BAND ROOM! The room had four stepped levels all focused down to the conductor. This was a well-designed facility. I loved the design of the VCMS music wing. And now I was going to be in this environment for a good part of the week.

I still had my elementary school fifth graders to teach at Skinner and Center Road schools, but they were combined into two days so I could be at VCMS for three full days. My middle school schedule would consist of "pull-out" sectionals (small classes of students who played like instruments, and who reported once per week out of an academic class). The schedule would rotate so that students would not be pulled out of the same class each week. Ideally it would be once out of each five or six weeks.

I would have two bands, seventh and then eighth grade groups. This was an environment I loved—busy, productive, and stimulating!

This would be my first experience teaching seventh and eighth graders. Little did I suspect the challenges and rewards of teaching thirteen-and fourteen-year-olds. I gradually realized that these kids, although less mature than the ninth and tenth graders I had previously, were generally more malleable. I liked that. I could influence their relationship with music. Not only for the next few years but also for the rest of their lives. What a challenge and responsibility!

I also loved the fact that I knew these kids so well. After all, I had started many of them on their instruments back in the fifth grade. During the first couple of months the word was getting around that Kleiner was tough but fair. And they learned pretty quickly that I loved to kid around and try to make the work fun.

2

I loved the fact that so many of my students were so passionate about music. But there were a few who were quite hard to please when it came to the music we were working on. As I would be handing out new music, I would sometimes hear comments like "Oh, I don't like this music," or "I don't like Bach," or "Why don't we play pop music?" I devised a strategy to combat this. I explained to the band that I did not want to hear that kind of comment. I told them they needed to be open minded about a piece of music. "Experience the music through rehearsal and performance before you make a final decision on whether you like it or not," I would preach.

I would also tell them that I personally liked many different styles of music and would try to program "my music" and "their music." Then after each performance we would discuss the things they liked or did not like about the music they played. At times I would have them fill out a questionnaire. I believe these activities gave them the feeling that they had some input into what we played in the future. And this worked both ways. For me, I hesitated at times in programming "their" music, but I did, and it would turn out I would discover I really liked it. One example of this was when I programmed "Highlights from Chicago," which featured the group's very popular song "Colour My World." Many of my flute players already knew the famous flute solo from that piece. I developed a love for Chicago's music and am a huge fan to this day.

3

Passionate they were! This played out in the fact that, without fail, we would have an altercation during a band rehearsal once a year. I am sure this would evolve from incidents which occurred outside of my classroom, but for some reason playing music seemed to just enhance the passion in the potential combatants.

The first time it happened, I heard a noise and when I turned around there were two young gentlemen rolling around on the floor in mortal combat. They got up and before they had a chance to get into the fisticuffs mode, I said, "Gentlemen, if you would like to dance, wait a second and we will put on some music for you." That statement would stop them in their tracks. Their thoughts of dancing at that age was a fate worse than death. The tension in the room was broken and the combatants would think better of escalating things. I was so thankful I did not have to get in between them to break things up.

And then there was the day when I again heard a weird sound during a rehearsal. I looked up from my conductor score and saw a trombone slide sticking straight up in the air. Its player was flat on his back with his chair having slid away behind him, obviously an aborted attempt at trying to balance on the chair's back legs. But at the sacrifice of his physical harm, he made sure his trombone survived, intact! Of course, the rest of the band thought it was hysterically funny, and I did too. But I was the adult in the room, so I rushed over to see how he was with a concerned look on my face.

The young man's embarrassment was obvious. My lesson for the band was to refrain from the balancing act on the chair. Bad things could happen. But I complimented our acrobat for thinking about the welfare of his instrument ahead of his own. All is well that ends well.

> *"We are all masterpieces with various forms of restoration."*
>
> —JIM CARREY

15 -
THE FIRST OF APRIL

GIVING CREDIT TO WILLIAM SHAKESPEARE, it was not the "Ides of March" that struck fear in the VCMS band director, but it was, in fact, April 1st, more commonly known as April Fool's Day. I suspect these jokes were somewhat traditional at VCMS. It was something I was anticipating and eventually looking forward to.

It was April 1, 1975. I had actually forgotten it was April Fool's Day but quickly suspected something was amiss as the kids entered the band room and got their instruments out. I was sitting in the office with the door open, as I always did, waiting for the band to sit and warm up. But on this day there was a strange lack of sound coming out of the room. No one was warming up. I glanced up and noticed there was a trumpet player sitting in the flute section. The trumpet was being held by a member of the flute section. Interesting ....

My brain kicked into high gear and surmised there was a dastardly plot unfolding. I could read the band's thought process. *Let's see if Kleiner notices that none of us are playing the correct instrument.* I decided to play this situation for all it was worth. I entered the band room and walked to the conductor's spot, all the while having my head buried in one of my conductor's scores. "Ladies and gentlemen, let us begin with our tuning chorale," I said, keeping my head buried in the score. I raised my baton and gave the down beat.

What I heard next was a cacophony of noise I had never heard before. I looked up in horror but kept conducting. My plan was to wait them out and see what happened. Well, that did not last long. One by one they stopped playing while laughing hysterically. I feigned a mild heart attack and played up the drama. The band were confident they played a great stunt on Mr. Kleiner. I was not about to burst their bubble.

Fast-forward one year as the day rolls around again. I figured they probably would not try to pull the same stunt again this year. But, sure enough, they did. By that year I had split the band into two groups. They were divided equally by instrumentation and ability level. We had the "Blue" and the "White" bands, after our school colors. As a result, I had two shots at the same scenario and I again played right into their hands. They loved the laughs and my reaction again.

So forward again one more year to 1977. After two years of the "wrong instrument" stunt, I was wondering if they were going to try that again. I was on the lookout with eagle eyes!

As the White Band sauntered into the room that day, I started to hear a swell of sound that was completely normal. I thought to myself that they had forgotten what day it was. All looked normal as I took my conductor folder and baton out to my stand. I had forgotten my roll book and although I knew I had left it back in the office, I was not sure where. I went back to the office to find it.

I was not back in the office for more than a minute or so until I finally found the book. I ventured back to my stand and noticed that the handle of my baton had some sort of substance all over it. And then it hit me. Someone had put Crisco on my baton handle! I chuckled to myself and decided to play along once again. "Okay, folks, let's play" were my words as I jerked the baton upwards for the downbeat. Of course, I let it go at that point and the baton flew across the room and ended up in the back row. I had a "shocked" look on my face as the kids roared with laughter. And, thus, another successful April Fool's Day "high jinks" pulled on Mr. Kleiner. Little did they know.

Obviously, the word had gotten around and a few periods later when the Blue Band came in, the same thing occurred. Again, the joke was a huge "success."

In '78, the baton joke was becoming a tradition. I made sure I used an old baton that day in case it might snap, which would be no great loss. And by that year I had refined my baton throw so that it would not land close to anyone. No harm, no foul.

About the same time as that final Crisco incident, I happened to read an interesting book. It was about how one's body language could have an influence on others, namely the science of Kinesics. After my revelation years before that I could incorporate a certain amount of "acting" into my teaching, I was fascinated to read in this book that by using your body position, certain signals could be sent to your students.

I learned that if I stood straight with my feet apart and my arms folded, the kids would get a certain impression. I tried standing this way one day at the conductor's stand as everyone walked into the room. That posture gave me a serious "no nonsense" look. I was amazed how the group quieted down and sort of slinked into their seats.

For the rest of my career, I used this strategy on occasion when I felt it was necessary. For instance, at the beginning of a rehearsal, when we had a lot of work to do prior to a concert coming up and we could not afford to waste time. It never failed to work like a charm.

I always enjoyed working with this age group. If you showed the kids you were fallible and had a sense of humor, they loved it. As a result, they were much more amenable at that point to buckle down and work hard when it was absolutely necessary. More lessons learned and others relearned. Middle school kids were never dull or boring to teach. I loved it.

16 -
THE SHOW MUST GO ON

CONCERT NIGHTS WERE ALWAYS SO exciting for me. My students were finally going to perform the music we had been preparing for months. I knew from experience that on stage they would be super focused and actually be watching the conductor more than usual. Their friends and family were out in the audience and they did not want to sound bad.

The band would have had good rehearsals, bad rehearsals, and everything in between. There were many factors causing this, not the least of which was that the band was made up of adolescents who were going through a learning process. They were learning how to concentrate and focus on the task at hand, listening to themselves as well as the person next to them and the rest of the group. My task as their teacher was to guide them through rehearsals. If things were improving over time then I knew I was teaching them well. These kids at VCMS had adequate rehearsal time, which was a great advantage to all of us. Later in my career this would not be the case.

One particular VCMS concert night stands out in my memory. It was one of those evenings filled with anticipations by us all. I had a nice dinner at my home in Ellington and proceeded to get dressed in my conductor clothes. Jacket, white shirt, tie, and concert shoes. The concert was at our usual time of 7:30 pm on this Tuesday evening in the spacious auditorium.

I would be leaving the house at about 6:30 pm, factoring in a fifteen-minute drive to the school. The kids would be arriving at 7:00 pm for warmup and tuning. After dinner I started to feel stomach cramps as I dressed. They became severe quite quickly and I ended up spending significant time in the bathroom while nervously watching the time begin to ebb forward. Instead of leaving the house at 6:30, it was now 6:45 and I was still not ready to leave. My thoughts were *Okay, this is a mind over matter so I am done with this discomfort and must get to the school . . . NOW!*

Cheryll wondered if I was okay and I assured her all was well. I gathered all my stuff, got in the car, and started to drive. As I travelled about a mile down route 83 towards Vernon, another wave of cramps hit me like a ton of bricks. It was a horrible feeling knowing that I was in the car while trying to control my bowels. I had another few miles to the school and I knew I was not going to make it. Luckily, there was an Italian restaurant a short distance down the road. On arrival there I quickly pulled into the parking lot and practically ran into the building. The time was now 6:55.

As I sat in the bathroom stall going through the same situation I had at home, I watched the time clicking away . . . 7:10 . . . 7:15. I was imagining my band kids warming up in the room supervised by a couple of our volunteer faculty chaperones. There was no way of contacting anyone to tell them I was running late. No cell phones in those days.

The second round of cramps subsided about 7:20. I made it to my car and finally got to the school at 7:30 . . . concert time. I walked into the band room looking a bit pale but none the worse for wear. I felt all the eyeballs on me as I walked to the center of the room, thinking about how I was going to explain why I was late. I could feel the sigh of relief from everyone there. That gave me strength!

I summoned up the courage and began to explain what had happened to me over the past hour and a half. I tried not to be too graphic but fortunately everyone in the room knew exactly what I had gone through. I was brief and to the point, not wanting to delay the start of the concert anymore. I told the seventh grade band we would play the tuning chorale on stage as a warmup and do a quick tuning. I also made it clear to them that if I had to stop conducting at any point and momentarily leave the stage, they should sit quietly and wait for me to return. "Don't panic if I disappear. Keep cool and I will be back," I told them. They got a chuckle out of that and that is what I wanted. I wanted them to relax. The seventh grade band proceeded to the stage while the eighth graders waited for their portion of the program.

I followed the band down the hallway with my scores and baton in hand. Suddenly I felt that evening's familiar feeling once again. I could not believe it. I thought I was over this. I made a beeline back to the faculty bathroom. Meanwhile the kids were seated on the stage waiting for me, as was the audience. It was another five minutes until I made it out on to the stage. By then the looks on my students' faces showed much concern.

It was now 7:50. Before we began, I had to give the audience an explanation and apologize for the delay in the start of the concert. I did so and tried to make light of the situation. Like the kids, the audience was sympathetic. They seemed at once to all think in terms of "Been there, done that!" It was a blessing that I did not, in fact, have to leave the stage during any point for the rest of the evening.

The concert was great. The students had performed up to expectation. Music had triumphed over Mother Nature, thank goodness.

17 -
RECOLLECTION VI – SUNY FREDONIA, 1966–70

I ULTIMATELY CHOSE SUNY FREDONIA for my undergraduate study in music education. Fredonia is a lovely town located in Western New York State. The Fredonia area is known for its grape vineyards, and it is not surprising that you can smell the aroma of grapes when the wind blows a certain way off of the nearby Lake Erie. All of us from the incoming Class of 1970 got a preview of campus life there during a three-day summer orientation. Then it was back home to pack and get ready for the trip back in September. I had chosen Fredonia upon the recommendations of Gerry Burakoff and J. David Abt. Both men were alumni, and Burakoff raved about the clarinet professor there, Dr. William Willett. I valued the advice of my Hicksville teachers, and so I ended up getting on a bus for the campus, which left from the Hicksville train station. It turned out that Hicksville was the Long Island location of the Fredonia bus. Very convenient.

As I found out travelling up to the orientation a month before, it was a long bus ride. The trip was 450 miles, which took about eight hours. There was much excitement during that initial trip. Lots of "buzz" was coming from the students. I sat next to a shy fellow named Frank. We immediately struck up a conversation and this began a friendship that would last all four years of our schooling and beyond. Being future roommates as well as student teaching together were in the cards for both of us. What we all didn't realize at the time was that this bus ride would be the first of approximately thirty-two round trips over the next four years! Too bad they didn't give us "frequent bus rider miles."

To summarize my freshman year, I can use only one word—eventful. I experienced the normal feelings about being away from home. At first there was a certain homesickness, then, as I became used to my new surroundings and more involved in the daily routine of attending classes, studying, and practicing, those initial feelings vanished.

A planned visit by my parents and sister during October was something I was really excited about. When they arrived that Saturday morning, after the usual hugs and kisses, they told me to look in their car. Lo and behold, there was my girlfriend Liz hiding on the back seat. I could not believe they brought her with them. My heart leapt as I saw that familiar lovely smile. To this day that was one of the best surprises I have ever had in my life!

By the time the much-anticipated trip home for Thanksgiving had arrived, I had already played my clarinet on a recital and had a symphonic band concert under my belt. I had been placed in the solo chair first clarinet with that group, which I found out was an unusual situation for a freshman. The Wind Ensemble was the premiere wind group, so I set my sights on someday playing with them. In the meantime, Dr. Herbert Harp did a great job with the symphonic band.

Membership in the Festival Chorus was a requirement for all freshmen and sophomores. It was a large group of about two hundred voices. And I was actually the first chair bass! I bragged about that to my family and friends but eventually had to admit that the only reason I was in that seat was that I was the shortest member of the bass section, as we sat in height order. Oh well, I tried. The chorus was known for singing large choral works often with the Buffalo Philharmonic, in Kleinhans Music Hall in Buffalo.

After performing Mendelssohn's *Elijah* during our first on-campus concert, an emergency meeting of the group had been called. There had been a breakdown of communication between the university and the Buffalo Phil over a holiday performance of Handel's *Messiah*. Our conductor, Harriet Simons, explained the situation, telling us that she had agreed to have us sing the work in Buffalo. But with about half the usual rehearsal time she only wanted those to participate who had sung the work before. The smaller Messiah chorus was chosen by audition. I had only heard the work a few times when it was performed by the Hicksville Community Orchestra and Chorus. I loved the work. I could not pass up this opportunity.

I got the music, rehearsed it, and went and auditioned, and by the grace of God, I was selected! I had the HHS music faculty to thank, especially Tom Buttice and Chuck Arnold for helping me become a better sight singer. I could hear my intervals even while reading bass clef and could hold my own with other singers who had much better voice quality than I did. But I could sing in tune and read the music.

The Buffalo Phil conductor, Lukas Foss, came down to campus and rehearsed with us a few times. He was quite the character and a bit hard to follow, but his enthusiasm for the music immediately rubbed off on all of us.

It is hard to put into words how the Buffalo performance affected me. It was inspiring and amazing. It was one of the most profound musical experiences I would have up to that point in my life. Between the concert in Buffalo and my experiences with my clarinet lessons with Dr. Willett and the symphonic band performances, I was a happy camper. And things only got better.

My classes were challenging but I was learning a lot. I was not a fan of getting up for an 8:00 am class every Tuesday, Thursday, and Saturday. But Saturdays were made easier knowing I had a 9:00 am band rehearsal. And, of course, one got used to the snowfall once the winter months rolled around. Snow squalls came in off Lake Erie almost daily. You had to dress accordingly every day.

One Friday night we were hammered with 20 inches of snow. Classes were rarely cancelled so I trudged out of my dorm to walk over to my 8 am Physics lecture. I could barely get the dorm door open. I stepped out into the snow drift, which was up to my waist. I walked in snow drifts all the way since nothing had been plowed at that point in the morning. There were about twenty of us there in the lecture class out of about one hundred students. The Physics professor thanked us for making the effort and took note of who had showed up. We all knew we had received many "brownie points" that morning.

Dr. Willett was the conductor of the Fredonia Orchestra. I admired his conducting talents and picked up many pointers just by observing his baton technique. Hearing Respighi's *Pines of Rome* under his baton was an inspirational experience I will never forget. A brass choir in the balcony that he was conducting simultaneously with the musicians in front of him was an image I would never forget.

In addition, Dr. Willett's teaching was really helping me develop as a clarinetist. But, at the end of the school year, he told me he was leaving Fredonia to take a position at the Indiana University of Pennsylvania. I was disappointed for sure but was excited for him. This was the first time I had begun to think about what a change of scenery at a different school or even a career change would be like. Little did I know I would be dealing with those issues in my professional years to come.

During the next couple of years, I became a member of the Wind Ensemble and eventually the orchestra. The Wind Ensemble would tour a portion of New York State each spring. I found it so much fun to perform at area high schools with such an accomplished group. Dr. Donald Hartman was our conductor and he was a gentle taskmaster whom we all adored.

When I found out we would be touring Long Island, I contacted Gerald Pellerin at Hicksville High School. Gerry contacted Fredonia and set up a stop for us to perform. I was thrilled. I would be back on the same stage where I had experienced so much in the past. The concert was like a dream come true.

Playing in the Fredonia orchestra under the baton of Harry John Brown, the former conductor of the Milwaukee Symphony Orchestra, was my first sustained experience in orchestral clarinet playing. Orchestral playing was a different world. I loved the challenge and the literature. Playing the solos in Rimsky-Korsakov's *Capriccio Espagnol*, as well as the wonderful Spanish melodies in De Falla's Suite from *The Three-Cornered Hat*, was a challenge I relished.

Brown had us meet once a week to read orchestral literature. I will never forget the evening we read through *Death and Transfiguration* by Richard Strauss. During the closing bars we could all see the tears running down Harry John's cheeks. Our reading of that great work had really touched him. And it did me as well.

The college concerto program was held each spring to give outstanding musicians the opportunity to solo with the orchestra. At the urging of my clarinet teacher, Dave Sublette, I auditioned for a spot on the concert on the "Premiere Rhapsody for Clarinet and Orchestra" by Claude Debussy. Things were a bit dicey during the audition since my accompanist Martha was pregnant and it seemed like she was going to give birth any minute. But if she wasn't deterred by that, I wasn't going to be either. I was so glad she hung in there since she was an amazing player.

I played the piece by memory on the stage of the big concert hall and it was nerve-wracking at first. The hall was empty but I knew there were four judges sitting out there whom I could not see. But I was able to conquer my initial nerves and the audition went well. I found out the next day I had been selected! I was going to dedicate my performance to Gerry Burakoff, who first introduced me to the Rhapsody, as well as Dr. Willett, who studied the work with me during my freshman year.

My family came up from Long Island for the concert. I had never played a long work from memory, but Harry John encouraged me every step of the way and gave me the confidence I needed. I actually had less nerves playing the piece in front of about a thousand people than I did at the audition! The performance was a tremendous highlight for me.

My music education classes were a great help prior to my student teaching. Lots of philosophical discussions about education and how to teach kids. But the real revelations came when a local high school band director came in to lecture us one day. Mr. John Krestic taught instrumental music at Hamburg High School, a suburb of Buffalo. Referring to our music education Methods class professor, Krestic whispered to us, "Don't listen to him. Let me tell you how it really is out there." And subsequently over the next two hours we all learned the difference between the real world and the "ivory tower."

Our class got to observe a few school systems in action, including Mr. Krestic's school. That was so helpful to get us more relaxed as we were about to head to our assigned student teaching locations. My old friend Frank and I would be going to Maryvale High School in Cheektowaga, a suburb of Buffalo.

SUNY Fredonia had been an invaluable experience for me. I had made the right choice, but, perhaps, the most wonderful outcome of all was meeting a lovely flute major from Lewiston, NY, during my sophomore year. This young lady and I have been together ever since. Cheryll and I got married after I graduated and she had finished her master's degree. We have been married for over fifty years! Thank you, Fredonia, for everything!

18 -
BOX SCORE BOMBED

I WAS ALWAYS A FAN of yearbooks. My high school yearbook is undoubtedly one of my prized possessions. Those pictures tell the story of my youth in so many ways. I have spent many hours over the years perusing through its pages. VCMS gave each faculty member a copy of the school yearbook during the final week of the school year. I thought it was a nice gesture. Since I would be signing many yearbooks during that week, why not have my students reciprocate?

I sent my book around the band room and looked forward to seeing what the kids wrote. The book made its way around the band room as I signed several of the students' books. This process ended up taking more than one period, so we were into the second day of this activity when the book signings were done. I was enjoying the student comments as I thought I would. What an intelligent and thoughtful bunch of comments! I just could not stop smiling until I arrived at a page with a baseball box score, which had been cut out of a newspaper and pasted on the page.

To give some background: I was born in the Bronx, NY, and lived for the first two years of my life a few blocks from the famed ballpark Yankee Stadium. My dad tells me I actually attended a few Yankee games with him before we moved out to Long Island. I was inevitably a Yankee fan from the get go. After settling in Connecticut many years later, I found myself teaching in what was, for all intents and purposes, Red Sox county. Connecticut was actually somewhat of a dividing line between Yankee and Red Sox fans. Yankee fans were more prevalent in southern Connecticut, and the north central area of the state was more populated by fans of the Red Sox. My "Noo-Yawk" accent gave me away as far as my allegiance was concerned. I eventually lost most of the New York accent over the years, but in the '70s it was still quite noticeable.

During baseball season the Yanks–Sox rivalry was quite a sticking point between myself and a few of my students. It was a "gentlemen's disagreement." It was polite yet fierce. Both teams were stocked with great players and would take turns beating each other throughout the season. The weekend before yearbook week, the Red Sox had pummeled the Yankees during a three-game series up in Boston. And thus the newspaper box score covered a whole yearbook page, listing the statistics from two of the games. During those two games the Sox outscored the Yanks 23 to 8! The Red Sox hit a combined 11 home runs during the three-game rout. That weekend in baseball lore was known as the "Boston Massacre."

The caption under the box scores read, "From us to you! Advice: Red Sox Burn you! Yankees rot!" It was signed by four young gentlemen calling themselves the "Red Sox Fans." I thought this was so clever. They really got me good. There was some consolation though in that I did get a few comments from a few other students. There were comments from them such as "Red Sox rot" and "The Yankees will win!"

Another day in the life of a middle school teacher. I was enjoying grades 6 through 8. Challenging ages for sure, but I was loving every minute.

19 -
THE TROUBLED ONES

AS MY CAREER PROGRESSED, THE realization that not all of my students would like my methods and teaching style continued. Most would adapt readily to a strict rehearsal routine tempered with "tough love." I knew from experience that if the doubters would hang on at least until the holiday concert, the band's success would win them over. Things got easier for these kids with familiarity. And along the way I was learning that each student was a unique human being with different needs, and some needed more "TLC" than others.

My low brass section often needed more attention and the aforementioned care. It was odd at times when that section of the band seemed to breed more problem students than the rest of the group. One young fellow by the name of David was absent from school frequently. Out of curiosity, I asked his guidance counselor one day about this. "Where had David been recently?" I inquired. "He has missed several band rehearsals over the past month."

The counselor said, "I have been meaning to talk to you about him and I am glad you stopped by." I immediately thought to myself the worst, but the following explanation really floored me. "He has been having some tough times at home since the beginning of the school year. His parents have split up and it has been tough on him. He has been getting into trouble in school and his mom has been in school here on more than one occasion. Jim, I want you to know that his mom told me that the only reason he wants to come to school right now is the fact that he is in your band."

"Wow, that is really good to know," I blurted out. I related to her how he got into a scuffle during a band rehearsal about a month ago, but as soon as I intervened, he backed off and cooler heads prevailed.

"I realize now I should have told you, especially knowing that he had been in trouble elsewhere in the school," I admitted to her.

After the meeting I felt bad I had not reported my concerns about David, but at the same time I felt a new responsibility for him. He was a troubled kid to whom I now knew how important band was. I started to think about other kids who might be in the same boat. After all, being thirteen or fourteen is not the easiest time for a youngster. From that day forward I always made time for David. And I noticed that with that extra attention in my class, he started to exhibit leadership potential in the low brass section.

Ironically, I had the pleasure of having another fellow by the name of David a few years prior in my VCMS band's trombone section. This fellow was an all-star member of the trombone section during the two years I had him there. A future member of the Connecticut All State band while at RHS, this kid went on to be a professor of music at Kent State University. David Mitchell, we remember you fondly!

2

Another troubled one appeared earlier in my VCMS tenure. His name was Larry and he was a talented member of my low brass section at the time. Good baritone horn players were a great asset to any band. But Larry was a challenge to say the least. He was good looking and witty, and he knew it. He was quick to interject comments during rehearsals. It was obvious he wanted to be the center of attention, at least in the low brass section. And I will be the first to admit that I cut him more slack than I should have because he was a good player. I mistakenly put up with his high jinks for his seventh grade year, hoping he would grow out of those shenanigans by grade eight. But that was not to be. He had gotten worse. My comments about his behavior on his report card had evidently fallen on deaf ears at home.

By this time, he had a buddy in the section, a trombone player named Paul. Paul was a good kid, quiet, polite, and quite unobtrusive. But he had fallen in with Larry and thought his new friend's actions during rehearsal were quite amusing. His reactions to Larry's antics were starting to affect the entire right sight of the band. I was losing their attention and rehearsals were suffering. As a result, after a particularly contentious session I told Larry and Paul to stay after rehearsal for a chat. I read them the "riot act" as calmly as I could. "Gentlemen, your disruptions and inattention are not setting a good example during rehearsals. You occupy an important section in the band as low brass players, and we need you to be the best you can be. Do you understand?"

I expected their reaction to be one of apology and remorse. But that is not what I got back from them. What I did get was laughter in my face. They literally walked out of the band room laughing! I was so taken aback by their reaction. I am sure Paul would not have reacted that way ordinarily, but since Larry did, he joined in. Big mistake!

Later that day I went down to the Guidance Office. I explained what had occurred and their counselor was not a happy camper. "That was an unusually disrespectful reaction to what you said to them," the counselor said in shock. I had already decided what I wanted.

"I want them removed from band."

"No problem; I will get in touch with their parents," she answered. That was the first time I had ever requested a student be removed from my class.

In fact, the decorum during rehearsals improved in short order. The word had gotten around among the other band students about what had happened. The example had been set. To be honest, it took a while to get over that reaction from those two kids. I had never had students laugh in my face.

I did not anticipate any fallout from that episode, but something strange happened at the Spring Concert a few months after that incident. The concert was nearing conclusion, and the combined bands were on stage getting ready to perform a medley of patriotic tunes along with the chorus. Our principal was on the stage thanking the audience for attendance and the students on and in front of the stage for their efforts. As I stood back stage waiting for his remarks to conclude I heard a rustling of the curtains behind me which startled me. "Someone back here?" I thought. I walked over to the curtain that was still moving, looked behind it and saw my "friend" Larry lurking around. He saw me notice him and he hurried out the stage door and was gone. He had been in the area of a fire extinguisher hanging on the back stage wall. *Hmm, I thought to myself, was this going to be a repeat of the RHS fire extinguisher attack on me from a few years ago?* The thought crossed my mind that perhaps Larry had gotten the idea from Tom or his cohorts. Where else would he get the idea to get back at me with another water bath?

How cool would that have been to soak Kleiner with water before he had to go back on stage. Fortunately, there was no harm done and I did not pursue the matter further. It might have been just my imagination, although I did not imagine Larry being backstage. He had been there. I saw him.

But I realized a few years later that this incident backstage at VCMS was no accident. My house in Ellington was "egged" on two occasions. We did not live far from the Rockville town line. I wondered who might have done that. It was quite an annoyance. Then one night I was awoken by the sound of a car radio in front of my house. I looked out the window and there was an old blue van sitting there. I could hear laughter inside and there was the unmistakable smell of marijuana in the air. I could see Larry, now a high school kid, sitting on the driver's side. So, he knew where Kleiner lived and thought a bit of harassment would be fun, especially at 3:00 am.

I watched him and his buddy for about five minutes. I was going to confront him if they made any approaches to the house on foot. But the van eventually pulled away.

I had another "visit" from the blue van a few weeks later. By that time I had confirmed that the van was in fact the one he drove to school every day. The same incident played out a second time. I was about to call the police, but one of my neighbors beat me to it. I watched the van pull away quickly, but he was pulled over at the end of the block by a police car. I assume Larry was busted for pot possession among other things. I guess that convinced him to leave me alone, for he never tried anything like that again. His fun harassment of me got him a police record. Careful what you wish for.

3

Returning to the VCMS year in question, there was some good news for Larry's buddy Paul. Paul's dad came to see me at VCMS after school one day towards the end of the school year in June. He apologized for his son's actions during the laughing incident. "Mr. Kleiner," he said, "Paul feels very bad about how he behaved over the course of the past year during the band rehearsals. He is also very sorry he was so disrespectful to you. I am asking today if you would consider letting him reenter the band program in the fall at Rockville High School."

I told Paul's dad that I would agree to letting him join band again knowing that his parents would be on his case. His dad was so thankful. If Larry had come to apologize at some point or perhaps his parents had done something similar to what Paul's dad had done, I would have also given permission to have him reinstated in band. In retrospect I should have followed up with his parents about the whole situation. I know his guidance counselor had certainly done that. That was a lesson learned.

I felt with these experiences I learned to treat each of my students as individuals. Each had their own back story. These experiences, both good and bad, were placed in my memory bank and came in handy down the road in my career.

20 -
MEMORIES AND MEMENTOS

THE KIDS AT VCMS WERE bright, spunky, inquisitive, feisty at times, and supremely talented. I could not have asked for a better bunch. I was quite comfortable with the age group. They had benefitted from effective teaching in the lower grades, and I was the beneficiary of that. My former students and Bill's as well, all well prepared. There was something to be said for knowing where these kids had come from and what they had been previously taught.

During their years at VCMS these kids were challenged often and usually rose to the occasion with flying colors. Guest conductors like Dr. Moshe Paranov, co-founder of the Hartt School of Music, as well as Dr. Alan Gillespie, band director at the University of Connecticut, inspired my students during those years.

The VCMS bands performed at the Connecticut Music Educators Association (CMEA) annual conventions as well as at the Greater Hartford Arts Festival. Exchange concerts were still in vogue during those years, including a memorable concert with the Gideon Welles School band from Glastonbury. All of these activities would not have been possible without the support and encouragement of the school administration and staff.

At VCMS I loved the fact that the teachers were trusted enough to enter the school building on weekends to do extra work. I remember having a key to the outside door of the band room. The Vernon police had a direct link to the school's PA system and through that could hear sounds in the school. I would simply say, "This is Jim Kleiner, the band director, and I am inside the band room working right now." That is all I would have to do to prevent the police cars from pulling up to the building on a Saturday.

2

Included in the many memories of those days, the fruit sales had evolved into funding the Vernon Friends of Music Summer Musicals. I was fortunate enough to be the director and musical director three summers. We performed the musicals *Bye Bye Birdie*, *Flower Drum Song*, and *How to Succeed in Business Without Really Trying*. I was gratified and proud that so many of my middle school students joined students from RHS in these experiences. They took part in all aspects of those productions, from acting to stage crew to orchestra pit players. Talk about a worthwhile project for one month each summer! And, this was before the days of central air-conditioning. That was dedication!

I know I keep saying this, but my experience at VCMS was professionally a high point in my teaching career. I loved the band picnics, the faculty–student basketball games, and the student helpers in the music office volunteering to do just about anything to help me. And yes, folks, the main attraction was my wonderful personality . . . . Okay, maybe that is stretching things a bit.

To top it all off, at each spring concert, it was a tradition at VCMS for each band member to chip in fifty cents for the director's gift. It got to the point where they would call my wife and ask her, "What does he need?" I remember receiving gifts like a golf bag, binoculars, and an electric metronome. All were gratefully appreciated. But one gift stands out.

After the conclusion of the '79 spring concert, the band officers came out on stage with a thin, rectangular gift-wrapped package. I opened it to reveal two Connecticut license plates that had the letters "KLEINR." I was floored! One of the band parents had gone to the Department of Motor Vehicles and ordered the set of plates. At his request, my wife had pulled the registration out of my car, unbeknownst to me. Good thing I had not been pulled over by the police for any reason over those couple of days.

I carefully drove home, not wanting to break any traffic laws.

The plates were on the car the next day. I was still in awe of what the kids had given me. But there was good news and bad news. I loved the thought of my name on my car's plate. But the reality set in when I realized that as I was riding around town, I was hearing cars honking at me. I was no longer an anonymous traveler on the roads of Vernon. Oh well, such was the price of fame!

> *"To the world you may be just a teacher, but to your students you are a hero."*
>
> —UNKNOWN

21 -
RECOLLECTION VII – THE WILLETT CONNECTION

CHERYLL AND I GOT MARRIED after I graduated from Fredonia during the summer of 1970. She had graduated the year before me and had gone to the Indiana University of Pennsylvania for her master's degree in music education. Dr. Willett was the chairman of the Music Education department at that university and helped her get an assistantship.

In the fall of 1970, I was not sure what my next step would be. Would it be graduate school for me or trying to find a teaching position? But, as fate would have it, Dr. Willett took a position at the Hartt School of Music, part of the University of Hartford. Hartt was one of my choices for undergrad school years before. My first thought upon hearing the news about this man, with whom I had studied clarinet at Fredonia during my freshman year, was that Hartt would be a great place to pursue a master's degree and I would be back with one of my favorite teachers.

I placed a call to Dr. Willett; he encouraged me to apply. In the back of my mind, I harbored the thought that I might have the chance to once again study clarinet with him. When I broached the subject, he explained that he was not part of the Applied faculty, but he would inquire as to whether it would be possible for him to take me as a clarinet student.

A week later he called back and sounded quite excited. He told me that the graduate school was going to be offering a new degree that fall. It would be a master's degree in music education with a performance emphasis. And if accepted I would be the first grad student in the program. And on top of that, the school administration gave him permission to take me on as a clarinet student. I was really excited to hear that news. Of course, I had an entrance exam and audition to pass. First things first.

The exam was fairly routine, but the audition was not. I played for a small group of faculty that day. I did not know who these people were at first. It was better that way. Little did I know that I was playing for Don Mattran, conductor of the Hartt Wind Ensemble, Arnold Franchetti, distinguished composer in residence, and Dr. Moshe Paranov, head of the Hartt School.

After playing an étude and portions of solo literature, Mattran gave me the clarinet part to the Symphony for Band by Hindemith. This was my sight reading. I assured them I had never played this piece, although I had heard the work in performance in the past. Luckily my sight-reading skills saved the day.

I was accepted into the program and Cheryll and I got an apartment in East Hartford. She got a teaching job in Windsor and we settled in Connecticut. It was a position teaching junior high general music, a "tough gig." I give her a lot of credit for going through that challenge during her first year of teaching. In the meantime, I began my graduate studies in a new and challenging environment.

I found myself as the solo chair clarinet in the Hartt Wind Ensemble under Don Mattran. At the first rehearsal he introduced all the new students, and when he came to me he said, "Jim is a top-notch player!" And on top of that I was playing second clarinet in the orchestra under Dr. Paranov and Dr. Marijosius. I had a strong feeling I was in store for some great musical experiences.

Within a month of beginning my lessons with Dr. Willett, he signed me up to play for musicianship class. This class was held once per month in Millard Auditorium and the audience consisted of the entire school of students and faculty! Gulp! What was it I signed up for?

I played the Debussy Rhapsody by memory in front of the Hartt School. Dr. Paranov was off to the side of the stage to critique the performance afterwards. I was glad the piece was still in my head from months before at the Fredonia concerto program. My accompanist was wonderful and I got through the piece, but not everything was as good as I had hoped. Some of the runs were a bit sloppy. But

"Uncle Moshe," as the students lovingly referred to him, was kind. His comment that stood out to me was "That was Debussy's style; blurring the tonality was his goal." Whew! I had survived.

2

The experience that had the most profound effect on me was the visit to the Hartt campus by the distinguished American composer Aaron Copland. I had started to work on his Clarinet Concerto while at Fredonia. Copland was to conduct the Hartt performing groups as they performed some of his works. And Dr. Willett was going to perform the Clarinet Concerto of Copland with the composer conducting the Hartt Orchestra.

During our first couple of months of lessons, Dr. Willett was going down to New York City to work on the piece with Copland. My teacher could get my questions about the work directly answered from the composer himself. Ever since then my copy of the Concerto has contained the composer's suggestions.

Copland's week on campus finally arrived and I was so excited that he was going to conduct the Wind Ensemble in his piece entitle "Emblems." I was in awe at the first rehearsal sitting right next to the podium while he conducted us. At one point we took a fifteen-minute break. Copland came off the podium and came over to me. He proceeded to ask me about a passage in the clarinet part that was very high and a difficult spot for our section to navigate. He said, "Jim (he knew my name?), are these two lines manageable for you folks?"

"Yes, Dr. Copland, we can do this. We just have to work out the best fingerings, but it's not a problem," I replied.

"Okay, good," he answered with a big smile. Later I realized why he knew my name. It was because the day before I had brought in my copy of his book, *What to Listen for in Music*, and had asked him to autograph it for me. He had asked me my name at that time. He wrote in my book, "For James Kleiner, Aaron Copland 1971."

Our performance of "Emblems" went very well and the composer was pleased. The next day, during the final concert he conducted his

Clarinet Concerto. I was not playing in the orchestra for that since the accompaniment was for harp, piano, and strings. The concert was sold out and I did not have a ticket! I was distraught and called Dr. Willett. He told me, "Don't worry, Jim. Just meet me outside the outer stage door at 1:45 pm." I made sure I was there even a bit early and the door opened right on time. I did feel guilty about sneaking in to hear the performance. Especially being in cahoots with Dr. Willett!

I stood backstage for the performance and peeked through the curtain. The performance was superb and I was right there when Dr. Willett and Copland came off stage after thunderous applause. The scene I witnessed next, I would never forget. Copland was urging Dr. Willett to be the first to go back on stage for the curtain call. At the same time Dr. Willett was insisting that Copland go out first. It was tugging and pulling for a moment and then both men burst into laughter.

The composer won the good-natured tugging match and Dr. Willett finally went out first, followed by Copland. "Bravos" were cascading all through Millard. I had witnessed a deep, mutual respect that two wonderful musicians had for each other. And, what was even better was that these two men were music idols of mine.

3

The final hurdle to receiving my degree, aside from the six-hour comprehensive exam, was the recital. As part of the degree with the "Performance Emphasis" tag, I was required to play a full public recital in lieu of writing a thesis. I would receive 8 graduate credits for the recital preparation and performance. It would be judged by a three-person panel. I set up a practice regimen to get me through this. I would practice from 8 am until noon each day, prior to attending my afternoon and evening classes.

Dr. Willett suggested a program I really could "sink my teeth into." I grew to love this literature. Of course, it would include my signature work, the Debussy Rhapsody, along with the Sonatina by Clyde Duncan, the Sonata No. 2 for Clarinet and Piano by Brahms, and finally the Clarinet Concerto of Carl Neilson. I enjoyed the challenges presented by this music, especially the Neilson Concerto, which was eleven pages of black notes. Musicians out there know what I mean. It took me four months before I could play that piece from beginning to end without having to stop!

As the recital date approached, I found out that Dr. Wilheim, Hartt's notorious music history professor and taskmaster, was to be on my judge's panel. I had already been a student of Dr. Wilheim for his Baroque Music class, and he was tough as nails. He worked you hard, but you learned a lot. I was happy to learn that Henry Larson, one of Hartt's clarinet faculty, was also on the panel.

I was fortunate to have a great pianist as my accompanist, Clinton Adams. Adams had just recently performed the Brahms' Second Piano Concerto with the Portland, Maine, Symphony Orchestra. At our first rehearsal of the Brahms' Clarinet Sonata No. 2, I was really inspired by his playing. Adams admitted two things to me that day. The first was that the Brahms Sonata was one of his most favorite pieces of Brahms. The second was that the Sonata was more challenging for him to play than the Second Piano Concerto he had just performed! I was truly amazed at that.

In the end, all the preparation and rehearsal were worth it. The recital was a success. Afterwards, backstage I was nervous as I always was after the fact. Dr. Willett came backstage and had a big smile. He gave me the "thumbs up." "You're in, you made it! Doctor Wilheim actually applauded after one of your pieces."

The next day, in Dr. Wilheim's class, with his pronounced Austrian accent, he said to me in front of all the students, "Kleiner, you actually play quite well, but that Neilson is a terrible piece." Thinking back, I always felt that I believed Dr. Wilheim applauded for the Debussy. Just a hunch.

"Thanks for letting me learn from you."
—WRITTEN ON A PHOTO OF DR. WILLIAM WILLETT, GIVEN TO HIS STUDENT, JIM KLEINER

22 -
A "NO-BRAINER"

ROCKVILLE HIGH SCHOOL HAD BEEN blessed over the past few years with a wonderful band director in Ruth Ann King. She was a fellow clarinetist, an effective educator, and a great musician. She had been an early member of the exclusive club of female band directors around the country. I loved the way she taught—with a sense of purpose, expertise, and determination, sprinkled with a Midwestern sense of humor. Her students loved her style.

She had asked me to assist her with the RHS marching band during the '78–'79 football season and I was happy to do that. She had also asked me to solo on clarinet with the RHS wind ensemble during their spring concert. Ruth Ann had become a good friend. My wife and I even drove out to Indiana the previous summer to visit her and her family.

A definite highlight of that trip was hearing the Carmel, Indiana, high school band in rehearsal. Her brother was one of the band directors on the Carmel staff. As we approached the school and parked the car, I heard this impressive sound of a band playing the Finale from Tchaikovsky's 4th Symphony. They were absolutely nailing it. But instead of taking a left turn into the building and proceeding to what I assumed was the band room, we turned right, around the corner to the football field. There was the band standing in formation and playing the music by memory! My jaw dropped.

Was this high school band a typical Midwestern group? From all I could gather in later years, I came to realize that this was fairly typical. Music education in the Midwest was alive and well.

2

Another memory of my collaborations with Ruth Ann was the time she asked me to be a chaperone and guest conductor on her band's trip to Walt Disney World in Orlando, FL. We stayed in North Carolina during the first night of our bus trip. The high school parents in Fayetteville were really great in hosting our kids for the night. Before we headed on our way, we would be performing at the high school during an assembly the next morning. I was a bit skeptical about performing for the school. With the repertoire we were going to play, including Haydn Wood's *Mannin Veen*, which I was conducting, I was questioning in my mind whether we could keep a school-wide audience's attention for forty-five minutes.

We arrived at the school as the Rockville students were being delivered by their host parents after the overnight. There were plenty of relaxed and happy faces. I had a good feeling about that, which carried over into the assembly. The Fayetteville High School students filed into the auditorium in an orderly manner with virtually no sound. It seemed like they had assigned seats. Those kids sat silently through the entire program. That was impressive. I am sure this was a product of a tough administration, faculty, and a great group of parents.

The rest of the bus trip down to Florida was full of good feelings and satisfaction in knowing that we had performed well in front of an appreciative group of high schoolers.

Upon our arrival in Orlando, the band prepared for being a part of the Walt Disney World daily parade. What a thrilling experience that was! To march around that famous park in front of all those people was awesome, to say the least. The rest of the day was full of fun and awe, despite the light jackets we all had to wear due to the temperature being in the upper 50s.

The following day the band performed at an outdoor venue in Orlando.

Again, I had the chance to conduct my piece. I felt very comfortable in front of these impressive high school students, many of whom were my former students. I was secretly hoping I would get the opportunity to conduct the RHS band again someday. And it was satisfying to know that Ruth Ann had included me in making many of the decisions during the trip. Perhaps there was a reason for that?

3

In early July of that year, the music staff had a summer meeting. But prior to that I had received a phone call from Sam asking me to meet him at RHS a few days before the meeting. I wondered what this was all about, and of course I assumed the worst. Sam could be quite blunt at times, and I had already been reprimanded by him a few times over the years. I did not always agree with his critiques, but I tried to be respectful. I had a great admiration for what he had accomplished in his teaching career. After all, he was the old vet and I was the new guy on the block. I tried to learn from him.

After we sat down, he got straight to the point. He told me that Ruth Ann was leaving the RHS job to take a job down at Old Lyme High School, which was a Connecticut shoreline community. I was really surprised and immediately thought, *What a loss for Vernon*. And, in the next breath Sam said, "Jim, how would you like to take the RHS band job?"

I did not hesitate and said, "Of course, I would!"

So that was that. Sam would announce the job change at the impending meeting. I agreed not to say anything until then. I drove home with all kinds of thoughts going through my head, some joyful, some fearful. Was I up to the challenge? I came to the conclusion that I could do this job. The decision to go to RHS was a no-brainer.

In the midst of all this euphoria, I realized that I was leaving a teaching environment I loved being a part of. I was so comfortable being a part of VCMS. I so enjoyed my colleagues and students. On the other hand, as far as the students were concerned, I realized I would have another chance to be their teacher over the next couple of years. And the kids at RHS, I knew very well.

At the staff meeting, Ruth Ann thanked everyone and said her goodbyes. And there was more news. Bill was going to become the band director at VCMS. I could think of no one more qualified to do the job. The VCMS would be in good hands.

August was spent in preparation for the upcoming school year. I combed through the RHS music library for band, jazz concert band, the Wind Ensemble, the Jazz band, a chamber music class, and finally an electronic music course. My planning was going well on all fronts except the marching band. I was in somewhat of a panic mode over that group.

I had never planned and executed a halftime show on my own. But I did have the experience of being the marching band assistant for Ruth Ann during the previous year. The first football game was the third week of September. I knew this group's membership was of students who were doing this on a voluntary basis. They would have to rehearse after school and on Saturday mornings. The angst was there, but I was so enthusiastic about the rest of the job that nothing could stop my feeling of excitement for the upcoming school year. I could not wait for the first day of school.

23 -
A REALITY CHECK

IT IS SEPTEMBER 1979 AND I am sitting in the band office at RHS after a morning of teacher meetings. I had just received my class rosters. So many familiar names. I was settling into my new office nicely. The band room, which was built a few years before I had arrived, was part of a new addition to RHS. The facility was spacious with a few practice rooms and adequate instrument and music library storage areas. The band room back door opened out to a large outdoor area, which led to the football stands and field. *Well planned* was my thought.

I learned I was to be host to a student teacher. I was experienced at being a supervising teacher for students from the University of Connecticut as well as from the Hartt School, having hosted several of them over the years. It was hugely satisfying to help guide and mentor these future music educators. And to "seal the deal," I had received a call from Dr. Willett about the prospective candidate. His name was Peter Boonshaft. Dr. Willett had nothing but good things to say about this young gentleman. If Bill Willett felt that way about a student, then that was good enough for me.

I received a phone call from Peter that evening. He sounded so enthusiastic and had a great personality, which further convinced me he would fit in well at RHS. It would be a week before he would begin his tenure with us. I was glad he would be here soon. No harm in "jumping right in."

2

School day number one began for me with one of my weekly teacher duties. I had been assigned hall duty and cafeteria duty—I was not looking forward to either. Since I was a teacher of a "special," as any arts course was called during my career, duties were part of my daily regimen. Other teachers were assigned them as well, but I always felt we in the arts seemed to have them in abundance. Maybe it was just my imagination.

I monitored my first hall duty, which was particularly busy due to so many freshmen combing the hallways still learning the lay of the land. However, since I had the hallway between the school library and the music area, I was back in front of the band room in time for the concert band rehearsal. The band membership included mostly students I had recently taught at VCMS. What a nice reunion it was with these kids! I could not believe how much they had changed, even in a few months. That was something I always enjoyed, watching kids grow both physically, emotionally, and cognitively right before my eyes.

My electronic music class was next, a small class of nine kids, none of whom I knew from the past. Lots of long hair and seemingly aloof behavior. I felt their attitude as they walked into the room. They were saying as a group, "Okay, man, let's see if you can teach me something!" *Oh well, this is different*, I thought. *I have a class of kids who just needed to fill up their class schedule.* But the good news was that I would be taking them on a creative journey, and perhaps some of them might surprise me. We will see what happens.

Jazz band was next, but not until I had my planning period. I was glad I had this break at this point in the day, knowing that my morning coffee and breakfast would usually be catching up with me at this hour. One thing I had already learned about education was that bathroom breaks were not a scheduled occurrence. You had to watch what you ate and drank so as not to be in a bad way in the middle of class. At least I did. Leaving your students unsupervised was not an option. Glad I was still in my twenties!

I was excited to have this group of jazz-ers on a daily basis, and as I took attendance, I discovered the instrumentation of the group was almost complete, except for the lack of a bass player. Luckily there was a local church minister who was recommended by a student in the group. I called the gentleman and invited him to sit in with us.

His name was Tom Johnson. He agreed to help us out and ended up being an invaluable resource. He brought with him a few jazz band arrangements he had done. They were wonderful and we ended up using them. My favorite was and arrangement of the Earth, Wind & Fire classic, "After the Love Has Gone."

Lunch followed, and as much as I did not think I could scarf down food in twenty-two minutes, I knew I had to get to the lunch duty that followed. Chamber music class was next and I had a class of fifteen kids. My challenge was to find arrangements for heterogeneous groupings of instruments. I would also be an arranger, but I did have a course in orchestration during my college years, so the task did not seem that daunting. And now, last period was approaching where I would meet the Wind Ensemble, now as their director.

I don't know what I expected with this group that first day. A couple of kids smiled at me, but for the most part it seemed like the fact was they didn't even notice me. They chatted among themselves as I took attendance. As I started to speak to them, I suddenly got the strong impression they were not particularly excited to see me. I thought, *Come on, guys, remember me? I was the guy that had just conducted you and chaperoned you during your Florida trip last spring.* But the reality was it had been two or three years since they had seen me in front of their class as their teacher.

It dawned on me in an instant. Sure, they knew who I was, but they missed seeing Ruth Ann up in front of them. Sure, why wouldn't they? How could you not develop loyalty and affection for a teacher like her? I could not blame them. If I were them, I would have felt the same way. My feelings of disappointment morphed into realizing the reality.

In retrospect, those minutes in front of the wind ensemble on day one of the RHS job would benefit me for the rest of my career. What I did not realize at that moment was that I would be in this same position multiple times in my career. That day was a reality check and a blessing in disguise.

24 -
ASSIGNMENT: MARCHING BAND

THE SCHOOL YEAR GOT ROLLING and I became more accustomed to the physical and mental grind of being a high school band director. I was usually one of the last teachers to leave the parking lot after school each day, and that was saying a lot. I never met many teachers who would leave the school after the designated half hour we were required to stay after dismissal. But I was still one of the last! I quickly realized why I would be dozing on the couch at home at about 7 each evening. High school instrumental jobs were not for the faint of heart!

The first order of business was the marching band, and I found I was putting in countless hours planning the show, picking out music, and holding after-school rehearsals. The hours were mounting up quickly and frankly were getting in the way of the preparation for my five regular classes.

I was well aware of the fact that my stipend for marching band for the year was $375. I thought that was somewhat low, so I began to call some surrounding high schools' band directors to find out what their stipends and duties were. I began with my grad school buddy John Erskine over at Bloomfield High School. His stipend was $500. In addition, he received days off equivalent to the time he put in. John told me that his band only sat in the stands for home games. They also represented the town at the Hartford Memorial Day parade. Those facts showed a better stipend for less time and preparation. And complimentary time off to boot!

During the next few days, I made the rest of the phone calls and compiled the following list:

Ellington HS – Stipend of $700 for four parades, no football
Glastonbury HS – Stipend of $1,000 for five home games (playing in the stands) and 2 parades
South Windsor HS – Stipend of $1,300 for all home football games and one after-school weekly jazz band rehearsal
Enfield HS – Stipend of $1,000 for all home and away football games
Granby HS – Stipend of $1,000 for parades and other extracurricular musical activities. No football team.

It was too late for this year since the contracts were negotiated already and signed between the Vernon Education Association and the School Board. Oh well, I guess you live and learn. But at least I had some "ammo" for the next contract in two years. I figured I had done my homework.

2

I picked out some marching musical arrangements and devised a simple show, incorporating marching on the field and playing a few numbers in formation. This is what we worked on initially. The band itself would consist of about fifty players plus a flag squad. And the dance team would do routines on the sidelines to our music. We would provide pep music for the game from the stands.

Peter Boonshaft began his student teaching with us the following Monday. I found Peter to be a bright, enthusiastic guy who was full of ideas right off the bat. This kid was the "real deal." As we chatted over the next couple of days, I realized that he not only had skills in conducting but also, to my delight, had marching band skills.

"Mister Kleiner," he said, "since you have a somewhat limited rehearsal time, how about letting me design a show for you? We could add to the show each week, incorporating new music and moves each time. We can keep the rest of the show and add on as the weeks progress." The more I thought about what Peter was suggesting, the more I loved that concept.

So, away we went. Peter's job was to teach the show incrementally, beginning with a sideline formation with fanfare and building off of that. The show increased in length and became more polished each week. This strategy worked wonders for the band members' morale. The people in the stands loved it.

3

The date was October 3, 1979. We had ventured out on the football field for one of our after-school rehearsals. It was about 3:00 pm and we had been on the field for about twenty minutes when I noticed the sky to the northwest becoming ominously dark. And the clouds were definitely coming our way. It was one of those situations where you were trying to play weatherman while realizing that the rehearsal had a long way to go. Saturday's game was imminent. There were lots to refine before then.

I stalled as much as I could, and then Peter asked me, "What should we do? Stay or go?"

Just then there was a big clap of thunder. We had been hearing thunder in the distance, but this one was close. I had not seen lightning up until that point but was looking up to the sky when the heavens opened up.

We were about 100 yards from the band room backdoors, so we shepherded the band members under the football stands to avoid the instruments from getting soaked. The brass and percussion could have survived this downpour but not the woodwinds. We would be risking massive instrument repairs. We huddled under the stands, still getting wet to an extent with the wind increasing.

Suddenly a huge bolt of lightning struck nearby and there was a thunderous boom. My whole life passed in front of my eyes. Here were sixty souls standing under metal football stands in the midst of an electrical storm. I looked at Peter and yelled, "Let's go!" We all made a run for it across the grass and tarmac. As if by a miracle, the rain actually started to let up a bit so we could better see where we were going.

One of the custodians had already opened up the band room's double back doors. Most of the woodwind players had instinctively shielded their flutes, clarinets, and saxes as best they could. One young lady tripped, fell, scraped her knees, and needed attention with some tissues. But other than that mishap, we were safe! Thank the Lord.

Band parents were already arriving at the school to pick up their kids as Peter and I sat in the music office. We were in a slight state of shock and dripping wet. We got a bunch of paper towels from the custodian and wiped down all the instruments after telling the kids to leave them out of the cases. The enormity of what we had just been through was hitting both Peter and me. We were realizing the responsibility of supervising a group of young human beings. That responsibility was huge.

That evening, the lead story on the Connecticut news programs was about the tornado that touched down in Windsor Locks, about 15 miles from Vernon. *Holy cow*, I thought. *That could have been us!* This tornado, which was later found to be an F4, had damaged about a 15-mile stretch of commercial and residential buildings. There were three deaths, five hundred injured, and $442 million in damages.

As I lay in my bed that night, I imagined the worst. There could have been injuries or worse if that tornado had come over us out on that field. And it probably would have been the end of my teaching career.

25 -
STEPPING HIGH

I WAS PLEASANTLY SURPRISED AT how much I was enjoying the marching band. Peter's involvement definitely had an impact during that football season. Since I was a huge football fan myself, the game days were exciting to me on many levels. Rehearsals were lots of work and planning, but my students really contributed with their positive effort.

Unfortunately, two major impediments cropped up along the way. On the Saturday morning of the second home game, we all arrived at the back of the band room area which was secured by a large fence. The fence gates were locked most of the time on weekends and evenings. However, it was always open for the marching band's access when we needed it.

We had a two-hour block of time to polish up our show on the field before the football team took over for their warmups. We all had the added incentive that after our rehearsal we would have pizza delivered for our pre-show food. But, on this day, the fence was locked.

I had asked for a key in anticipation of this situation so as not to have to rely on a custodian inside the building to remember to come out and open up the gate prior to 9:00 am. But there was a general reluctance by the school administration to issue a key to a building entrance to staff members. Most of us no longer had that convenience. At this moment then we were locked out. There was no access to the building from any other entrance. There was no custodian in sight. My thoughts were *Perhaps, he had an emergency in the building and would be here momentarily*. No such luck.

At about 9:20, a father of one of the band members volunteered to make a few phone calls. After about another twenty minutes the custodian came out of the band room and opened the gate. He apologized and claimed he was not aware that he had to open the gate for us. He said he was filling in for someone else and didn't usually work on weekends. This was just the situation I was afraid of. And don't tell me that the football coaches didn't have a key to the building. Fat chance of that.

We therefore lost the first hour of our rehearsal. And it had to be the game against New Britain HS. The "Marching Hurricanes" were going to be here sharing the halftime show with us. NBHS had a reputation for having a top-notch marching band. But I had heard it was at the expense of the rest of their instrumental program.

The game progressed through the first half and we took the field to do our show. The crowd seemed to have a positive response to our evolving show. I was a bit apprehensive because we had lost half of our rehearsal time that morning. But, despite that, things went very well. The kids came through. I could see the faces in the stands and felt quite good about how the band sounded and looked. It was only fifty players, but what a sound!

As our last number was drawing to a close, I heard a huge wall of sound coming from the NBHS band who was lined up under the far goalposts. Instead of waiting until we were done with our show, they started their entrance routine and began to march on the field. We were being drowned out, and Peter and I were in disbelief. It was obvious this 120-piece band was "blowing us off the field."

As we exited, no one could hear our final notes. That was bad enough, but what had replaced our sound was a loud and out-of-tune sound that seemed to me like an elementary school band. Their sound seemed misplaced accompanying their impressive marching technique.

In the meantime, I was livid. My thoughts included *What did the people in the stands think of this band? Did they think the volume was impressive? Could they tell the musical difference between the two bands?*

As their show continued, Peter and I looked at each other and shook our heads. After the "Golden Hurricane" band exited the field, they immediately went to their buses and departed. It was a good thing they left quickly because I was planning on going over to their band director and giving him a piece of my mind. I felt like punching him in the nose! I actually felt sorry for his students. His band was all glitz and no substance. Anyone who knew anything about music knew this was the case. But did the average person in the stands realize this? I was convinced that many Vernon parents certainly knew the difference, based on the quality of the Vernon music program over the years, but did our superintendent of schools and school board?

2

We had a couple of weeks to plan and rehearse for home game number three. It was a game against one of the best high school football teams in the state, Bloomfield. I had been assured by the head of the custodial staff that we would not again experience being locked out of our room on a Saturday morning. This was good. He also said that because we were blurring the football lines as we rehearsed before the Saturday game, we were not to step on the lines. Wait . . . what? We can rehearse on the field only if we don't step on the lines? When I told that to Peter, he thought that was hysterical. A future meeting with the custodial head seemed to be inevitable.

The game at hand with Bloomfield turned out to be a rout for the visiting team. RHS could not beat the number one team in the state. About the only thing the Rockville fans had to cheer about was an ever-improving band halftime show. We even had inserted a humorous square dance routine in the show where the band members put down their instruments and sang and danced together. They had a ball doing that and the fans loved it.

After the game finished, the RHS "victory" bell started to ring. It was a large iron bell around the corner between the school and the parking lot. Rockville would go down and ring the bell after each victory. But they lost his game and the bell was ringing. It was obviously being rung by the Bloomfield team as they returned to their buses. The Rockville players immediately started to race around the corner to the bell. The coaches tried to stop the team but it was too late. I yelled to the band to "stay right where you are!" I did not want kids with instruments to get caught up in "God knows what."

I saw two policemen running around the corner as well and one looked like he was calling for backup on his radio. My task was to keep my kids away from any tussle. Later we found out that the coaches for both teams managed to defuse the situation. The Bloomfield team was quickly ushered onto their buses without incident. The incident could have been much worse if not for some quick-thinking and fast-running adults.

The anticipated meeting between Sam, the head of the custodial staff, and me came a few days later. I explained, "If you want the marching band to go on the field and do our show, we have to be able to use the lines as guides for our marching." The compromise was that we would be able to use the football team's practice field. They would make sure the lines were fresh and clear. I would have objected more to this if I had realized that the practice field was not manicured in the same way as the main field. The band kids were tripping at times over clumps of grass. And, the lines were not always clear. But we had no choice but to live with that. When it came to being on the football field, we were second-class citizens.

3

There was one home game left during the final three weeks of the season. In a weak moment, I agreed to have our band perform at an away game. I thought it might be interesting to see how the kids react to playing on foreign turf. It was at East Hartford, which was not a long bus ride.

The morning of the game it was raining steadily, so I decided we would not perform in the rain. We did not have rain ponchos for the uniforms and I did not want the instruments to get wet to any degree. The day's forecast was for a complete washout. I notified the "powers to be" that we would not be making the trip. I explained my concerns and everyone agreed, except for the dance team coach. I apologized to her and assured her we would do our best for them at the final home game.

The football season came to a close and we had the uniforms cleaned as we ventured towards the holiday concert in December. We had survived what I assumed would be the first of many football-show seasons to come.

26 -
THE WINTER CONCERT

HAVING SURVIVED THE MARCHING BAND season, I felt a huge load off my shoulders knowing that I could now devote my time to the regular RHS performing groups. I knew we had a couple of parade commitments coming up in the spring, but that seemed like a long way off. I was about to make a final selection of works for our December 17 concert.

In looking back at programs from the previous few years, I saw an emphasis on music on the lighter side. Holiday music was always featured. However, I had tended in the past to program some music that also had more musical significance. I never wanted to miss an opportunity to give my students a well-rounded experience of music of all genres.

As a result, I hoped to play music for everyone to enjoy, regardless of their preferences. My greatest influence in that regard was my mom. When I was in high school, she never missed a concert. She would inevitably say, "Make sure you play something peppy." I would always chuckle at that, but in the final analysis, she was right. Don't forget the "toe tappers" out there. Marches would always fit the bill in that regard. I don't ever remember programming a concert without including a march.

Peter was doing a really good job working with both bands. The first week he observed me running rehearsals with both groups. I got a kick out of Peter's comment after one rehearsal in which he asked, "How do you do that?" He was referring to the professional ambiance of our rehearsals. "Peter," I related, "those kids have been through the concert wars with me in the past. They know they will perform to their best capabilities if they work hard in rehearsals."

After watching these initial rehearsals, Peter was noting the band's strengths and weaknesses. I know this now in retrospect after many years of watching him conduct bands at every level. He chose an arrangement of "Elsa's Procession to the Cathedral" to work on with the Wind Ensemble. The kids really took to this piece. I was hearing them really put their heart and soul into this music. And Peter was inspiring them to do so every step of the way.

I was concerned that "Elsa" might not fit into the Winter Concert because the bands were already performing enough "heavy music." I told Peter this and his reaction was "Gee, that's a bummer." I felt bad seeing how disappointed he was, so I told him I would think about it.

A couple of days later my wind ensemble officers asked for a meeting with me after school. I was not sure I knew what they wanted to talk about. The meeting began with them talking about how much they loved playing "Elsa." They thought it should be included in the concert. I was so impressed at the way they made their case. They were calm and deliberate in their argument. The way they described how the music "stirred their souls" won me over. "Okay, gang, you have convinced me. Let's add the piece to the concert," I said. They left the meeting all excited, and the next morning when I told Peter what they had done and what my decision was, he was elated. "Let me buy you a coffee!" he exclaimed as we walked down to the cafeteria.

Peter was totally immersed in our program, and I loved seeing that. The tables seemed now to be turned. I was the one observing his rehearsals with the wind ensemble. And I was taking mental notes about the things he was doing. I had made it a habit over the years of watching other conductors work and picking out the things I liked and disliked. And in Peter's case, I had him in my own rehearsal room every day to enjoy. Could a supervising teacher learn from a student teacher? Of course!

Rehearsals in the auditorium took getting used to again. It had been four years since I had a band perform in that echo chamber. But

I knew from past experience that the audience would soak up some of the echo. The acoustics didn't seem to bother Peter. He just "went with the flow" as I was doing.

The big night arrived and the auditorium was full. All the performing groups were outstanding. And guess what piece was the hit of the concert? That's right, "Elsa's Procession to the Cathedral." Peter's rendition with my students received a standing ovation. I had goosebumps. What a treat to have a student teacher like this in our midst! And thanks to Bill Willett for steering him towards RHS.

The concert had concluded with the wind ensemble and chorus performing the "Hallelujah Chorus" from Handel's *Messiah*. There was a distinctive glow around the music department for days afterwards. As we adjourned for the school holiday vacation, I knew Peter would be back in January to guest-conduct our jazz ensemble.

What could we play in the spring to top this performance? Well, plans were in the works.

27 - EXCITING PLANS TAKE SHAPE

WE WERE ALL SORRY TO see Peter leave us. However, we all knew he was on to bigger and better things. I finalized a "plan of attack" for the RHS program during the winter and spring months. I had a pretty good handle of what level of music the bands could handle. I had in the back of my mind a few pieces we might try, including the "Symphony for Band" by Vincent Persichetti. I was familiar with that work from my days at Fredonia.

The piece was definitely a college-level work, but I loved giving my students one real challenging piece on every concert. I thought I would focus on the first movement. There would be so much to learn tackling that music. But I had confidence this group could do it.

The idea of taking part in an adjudication festival in the spring was ever present since the beginning of the school year. I scoured the festival list, focusing on the Eastern seaboard. I found the Six Flags Festival for bands based out of New Jersey. I thought this event would be perfect. I signed up for the wind ensemble and sent in the entrance fee from our band fund. I knew we had some fundraising in our future.

With the help of the Friends of Music, who committed funds for us from the fruit sale, we took on another fundraiser and sold beach towels with "RHS Band" printed on them. Another idea surfaced that we could have a "play-a-thon." The band officers took the lead with this. They acquired a venue and we set a date.

It was scheduled to take place from 7:00 pm on March 8 and would conclude at 11:00 am on March 9. We separated the band into three groups, with two playing together for an hour while the third group would rest. I had recruited Bill and my friend George Sanders, trombonist with the Hartford Symphony, to help me handle the conducting duties. I brought a supply of music for us to use, hoping it would be enough.

During the sixteen hours, I was amazed at everyone's stamina, including my own. The students worked hard for the hourly donations they were being given by friends and family. Food was donated by a local pizzeria as well as by parents. We all tired physically as well as mentally over the course of the time, but that did not matter. We made it through the night and the next morning. It was such a bonding experience for the band members—one we would not soon forget.

We raised a few thousand dollars, including a few generous donations from local businesses. The people of Vernon really came through for us. We had money for our trip. It was on to Six Flags!

28 -
A PARALLEL UNIVERSE

WHAT EXCITING TIMES AT RHS during the first half of the '79–'80 school year! Fundraising, concert and parade planning, and the impending adjudication trip to New Jersey. All keeping us busy and motivated. And on top of that, I had two enthusiastic student teachers from the University of Connecticut. Cathy and Joanne arrived in January.

They took one look at the music office on their first day and encouraged me to go down to the cafeteria for my lunch duty a bit early. I thought this was odd, but I went along with their request, stopping off to get a cup of java on the way. When I returned about an hour later, I had trouble recognizing my office. It no longer looked like a tornado had blown through. Instead, it was neat and organized. You could actually see what the top of my desk looked like. I was an organized band director again thanks to my UCONN student teachers!

However, behind the scenes it was a different story. I was dealing with the fight to convince the administration to bring the band director stipend up to be more in line with other area high schools. Based on the information I had gleaned from the local high school band directors, I drafted a letter and sent it to the chairman of the Vernon Education Association negotiating team. In the letter I made my case about the number of hours in preparation, rehearsals, game day commitments, and other activities such as parades.

I also mentioned in the letter that our new superintendent of schools, Dr. Sidman, had made it clear to other staff and parents that he wanted RHS to be the number one marching band in the state. The Massachusetts school system he had previously headed up was well known for its high school marching band. Initially, I thought that his influence could be a positive for our marching program and the stipend as well. I was sure he would understand what it takes to have a solid marching program. But as it turned out, I was wrong.

I sent the letter in early January. Later that month I met with our principal to review what the formal grievance procedure was in case I needed to go down that route. In February I met with the VEA president, Pat Brown, and laid out my concerns to him. He was familiar with my letter to the negotiating team. Pat was in agreement with my concerns. "We have to get Vernon's marching band stipend up to the level where it belongs." My spirits were buoyed by that statement. The final step was to meet with Dr. Sidman.

We met in early March. He and I exchanged pleasantries, and he asked me how the plans were going for the concert adjudication trip. I brought him up to date on how things were going. He seemed to enjoy my excitement. Then, our discussion turned to the marching band.

"Why isn't the marching band a larger group?" he inquired. I honestly don't think he realized that the marching band was a voluntary group that met after school. I thought to myself, *Sure, if all we did in the fall was marching band, we could have all the kids in the band and rehearse during the school day.* I knew that but did not want to share that with him. This would go against the long-time philosophy of the Rockville High School band program.

Although, I did tell him about the volunteer status of the marching band. I added, "We have an extensive concert program in both the fall and spring. Marching is one facet of the overall program. I have two concert bands, jazz ensemble, chamber music, and electronic music classes each day."

"That is quite a schedule, Jim," he remarked.

I reminded him, "And on top of that, the marching band is quite a time commitment both in the planning and rehearsals during the fall months." I thought I was making a good case for a stipend increase.

"Well," he intoned, "I am informing you that next fall your

marching band will be playing at both the home and away games."

"So I assume the stipend will be raised for doing all the football games?"

"No," he uttered. The conversation paused momentarily and then he followed with some words I absolutely did not expect. As he suddenly pointed his finger at the door, he said, "And if you don't like it, THERE'S THE DOOR."

My heart sank as I was shocked to hear him say those words. His words echoed around my brain. The reality of that statement hit me like a ton of bricks. I gathered myself and left his office, not saying a word.

On my way home, I literally shook. My thoughts were *This administrator really does not have a clue about the history and tradition of the RHS music program.* Countless honors, concert performances on state and national levels. Undeniably one of the top high school music programs in Connecticut. "Now the emphasis is going to be steered towards marching?" I could not stop thinking. I knew in my gut that this was not what I had signed up for while taking this job.

I had to calm down and assess this situation. The last thing I wanted was to let on about what had happened in the meeting. I kept a lid on things. I had a potentially great spring coming up. This incident was not going to spoil that.

"It seems such a waste of time, If that's what its all about. Mama, if that's movin' up then I'm movin' out"

—Lyrics for the song "Movin' Out" Billy Joel

29 -
PONDERING THE FUTURE

MARCH CONTINUED WITH THE ST. Patrick's Day parade in Hartford. The day of the parade was a typical March day—windy! I didn't think much of that, although I remember one of our fall football games in which our flag squad really experienced a tough afternoon. The flags were acting more like sails and those kids were really pooped when the halftime show was over. They had fought their flags so as not to be launched into the air!

The parade turned out to be a nightmare. The wind was howling up and down the Hartford streets. Students carrying the larger instruments were feeling the effects of the wind. As the band was turning a corner onto Main Street during the final moments of the march, all of a sudden the percussion section's "street beat" ceased to exist. It took me a few seconds to realize that all I was hearing was the band members' footsteps on the pavement. The sound of the percussion section had vanished. I turned around to see the entire drum line on the right side of the street. Both bass drummers were on their knees, but they kept control of their drums. They had been blown by a large wind gust off the parade route as their drums caught the wind. I motioned to our drum major to halt the band.

This was one of those moments when I realized how focused the kids were. The drum line quickly composed themselves and took their places back in line as if nothing had occurred. The flag carriers did the same. We even got a round of applause from the crowd! What a group. We continued on the parade route none the worse for wear.

2

The next week after school, one day my office phone rang. It was John Erskine, the music supervisor from the Bloomfield public schools. He just wanted to let me know that he had a job opening in his department. The junior high band job had opened up. "Jim," he said, "if you know of anyone who might be interested in that job, let me know."

I did not hesitate with my reply. "John, I know someone who is interested in that job—me." There was silence on the other end for a moment. I continued, "Tell me what the position entails."

John sort of stuttered a bit, "The position is split between the junior high and middle schools. It would involve having a band at each school plus teaching pull-out lessons."

My reply was "John, I am very interested in that position."

John paused for another moment and then said, "Jim, I have about ten resumes on my desk right now. If you can get yours over here in the next couple of days, I will put all of these aside and yours will go to the top of the heap."

I was thrilled at John's reaction. I had always admired him as an educator. His program in Bloomfield, including his Bloomfield High School band, of which he was the director, in my opinion was one of the top five programs in the state, along with Rockville. John and I had done our master's degree program together at the Hartt School. I had known him for several years. I had heard his band in the past when they had performed at CMEA conferences. They were amazing.

Two days later I made an appointment to meet with him at the Bloomfield Board of Education office. It was great to see him. He gave me more background on both schools. I handed him my resume and he told me he wanted to come to RHS and observe a band rehearsal within the next couple of weeks. It seemed like things were happening so quickly.

Joanne and Cathy were such a huge help in keeping me on task during those unsettled times. They were a huge help with all kinds of things. They certainly made my life easier. I gave them ample opportunities to gain experience by having them work with my ensemble and other classes. They were doing great, and the kids liked them. Don't think I wasn't fortunate to have such a quality of student teachers this school year. In fact, I had been so fortunate at VCMS as well with a bevy of wonderful future teachers from Hartt School and UCONN.

3

John showed up at RHS for an April 17 morning rehearsal. He sat quietly as I rehearsed the Wind Ensemble and I could see his face break into a smile on a couple of occasions. That gave me great hope. I knew that John and I were musically on the same page. Afterwards he and I went down to the cafeteria for coffee while Joanne and Cathy ran the concert band rehearsal.

We sat down with our cups of java and John looked at me and said, "Jim, the job is yours if you want it."

I answered breathlessly, "Yes, John, I do want it. I like everything about it." It was a done deal.

We ended our discussion comparing notes on our upcoming trips. John was going to a band festival down South next year with his high school band. "You want to go with us?" he asked.

My reply was "Sure, I am there!"

The die was cast. With a handshake I committed to take the Bloomfield position starting in the fall. I had given it much thought and had many discussions with Cheryll about this move. The decision was not an easy one. I had been grappling with the notion that if I left the Vernon position, I would be missing out on future years with these students for whom I had such love and respect. But I could see what was coming down the road. The writing was on the wall. More marching band and less of everything else. To be honest with myself, I did not feel that I had the background or the motivation to get involved with that kind of program. I was not cut out for that. I am sure they could find someone who was. If I could continue to be a part of another music program of high quality, why would I not want that?

I had to now put aside these future plans for the near future. I was excited for this new opportunity, but I also knew I had in front of me at RHS what was potentially the most exciting couple of months of my career.

> *"A bend in the road is not the end of the road unless you fail to make the curve."*
>
> —HELEN KELLER

30 -
THE TRIP, BEFORE AND AFTER

ONE OF THOSE EVENTS I was so excited about was having my students perform at various functions around Connecticut. Both the percussion ensemble and flute quartet would be performing at the CMEA conference at UCONN. RHS also had students from the wind ensemble and chorus participating in the All-State Festival, which meant I had to be at the CMEA conference for three days. The conference and All-State were always held in conjunction with each other. The students' teachers had to be there with them. Watching them in the All-State ensemble was a treat for me.

The RHS wind ensemble spring concert was scheduled for Sykes Auditorium on Tuesday, May 6. The concert band would be performing on May 27 after the wind ensemble returned from their trip. The first half of the May 6 concert would feature the three selections we were going to play at the Adjudication Festival at New Jersey's Glassboro State University. The second half of the concert featured my talented tympanist, Brian Prechtl, along with a brass sextet in the "March for Timpani and Brass" by David Heisinger. Then we would have our great set drummer, Brian Wind, play the "Concerto for Drum Set" by Carroll DeCamp. We would then close the concert with "Mars" from *The Planets* by Gustav Holst.

I remember the performances at that concert like it was yesterday. And, the acoustics in Sykes Auditorium enhanced everything. We gave out the band awards and went home to get some well-needed rest before we left for Six Flags two days later.

2

The morning of the trip I was pleasantly surprised that Dr. Sidman and Sam met us as we loaded the buses. I thanked them for doing that, knowing that several weeks ago, Dr. Sidman and I had a not so particularly good conversation. Did Sam find out about that meeting and perhaps was trying to smooth things over between us? However, I quickly forgot about all of that as we boarded the buses and began the trip. Everyone was so excited, including our chaperones, who included Cheryll, my brother and sister-in-law, and a few sets of parents.

To sum up this experience with my students, I would say that all the preparation, rehearsing and logistics for this major trip were absolutely worth it. Things really could not have gone any better.

Musically, the wind ensemble played with expertise and acted classy the entire time. The only glitch was at Six Flags, where I had to hide from my students so they wouldn't drag me on to one of the monster roller coasters. Coasters were not my thing. The kids did manage to take a collection and buy a monogrammed wine glass with my last name inscribed on the glass. They presented it to me after we got back to the school. I was quite touched by their thoughtfulness.

On the Friday of the trip the judges gave us an "Excellent" rating for our performance at the college. On Saturday we performed at a noon concert in Philadelphia at the park where the Liberty Bell resides. We had a nice lunchtime crowd, and it was a beautiful spring day. Afterwards we did the "tourist thing" and toured Philly. All of us slept well that night for sure.

On the way back to Connecticut we had a stop in New York City planned. I had been looking forward to seeing the new musical by Stephen Sondheim, *Sweeney Todd*. We were able to get orchestra seats for the Sunday matinee performance. George Hearn and Dorothy Louden were in the lead roles. From the moment of the first downbeat until the last note, I was enthralled with the production. The show began with a screaming factory whistle which scared the living daylights out of all of us. Two and a half hours later, the show ended with the ghost of Sweeney exiting through a door at the back of the stage and slamming it on the final note.

After that jolt, I felt as though I needed assistance in getting up and leaving the theater. I had never had that kind of a visceral reaction after the end of a show. The range of emotions I had after hearing all of that music was unusual. I became a Stephen Sondheim devotee from that day on.

3

Back at RHS I had other things on my mind. I took a personal day and went over to Bloomfield on Friday of that next week. I signed a contract to begin teaching in the Bloomfield public schools starting in September. I still did not want to make my plans public until after the band concert. The Concert band did so well in that performance. I was so proud of them, since, because of our recent history, I felt we had a special bond.

The day after the concert, I met with Sam and Eileen, the RHS choral director, and told them of my plans. Eileen was incredulous as to why I would want to leave. I came up with the fact that John and I had gone to Hartt together and were good friends. Sam seemed to be quite disappointed by the news of my leaving. He and I took a walk around the hallways of RHS during which he did his best to try to talk me out of my decision. I thanked him for his support and trust in me over the years. He knew of the Bloomfield instrumental music program and I sensed that he understood why I wanted to join the staff there.

I drafted a letter to the school board with a copy to Brian McCartney, the RHS principal, and delivered it to the board office on Monday afternoon, June 9. Now my task was to tell my students I was not looking forward to this in any way, shape, or form.

31 - TOUGH DAY

I DID NOT SLEEP WELL. The wind ensemble would be coming in period 2 and the concert band, period 4. I told the wind ensemble not to get out their instruments. Instead, we would be chatting about all the highlights throughout the past year. The kids had anticipated the rehearsal being on the graduation music, but I assured them we would have ample time for that.

I went through the year with them with as much of a positive tone as I could. I thanked them for many things, including the great way they comported themselves on our recent trip. I made sure to have them thank their parents for all their support this year. There were some funny comments about how I was hiding from them at Six Flags. We went back and forth about that, which relaxed all of us.

I noticed there were fifteen minutes left in the period. I thought I had better begin. "Ladies and gentlemen, I thought you should be the first people to hear this. I will not be returning to RHS as its band director next year. I will be taking a job in the town of Bloomfield as their middle school and junior high school band director."

There was dead silence and many jaws dropped in unison. "I want you folks to know that this was a professional decision on my part and has nothing to do with anything you have done. I am going to miss you folks and will never forget you." I started to choke up a bit. "Just relax for a few minutes and you can leave when the bell rings."

I headed to the music office. The silence was deafening. I was touched by their response. I tried to compose myself for a few moments and went out into the room again. I had forgotten to thank the seniors specifically for their support. "Seniors, thank you for being the backbone of this group all year. You did a terrific job in that regard. I, as well as the underclassmen, will miss you." I had said those words at the spring concert but wanted to emphasize that again. The seniors had been a remarkable bunch of musicians and people.

The bell rang. "See you folks tomorrow. We will be reading the graduation music," I said. They filed out and I had another chance to compose myself. The electronic music class came in and I gave them time to fine-tune their term projects. Before I knew it, it was period 4 and the concert band came into the room.

There was a murmur going on and I knew why. The word had gotten out. I could tell by the faces which kids had heard. "No instruments, folks; sit anywhere you like," I announced. Then the whispers started, so I began. I went through the same scenario as I had in the wind ensemble. The years' highlights, the thanks, and finally my news.

I should have anticipated a different response from these freshmen and sophomores. After all, I had been their teacher for most, if not all, of the past few years. Their reaction was different. I heard audible sounds of shock as I was telling them of my plans. As I did before, I told them to relax and chill until the end of the period. "We will sight read some new music tomorrow," I assured them. Time passed and then the bell rang. But not everyone left. And the dams burst.

Donna, our band president, came up to me, already in tears, threw her arms around me, and hugged me tight. She was such a sweet kid, and I was quite touched by her sincere reaction. I hugged her back and felt my own tears well up. I had started her on the flute when she was a fifth grader. We went back a long way.

I must have hugged about ten of them and not only the ladies. Some guys too. Fortunately, I had a free period next, so I had time to recover from that outpouring of emotion. I remember sitting in my office thinking, *I hope I never have to go through that again in my career*. Little did I know this would not be the last time by any means.

"To teach is to touch a life forever."
—UNKNOWN

32 -
A SMOOTH LANDING

THE VERNON FRIENDS OF MUSIC hosted a luncheon in my honor shortly after the RHS graduation. They presented my wife and me with a lovely mirror and a set of matching sconces, which hang in our home's entryway to this day. The timing could not have been better for our plans to drive cross-country for our tenth anniversary. It was a great way for both of us to get our minds off of school for a while.

We hitched up our VW Rabbit with our tent trailer rental and headed west. Out I-70 and six weeks later back east on I-80. Stops along the way included Denver, Las Vegas, the Grand Canyon, Yellowstone, the Devil's Tower (had to visit this landmark due to my being a movie devotee of Spielberg's *Close Encounters of the Third Kind*), and ultimately Los Angeles, San Francisco, and San Diego. We visited several friends and relatives along the way.

During this trip I "parachuted" back to reality. I landed on my feet! Nine years in Vernon had been a great learning experience for me. But I now found myself in another great musical environment. I would be working with John, whom I had always admired as an educator.

On August 28 was the Bloomfield "new teachers" meeting. In my case, however, new only to the school system. There were several first-year teachers among us that day, and you could see the nervous anticipation in their eyes. That reminded me of myself back in 1971 at that first Vernon faculty meeting. I knew what these new educators were thinking. This meeting was followed by the district and school meetings prior to the September 3 first day of school.

My new position felt like a bit of déjà vu. Bloomfield Middle School consisted of grades 6 and 7. My responsibility there was the Advanced band. This would be interesting since I had never taught sixth graders before. The Junior High band included eighth and ninth graders. Nothing new for me there. I would be teaching homogeneous (like instrument) lessons for these students as well. John actually set up my schedule so that during the three days I was at that school, I would have two planning periods per day. He knew from first-hand experience how much planning and preparation a band director went through. The extra planning time was a nice gift, especially during the times of the year when there were parade commitments for the junior high.

At the music department staff meetings, I was quite impressed with the experience of the music staff. They had obvious expertise I could tap into. I was in great company once again. At these meetings I found out about the high school band's planned trip to the Shenandoah Valley Band Festival in Virginia, which would be coming up in the spring. John invited all of us to help him with the fundraising and logistics and in return we could be trip chaperones. That sounded exciting. There was plenty to look forward to for 1980–81!

33 -
THE JOKE OF THE DAY

BLOOMFIELD JUNIOR HIGH PRINCIPAL MR. O'Hara was a tough Irishman who was a "no-nonsense" guy. He had to be strict in dealing with a very diverse school population. Many ethnic backgrounds, including a group of upper-class Caucasian kids from the Bloomfield Hills area. One day I overheard one of my horn players brag that he had eleven television sets in his house. Perhaps he was exaggerating a bit?

I had become aware before the first day of school that the decorum of the eighth–ninth grade band at the junior high during the past few years had left quite a bit to be desired. I suspect that John felt that situation by having some problems with his tenth graders during that time. I was determined to run a tight ship right from day one. I knew some of them were looking forward to pushing my buttons. I had my work cut out for me.

I told my band members what I expected at our first meeting. I could see some of them smile immediately. Of course, only the ninth graders had been in this band last year, so when some of them reacted, I got the impression they were glad to have some law and order. And yet there were those whose brains were in high gear already. I am sure they were thinking *We are going to make this guy's life miserable until he gives up and lets us do our thing*. But little did they know who they were up against.

The band had about seventy members and featured an instrumentation that covered all the bases in terms of instrumentation. The group even included a bassoon, which was a first for me. And I loved the fact that I had eight French horns! I liked the balanced sound of the group from day one. Thoughts of literature we might be able to play began circulating around in my head.

During that first rehearsal, out of the blue, one of my trombone players stood up to announce his "joke of the day." That threw me, but many others seemed to acknowledge that this had been a daily tradition from last year. Some students smiled, some rolled their eyes, and some did not know what to make of this. I decided to see where this would go. The kid went with a knock-knock joke, and fortunately it was harmless. Many chuckled, including me.

After band I spoke to the young man and told him I did not mind the tradition, but in the future this would be a joke of the week instead. He bought into that because I think he expected I was going to tell him he could not do this at all. I did tell him that the jokes must be clean or they would stop.

The "button pushing" began after a few rehearsals. Initially a few of our Bloomfield Hills kids were the disrupters. The kids in question seemed to be exhibiting the personality traits of self-centeredness and arrogance arising out of the late '70s. I learned later on in my career that in most cases these kids had been enabled by their parents from their early years. They had been called "spoiled" back in the '50 s and '60s. I had not seen much of this in Vernon, which is a tribute to the Vernon parents.

I guess it was not surprising that I began to get some flak from the parents of these instigators. I realized this when John and I went out for a beer after school one day and he brought up the subject of a parent who was concerned that I was being too hard on his son. John wanted to give me a heads up. I told him how this kid was a constant distraction during rehearsals. John said he would talk to his father, who was a prominent person in town. My thought was *This is what administrators do—run interference for their staff.* And John did just that. And as it turned out, this kid really settled down after those first couple of months. That had a positive effect on others in the band as well. Thanks, John!

34 -
TEACH AND LEARN

TEACHING IN BLOOMFIELD WAS PROVING to be professionally stimulating for me. Here was an opportunity to learn from a new set of teaching colleagues. They brought with them all sorts of educational knowledge. My principal at the Bloomfield Middle School was one such person. His name was Carmen Arace, and it was obvious he was well respected by his staff. He was the type of administrator who would make me smarter and more educationally informed each time I chatted with him. I thought, *Wow, another VCMS!*

BMS was an incredible learning environment for its students. No wonder the town of Bloomfield had been named a national "All American City" a few years earlier. I know the school system had a part in that.

The lessons in this building were going great. The Advanced band, consisting of sixth and seventh graders, was my responsibility. There was so much enthusiasm amongst this diverse group of students. And, I knew I would have these kids as students for the next two or three years.

On the other hand, the band at the junior high had its good and bad days. There was still an element of unrest at times amongst a certain number of kids. And yet I was sensing that even those kids were beginning to come around to my way of doing things.

A seminal moment in my relationship with that band happened unexpectedly during a November rehearsal. I was relating to them a story about a band experience I had in high school. I was trying to make an example of one of my fellow clarinet players. In the course of my story I said, "This kid pulled a boner and I knew the band director noticed it."

Now to put this in context, "pulling a boner" was a common phrase in the world I grew up. It meant you made a big mistake. But no, not in Bloomfield in 1980! That phrase had a sexual connotation I was not used to. As soon as I got those words out of my mouth the band instantly erupted into delirious, roaring laughter. It actually scared me for a moment. I quickly realized that what was going through my brain was vastly different from what was going through theirs. This was another "instant learning" moment for me. *How do I get out of this moment?* I thought. *Okay, I will go with it.*

I immediately clamped my hand over my mouth and acted like I was totally embarrassed. The kids loved this reaction and laughed some more. This was the closest I ever felt to being a Shakespearian actor. I proceeded into my best British accent, "Ladies and gentlemen, I am totally mortified." They laughed again. I had them! They had awarded me a moment where I could show them that I was a real human being.

It was another example I had experienced in my career where I found out how much humor can work to my advantage with my students. They had accepted me as a flawed human who could laugh at himself. I had achieved that ambiance with the kids in Vernon and now I had it in Bloomfield. This was priceless.

From that day on I felt we were both more relaxed with each other. And in only three months! We ended up having successful concerts with both bands at our winter concerts in January. They did not play holiday concerts in Bloomfield due to the wide variety of religious backgrounds in town. Now our attention was focused on the high school band trip.

Fundraisers had been going on since the beginning of the school year. I had not been involved in any of them until the hike-a-thon held in February. I thought that month might be a bit dicey in terms of weather but volunteered to help. The high school band members each took pledges, and that money would contribute to their own trip fees.

The day of the event was surreal. It was an "Indian summer" February day and the forecast was for a high of 70 degrees. We gathered at Penwood Park and proceeded on a 10-mile hike. I remember I was first struck by the weird sight of having no leaves on the trees while feeling the air temperature of a spring day. At least none of us had to wear winter clothes. But wearing shorts during February felt strange.

The walk was fun, if not a bit taxing for those of us who weren't teenagers. It was really a great opportunity to chat with many of the high school kids and to get to know them prior to being a chaperone on their trip. The road we walked on for the entire length caused my hips to feel exhausted due to the pitch of the road. I never thought about walking equally on each side of the road. Needless to say, I slept well that night.

35 -
MARCHING INTO THE ELEMENTS

THERE WERE A COUPLE OF marching commitments for the junior high band that spring. The first was the St. Patrick's Day parade in Hartford. Having marched in that parade with the RHS band the year before, I knew that time of year was not optimal for kids to be outdoors playing their instruments. You never knew what kind of conditions you were going to be facing. The memories of the previous year's parade with the RHS marching band were still fresh.

Nonetheless, we were preparing the Bloomfield JHS band for marching. It was unusually cold during the week leading up to the parade date. In fact, the forecast for the day of the parade was a high of 35 degrees with a wind chill at around 20. I went in to see principal O'Hara thinking I might be able to make the case that perhaps it might be too cold for the kids to be playing their instruments that day. I cautioned him about mouthpieces frozen on lips, frozen brass valves and slides, and nonfunctioning reeds.

My argument fell on deaf ears. "You are going to represent the school and the town of Bloomfield tomorrow in Hartford," insisted O'Hara. I left his office hoping it would snow, but no such luck!

We marched and the conditions were brutal. Even worse than the year before. However, we weren't the only band out there. It was so frigid, there were less people watching along the parade route than I could ever remember. We did play as much as usual since I did not have a surgeon marching along with us to pry skin off brass mouthpieces. The only casualty, besides some frozen human beings, was a plastic clarinet. Due to the temperature the cork on the middle joint failed and the lower half of the instrument plunged to the pavement. Several keys were bent and the bell joint broke into two pieces. Other than that, we survived and I was proud of the kids. I did not hear any complaints along the way.

Perhaps our principal knew the band members better than I did. I guess I give him credit for that. He and the people in town were happy and proud. What their young musicians had done was above and beyond the call of duty!

36 - ANOTHER ROLLER-COASTER RIDE

I WAS FREQUENTLY MAKING MENTAL notes about every aspect of John's spring trip. He hired a consultant to organize most aspects, from fundraising, to travel, to logistics. The Shenandoah Festival was held in conjunction with the Shenandoah University in Virginia. Participation included a concert adjudication as well as a parade. Aside from the preparation, there was a ton of equipment and instruments for them to bring along, not to mention the chaperones and students.

I watched the organizational details from afar and learned much about organizing a trip. I was gratified to observe that I had done most of the same things the year before with the RHS trip to New Jersey. In fact, John had picked my brain about that trip. He was looking to learn from my experience as well.

The trip ran like clockwork. The rules for the kids were laid out in detail ahead of time so that everyone would know what to expect. For instance, one of John's key rules was that students were to stay in their hotel rooms after curfew—no exceptions. I felt that was an effective way to avoid all sorts of problems. Our job as chaperones was to monitor and enforce the trip rules.

On the first overnight, one of the band members was found in his girlfriend's room. The curfew rule kicked in immediately. John called the kid's parents the next morning. He told them that their son was being put on a plane with one of the chaperones and would be arriving back at Bradley (Hartford/Springfield) Airport that afternoon. *Wow*, I thought. But that was the rule. The kid learned a life lesson. Rules are rules, especially on this kind of trip.

The band performed up to the high standards one expected from one of John's groups. The parade was tons of fun too. The townspeople in that college town were enthusiastic in supporting all of these school bands. It was their town tradition each year. And, the festival was a significant recruiting tool for the university. It was obvious that the townspeople were proud of their school and annual festival.

2

We all returned from the trip on a real "high." I was feeling really good about being in this town with this music program. The junior high band could be a struggle at times, but things were certainly improving, and as a result the level of music-making was on the rise.

One weekend as I was perusing the *Hartford Courant*, I read an article about how Bloomfield was considering closing one of their elementary schools. Since I did not teach at that level, I did not really pay much attention to that. However, the next week the Town Council voted to close the Metacomet Elementary School at the end of the school year. My first thought was *What happens to the faculty of that school after it closes?* It wasn't until mid-April that I found out.

The Bloomfield teacher's contract specified that in case of a school closing, there would be a "reduction in force." A RIF, as it was commonly called, would provide a vehicle for the closing school's teachers to retain their jobs. Which jobs would they be assigned? Good question. I found out through the faculty grapevine that an RIF would cause one person from each department to be laid off to make room for the displaced staff. The last person hired would be the first to be laid off.

I was that person in the music department. *You have to be kidding*, I thought. *I just got here!* The next day I got a call from John. "Jim, can you meet me after school today?"

"Sure, John, what's up?" I answered.

"I will tell you later. Gotta go now; see you at Brewer's Pub at 3:30."

I had a bad feeling all afternoon. When I arrived at the pub, John was as white as a sheet. The first word out of John's mouth was "SHIT."

I blurted out, "I am getting the ax, right? Last one in, first one out, right?" Again, John uttered "SHIT." I had never seen John so upset. He had tears in his eyes and I started to tear up myself.

"I can't believe this is happening, Jim," John blurted out between sniffs.

"John, it's not your fault. I guess I am in the right place but at the wrong time."

3

I was "clued in" as to what was going on behind the scenes a few weeks later by one of my music teacher colleagues. The elementary vocal-music teacher was close to retirement age. She had six months left to be fully vested for her teacher's state pension. John had plans to assign her to the junior high band job. Technically, he could do that. Music Education jobs in Connecticut were specified to be kindergarten through grade 12. Any teacher, no matter what their area of expertise, could be placed in any position at any grade level.

I knew John's reasoning behind this move. Perhaps the teacher would reconsider and retire at the end of this school year. John and I were hoping she would consider this, knowing what might be in store for her at the junior high. But she decided to stick it out. I honestly could not blame her for doing so. A full pension was important.

I was going to be out of job in a couple of months, just when I was feeling more comfortable and confident at my two schools. John had asked me not to say anything publicly to staff or students until things became official. They did the next week. The assistant superintendent of schools came into the junior high office and gave me an envelope. "I am sure you know what this is. I am very sorry to have to give you this," he said. After he left, I read it. It was a summary of the situation from the superintendent. The last couple of lines read: "This termination of your employment is in no way a reflection on your work, which has been greatly appreciated by the administration and the people of the Town of Bloomfield. Your last day will be June 23rd. All the best to you in the future."

As I told my students, after word was getting around, I made sure they knew it was not my decision to leave and my leaving had nothing to do with them. My colleagues were quite supportive and felt terrible. They took me out one afternoon during the last school week and we had some food and drink. We had fun but there was an undercurrent of sadness. I had tears in my eyes driving home and was thankful that Cheryll had a big glass of wine waiting for me.

June 23 came and went. I was unemployed.

37 -
GRAD SCHOOL DECISIONS

IT WAS A STRANGE SUMMER ahead. What to do? The first thing was a trip to the Connecticut Unemployment Office to do the paperwork to apply for funds. This was a new experience for sure. Things progressed quickly and I received my first unemployment check in mid-July. In order to receive the check, I had to show that I was job-seeking, which I was.

One day I saw an ad in the local paper about an opening at Ellington High School. I knew the town quite well, since Cheryll and I lived there for seven years. The high school had a part time position open for a band director. It was not full time. I would be teaching only three out of the five periods of the school day. I immediately put in a call to my friend Sal Ciccarella. He was the EHS choral director. We had a nice chat and Sal seemed to be excited that I was interested. He explained the job requirements, which included lessons, concert, and marching band. Sounded right up my alley! But a part-time position was going to definitely be a financial hit.

Again, as it had happened twice before in my career, I was hired quickly. My resume was strong and Ellington did not hesitate. Since this was to be a part-time job during the morning hours, I thought this perhaps might be a good opportunity to go back to school to work on a doctoral degree. That kind of degree would certainly make me marketable for a college-level position in the future.

I called Dr. Willett over at Hartt and we scheduled an appointment to discuss the doctoral options available. I had also considered applying to Yale University but heard there was a two-year waiting list for their doctoral programs. And, it would have meant a lot of commuting back and forth to New Haven, which was a forty-five-minute drive. Willett encouraged me from the outset. "Jim," he said, "my suggestion would be a DMA (Doctor of Musical Arts) degree."

We went through the course requirements and I noticed I would be eligible to play in the college groups such as the Wind Ensemble and Orchestra, but only if I passed the auditions. It had been about ten years, but I thought I could still compete with those young kids! I went through the application process and took the entrance exam.

It became official—I was a doctoral candidate! The classes all met in the afternoon and early evening, which meant I could teach my morning classes at EHS. I found out when the ensemble auditions were for the Hartt ensembles and made plans to be there. My clarinet was ready!

2

The day of the Hartt ensemble auditions I got caught in a traffic jam on the way to West Hartford, where the college was, and by the time I got to the school, the auditions were over. I had missed out. I could not believe it. I was standing in the hallway outside of the audition room with a dejected look on my face. At that point, Don Sinta, Hartt's well-known professor of saxophone, came up to me to say hello. I had known Don from my master's degree program a decade before.

"What happened, Jim?"

I replied, "Don, I missed the auditions. They are done."

Sinta then gave me some advice that would change my life. "Why don't you take some lessons?"

I thought, *Take some lessons? I give lessons, so why would I need to take lessons?*

Don continued, "You know, Charlie Russo teaches clarinet here and is a wonderful teacher."

I had heard of Russo from my old friend and Vernon colleague, Ruth Ann. She had taken lessons from him. He was the principal clarinet with the New York City Opera orchestra and was a much sought-out teacher in New York City. I stopped to see Dr. Willett on the way out of the building and told him I wanted to sign up for lessons with Russo. Willett thought that was a great idea. Thank goodness for traffic delays and the advice from Don Sinta!

My first lesson with Charles Russo was the next week. He was a nice man and seemed quite easy-going. He asked me to play an etude from the *Rose 32 Etudes* book. After I was done, he said, "Gee, Jim, that sounded really good. I don't know if there is much I can do for you." I gladly internalized the compliment but at the same time I was thinking, *Oh great, this is not going to be helpful.* But then Russo said, "But let's try something. Pull your clarinet inwards towards your body a bit and open your throat as if you were saying, 'Owwwww.'"

I did both and the sound that came out was totally different and amazing. He smiled and nodded. No words were necessary. After the lesson was finished, I was so elated. In fifteen minutes, he had changed my sound for the better. I could not wait to get home and start practicing.

Russo also told me to "put away the orchestral excerpt books." He wanted to study the Rose Etude books with me. Although I had been through those etude books, I was curious as to what his take on them would be. We explored them all during the semester's lessons. I had grown so much musically over the past decade, and with his help I was looking at these pieces through a different lens. This experience turned out to be a revelation for me. And, I am still in the midst of teaching these Rose Etudes today, forty years later.

38 -
ELLINGTON AND A FORK IN THE ROAD

MY FIRST IMPRESSION OF ELLINGTON High School was that it was a friendly environment. Part of this impression was fostered by my new student and colleagues. My colleague Sal was a calm and confident sort of person. He made me feel comfortable from day one and I appreciated that. I put aside the fact that the kids called him by his first name, which was something I was not used to.

The year started with several weeks of all of us getting to know each other. I was teaching two periods of class lessons as well as three band rehearsals during the week. All of these classes were held during the morning hours, which gave me time to travel to Hartt School of Music for my Doctor of Musical Arts classes. I felt comfortable with this schedule. Ellington was already proving to be a good landing place for me.

Early on in the school year, I was again reminded of how high school kids could get attached to their band directors. One of my tenth graders was a shy and quiet trombone player named Cassandra. I noticed that she began hanging around the band room during her free periods. And, she seemed to know when I was staying at school on those days when I did not have to go to Hartt. I used those days to catch up on work. Ellington was getting more hours out of me than they were paying me for. But I did not complain. The work needed to get done.

I began to see another side of Cassie that I hadn't seen during my band rehearsals. When we spoke outside of class she enjoyed talking. I sensed she needed an adult to talk with and I was him. One day I found an envelope on my desk which contained a letter. It was from her. In the letter she said that she enjoyed our chats and that I was like a father to her. That was not the first time I had a student say those words to me.

At the end of the letter, she asked if I would be willing to give her a ride home from school someday. This request was initially not foreign to me since I had, on occasion, given students a ride and in those days there was no stigma about doing that. It was a different world back then.

I thought about that request and the other things Cassie had expressed in her letter. I decided to go and have a chat with the EHS social worker the next day. I told Barbara that Cassie was a quiet kid who seemed to love band. She had been hanging around the music department frequently after classes and rehearsals. On the surface, she seemed like the typical "band rat" I had encountered over the years. And, of course, that was a phrase used by me with much affection. After all, I had been one myself during my high school years.

As I explained to Barbara, I was feeling there was something here more than just hanging around. I had a gut feeling that Cassie was harboring a crush on me. I knew the signs since I had seen them before. I was confident Barbara would know how to handle this situation. She spoke to Cassie the next day. Barbara had a follow-up meeting with me a couple of days later. She advised me to speak with Cassie and assure her that I would always be there for her if she had a problem. So, I did that the next day and all seemed to work out fine. I still had my dedicated trombone player.

2

One evening at home in early October I received a phone call from John Erskine. His words were "Jim, I just wanted to let you know that your old job in Bloomfield is now open. Would you be interested in coming back to us?" He went on to explain that the elementary vocal teacher that had replaced me had just handed in her letter of retirement. She had lasted four weeks trying to deal with my former bands and that was enough for her. That did not surprise me in the least. I had been an experienced band director and still had my hands full with those kids, especially early on.

Now John was offering me the position again. It was a tempting offer. It would be back to a full-time position, and certainly from a monetary standpoint it would be beneficial. But I had been enjoying my situation in Ellington and Hartt. I told John I had to decline the offer and I could hear disappointment in his voice.

The Bloomfield experience had ended up as a huge professional disappointment. I was appreciating the fact that I had landed on my feet in the aftermath. And in two different places no less!

3

For the most part the DMA program's courses were quite enjoyable. There were still so many new things to learn. I was loving my inspirational clarinet lessons with Charles Russo. He was recharging my love for the instrument. On the other hand, my Musical Styles course with my old friend Dr. Wilheim was taxing. It seemed none of us in the class could work hard enough for his standards. He certainly had not mellowed over the years.

One of our assignments was to perform in class. I chose the Mozart Clarinet Quintet. I knew how Dr. Wilheim was rooted in the Baroque Era, but he somewhat reluctantly let me play the Mozart. After all, the clarinet was not a popular instrument during the time periods that we're studying in class. However, during Mozart's time the instrument was developed and refined to the point that it was being included in the repertoire of composers.

To contrast the Musical Styles class stress we all felt, I was really having a great experience with my Independent Study course in conducting. This was a weekly one-on-one meeting at the piano with Dr. Mariosious. We would study several of the great masterworks and discuss interpretation and other concerns like string bowings. Dr. M would play and I would conduct. I loved the interaction with someone of his experience and expertise. I had played under his direction with the Hartt student orchestra over a decade before while

I was a master's degree candidate.

My final exam was an opportunity to conduct the present day Hartt orchestra playing Schubert's *Unfinished Symphony*. What a thrill that was! And I passed with flying colors!

In the meantime, Dr. Wilheim had assigned a term paper for the Styles class. My topic was "Tempo Variations during the Baroque and Classical Eras." I spent many hours in the Music Library listening to recording, looking at scores, and researching. After a while it seemed like I lived in the Music Library!

We all handed in our papers. A week later during our final class meeting, Dr. Wilheim was not happy. He proceeded to say that none of us had received a final grade. He had given everyone an "Incomplete" for the course. The implication was that our term papers were not finished and we had more to do. We were all in shock.

It was obvious he wanted each of us to make an appointment with him so he could "put us in our places." I had never worked harder on an assignment in my life. We all discussed the situation outside of class with much consternation. We all thought we deserved a grade for our efforts. Most of the class, including myself, were not going to meet with him. I thought perhaps the school would see this situation and intervene. They never did and I came out of that course with an "I."

I then found out that during my final semester I was going to have to take another Music History class with Dr. Wilheim. The only courses available were the same courses I took during my master's program years before. *I have to take the same class for a second time?* That did not make any sense to me.

I had serious discussions with Dr. Willett and Charles Russo about this situation. *Is this degree worth continuing under these circumstances?* They both encouraged me to follow my gut. It was my decision. I did not register for the next semester's classes. I was done.

4

Time flies when you are having fun, as the old saying goes. The school year at EHS progressed with a couple of parades and a spring concert. My band officers really did a great job for me and the rest of the band. My band president, Matt, was my solo clarinet and a great kid. He seemed to be a born leader and the other kids followed his demeanor during rehearsals. This helped result in few problems with discipline. The Ellington kids had a high interest in music. In the back of my mind, my thoughts were *I would not mind staying at this school for a long time, if not for the rest of my career.*

The school year came to a close and I was anticipating finding out if my position would be expanded to full-time. I say that because during the year I had met the superintendent of schools in the parking lot one day after school. He asked me how things were going and then said, "Jim, if you work hard there is the chance we might be able to expand your position for next year."

I tried to work hard all year and I was optimistic. Unfortunately, my optimism was derailed. In July I received a letter informing me that my position for the next school year would be trimmed from a three-fifths to a two-fifths position. The job's future was heading in the wrong direction.

Cheryll and I travelled to Long Island to visit my mom and her husband, along with my sister Joann. It had been a week after the disappointing news about my job. While we were at my mother's home, we happened to watch a show on TV that was all about the career of the future . . . computers! That show caught my attention for sure.

Back in Connecticut, there had been recurring TV ads for the Computer Processing Institute located in East Hartford. Their ad stated that you could receive a business computer programming degree in six months. We had a few family discussions about this over the next few days. My mother then made me an offer. She suggested if I was interested, I should call CPI and inquire about the courses. If I was ultimately interested, she said that she would pay for the tuition.

When we got back to Connecticut, I called CPI. Their pitch

was that with the city of Hartford being the "insurance capital of the world," the school had a 90 percent placement rate with their graduates holding a programming degree. The course was indeed six months and would basically guarantee a resulting programming job with one of the insurance companies. I had lots to think about.

5

As my second year at EHS began, I could immediately see that this position was not going to be sustainable with only two periods of student contact each day. The same amount of work was there: parades, concerts, lessons, and the like. But I would do my best and certainly, my experience would help.

We had the local fireman's parade right off the bat in early October, followed quickly by the Four Town Fair. At that parade, I was standing with the band as they were lining up to march. All of a sudden, a large coach bus pulled up. The bus door opened and a large man bounded out of the door near where we were standing. He came over to me, reached out, and shook my hand. It dawned on me quickly who this man was. It was none other than Connecticut Senator Lowell Weicker! His words were "How are you, young man? Best of luck to you and your students in today's parade."

I was stunned. One of our state's senators just shook my hand! Senator Weicker was a large man, probably about 6 feet 5 inches. My hand had felt quite small in his. He was obviously there to do some politicking with his constituents. None the less, meeting him was the highlight of my day. That experience topped off a great job by the EHS marching band. They had "nailed" the parade on a welcome day of beautiful weather.

Another highlight of that day was when I found out that our senior band president, Matt, had been accepted into West Point! He was the first student that I knew of who was going to attend one of the service academies. I was not surprised to get this news. If anyone would qualify to be accepted to West Point, it would be him.

6

The bottom line was that my attending CPI loomed as a possibility of again having a full-time job. I decided to take an interview. The interviewer's eyes lit up when we discussed the fact that I was a musician. He related to me that musicians made good programmers. Music is a language in itself. It made sense. I was told I had qualified for the programmer class based on the logic test they had given to a group of us prior to the individual interviews. And, my background in music seemed to have "sealed the deal."

After the good news, a couple of CPI instructors gave us a group tour and information session. The prospective class members were from all walks of life. In the process of chatting with some of them I learned that all of us had a common interest in computer science and were going through a career change. The afternoon classes were slated to begin next week. I signed up and committed to this change in career. I was somewhat nervous but excited.

I dove into the work at CPI. The two worlds of music education and computer programming were so different. The classes were all about learning computer languages, programming logic, and developing an eye for detail.

The six-month course concluded in early April and included a test given by the Hartford Insurance Group, also known as The Hartford. We all took the exam and I felt certain I had done well. Then, in the interview, the HIG representative took note of the fact that I was a musician. Thirteen members of our class of thirty-two were hired by The Hartford. I was one of them.

A few days later the company hosted us for an introductory tour at the home office location in the city of Hartford. During that session we were shown the "IBM" manual. We were going to learn how to program for the IBM 360 and 370 mainframes, using the languages we had learned at CPI, namely, COBOL (Common Business Oriented Language) and JCL (Job Control Language), among others. The IBM manual was going to be a valuable resource for us.

We were brought into a large room. All four walls were lined with a dozen or so long, three-tiered shelving units. There were dozens and dozens of thick black binders, each about 3 inches thick and labelled with computer lingo I had yet to understand. My thoughts were *You mean we have to carry around one of these huge binders all day while on the job?*

Someone in the group asked, "Which one is the IBM manual?" The answer blew my mind. "Ladies and gentlemen, look around you. You are standing in the midst of the IBM manual," explained the tour guide. The entire room was the manual! I thought, *So you wanted to be a computer programmer? Careful what you wish for.* But not to worry. It was then explained to us that only the "techies," as they were called, namely, the IBM experts, would actually be using this room. But we would have to become familiar with most of the manual terminology as we went along.

Phew! That was a close call. We already had enough to learn as it was. I was glad we had experts to help us out.

7

Unfortunately, the Hartford training class would begin the first week of May. And it was an all-day affair, so I was going to have to bail out of EHS before the school year was done. I hated the thought of doing that. Would my students understand? This would mean they would have a long-term sub for the final two months. I would miss the senior's graduation. I had no choice.

I submitted my notice of resignation to the superintendent. I told my colleagues and students as well. There was obvious disappointment on both fronts, which touched me. I had developed a true affection for my students. They were great kids. I was again leaving a school district with mixed emotions.

My final two days at EHS had a couple of significant moments. I was leaving the school during the late morning, the first day after my two teaching periods were done. I again ran into the superintendent of schools in the hallway. He pulled me aside and said, "Jim, we are really sad to see you go. We are losing a fine educator and person. Best of luck to you." I saw the sincerity in his eyes. He meant what he was saying. I got the impression that he had fought for me during the budget deliberations during the recent past. But he had lost the battle to enhance the band position. I have no proof of that but I just had a gut feeling.

Then, on my last day, I was called into the EHS principal's office. Principal Bob Ford sat me down and told me, "Jim, we are offering you today a full-time position for next year. It would be two-fifths band and three-fifths computer science." I was floored! The administration had known that I was attending CPI since last fall.

I was immediately caught off guard. I knew two things for certain: I had put too much time and effort to prepare for the position at The Hartford. I also did not feel I had the confidence to jump into three high school computer classes. I still felt like a novice in that field. I had too much to learn. As a result, I respectfully declined the offer. It was a nice feeling that the administration had tried to piece together a position for me. They did not want to lose me.

I was about to land on my feet again. But this time in the land of technology.

39 -
THE HARTFORD, A NEW WORLD

IF MY POSITION IN ELLINGTON would have been full time, with a master's degree, I would have made $18,500 during the 1982–83 school year. It was a well-known fact that Connecticut teachers were grossly underpaid in comparison to other occupations in the state. Teachers were paid on a series of steps, correlating to how many years of experience they had. Each town had its own salary scale and raises were given in compliance with the amounts negotiated between the teachers' union and the board of education. Ellington's pay scale was about average in that regard.

The reality of this salary disparity set in when I signed a contract at The Hartford for the entry-level programmer pay rate. I would be making $18,750. After twelve years of teaching, I was making a lateral move salary-wise. True, this was an entry-level position at one of the country's most significant insurance companies, but this fact did not shine a good light on the pay for educators in Connecticut.

Programmer training class was held at The Hartford's Hamilton Heights facility in the city. The school was a former mansion that had been converted into a training facility. It was impressive, to say the least. It included a cafeteria and fitness center. Talk about a "new world"!

The trainees were going to learn how to use the knowledge we had learned at CPI under the standards of the company. There were lots to learn over the next ten weeks.

On the first day of training, we were given a tour of the company home office building, located on Asylum Street in downtown Hartford. As we were listening to our guide as we walked down a large, centralized hallway, all of a sudden, I heard, "Hey, Mister Kleiner!" I turned around and saw this lovely young lady come bounding up to me. I recognized Pam immediately. She had been a student of mine at VCMS. "What are you doing here?" she excitedly proclaimed. I told her I was part of the new programmer training class and that I had left teaching. She was surprised and seemed so happy to see me. We made plans to get together for lunch once I got out "on the floor."

A few days later I was relating this story to one of my class instructors and he said he knew of her. She was a middle manager in one of the divisions at the Home Office. Obviously here I had a former student who was a bunch of pay grades above me. I made a mental note to tell her to call me "Jim" when we had that lunch together.

2

After the training classes completed, I landed in the Life Insurance Division located in a sprawling building complex in Windsor. On my first day there I found out about "flextime." This meant that as part of the data processing department, I could start my workday anytime between 7:00 and 9:00 am as long as I stayed consistent with that time. The work time requirement was 7.25 hours in addition to your forty-five-minute lunch break.

Forty-five minutes for lunch? I never remembered having that long to eat my lunch during any of my teaching years. It was always like twenty-five or thirty minutes at the most if you were lucky. And on top of the expanded time for eating there were coffee and goodies at the coffee wagons spread around the buildings. I had already gained a few pounds from the Hamilton Heights cafeteria and I was afraid this trend would continue. I decided to make an effort to use the Hamilton Heights fitness center a few times a week.

This was a bit of a drive from Windsor to Hartford, but I felt it was worth it. After these regular workouts I initially gained 5 pounds of muscle weight. The fitness folks said not to worry about that. Muscles metabolize faster than fat. And sure enough, over the next few months I lost 17 pounds and was getting into great shape. I also continued to play in an adult ice hockey league as I had over the past five years. Wayne Gretzky I was not, but it was an awful lot of fun.

This was the first extended period of my work life in which I was not around kids. I missed them, but on the other hand, I was enjoying working in the world of adults. I was in my thirties by this time and found I was relating well to people younger and older than me.

There was a particular older guy who I used to often meet at the fitness center while I was working out. The two of us would often be using side-by-side treadmills. His name was Don and we seemed to always have interesting discussions about kids and hobbies. He learned about my having come from the teaching profession and never could say enough about how he had so much respect for teachers. He seemed particularly interested in what it was like to be a teacher. On top of that, he and I were avid golfers. We always had much to talk about during our treadmill time.

One day I was at a Life Company staff meeting, and during this they showed a video about some up-and-coming innovations. The video began and there was Don on the screen with an introduction. The announcer introduced him as Don Frahm, the president of the Life Company! Who knew? And he and I were on a first-name basis!

3

The Life Insurance division spent two years at the Windsor facility while construction was happening in Simsbury. The sprawling new facility was opened and we all moved over there during the summer of 1986. By that time Cheryll and I had moved to South Windsor as a family of three. We had adopted a four-month-old little girl through the State of Connecticut adoption program a couple of years before and felt that South Windsor would be a great place to live. Its school system had a solid reputation.

As little Janet got to school age, I became a team leader of my work unit. I had migrated to the Application Support unit at Hartford Life. This unit worked three twelve-hour days and then had the next four days off. We were the watchdog for the production computer runs. I opted for the 7:00 am to 7:00 pm shift. The unit's staff rotated between Monday through Wednesday for six months and then Thursday through Saturday for the balance of the year.

This schedule enabled me to be at home for two or three days a week, during which time I could put Janet on the bus in the morning and be there for her when she returned home. Cheryll was teaching in Stafford, and this worked out well for day-care purposes. Working the twelve-hour shift for three days was easier said than done. In fact, most days after the three long days, I felt exhausted. I called it my "zombie day."

My career in data processing had lasted ten years at that point. During the last couple of years, I had been a part of the technical support area and was back to a normal five-day work week. We were always learning about the newest facets of DP and the company made sure we were up to date on all the latest stuff. However, as the new computer languages that were developed became more powerful, the need for programmers became less and less. One could see the writing on the wall.

4

A particularly momentous day occurred about seven or eight years into my tenure at the company. There had been rumors floating around for weeks about an impending job layoff. In the data processing division, the managers had been assuring us that we had nothing to worry about in that regard. And then the day came, known as "Black Monday."

Shortly after we arrived at our desks that morning, we were told to stay there and not turn on our computers. My first thought was *Uh-oh, what is this all about?* I knew something was not right when I saw the veteran employees quite nervous. The next instruction was that if our desk phone rang, we were to proceed to the manager's office. That did not give me "the warm fuzzies" either. Slowly, some phones began to ring.

The phone of one of my co-workers rang. He slowly went to the office. He was visibly shaking. Over the next half hour several people were summoned to see the manager. I was not one of them. My colleague returned to his desk, took his belongings, and was escorted out of the building by a security guard. He, along with several others, had been laid off.

I later learned that someone on the other side of the floor had suffered a heart attack after his phone rang. He was taken out of the building to a waiting ambulance by the EMTs. People being terminated were immediately escorted out.

My experience that day was something very new to me. Despite all the wonderful ways The Hartford treated its employees, this was the "dark side." None of us had "tenure" as I had once had as an educator. Here, you were at the mercy of the company. This was a reality check for me.

During the early '90s it was increasingly clear that programmers were not as valuable as they once had been. The software was eliminating the need for us. The writing was on the wall. I could see myself down the road as an unemployed programmer. Perhaps it was time to start thinking about teaching again. I could no longer ignore the fact that I was missing the kids.

40 -
A SENSELESS TRAGEDY

TO DIGRESS A FEW YEARS, back when The Hartford opened up the Simsbury Life Facility, I decided early on to walk around and explore the interior of the sprawling complex. Maybe as a result I might not get so lost when I had to get from one place to another. Not too far from my section of the data processing building, which had no windows and was supposedly "bomb proof," I came across a secretaries' desk. As I passed by, the desk's occupant said, "I know you. You are Jim Kleiner, who used to be the band director at Ellington High School."

"Yes, that's me," I responded.

"My name is Diane, and I am the sister of your former band president, Matt."

My first words after that exchange were "That is amazing. How is Matt doing at West Point?" Diane proceeded to give me a detailed update on how his military career was doing and then informed me that in a few days, Matt was coming in to visit her for lunch. She invited me to join them. I was so excited to see him!

The lunch was wonderful. It was so great to see him after several years and find out how he was doing. He had grown even taller and looked amazing in his dress uniform. His leave was almost over, after which he was going to be stationed at an Army base in Texas. We could not help but reminisce about the Ellington band for quite a while. He told me he was engaged to a young lady whom he had met in the band. Tina played the flute and I remembered her very well. *What a great match!* I thought to myself.

Matt came in a few months later to visit his sister again and I joined them on that occasion as well. What a treat to be in touch with a former student, especially a young man like Matt.

2

A few more months passed by and I was about to transfer to the Home Office complex in Hartford to join the technical support unit. I had expressed an interest in learning and working in the "nuts and bolts" unit of the DP area. This was despite the recommendation by my superiors to go the "middle management route" for my internal career path. I was being told that I had received positive reviews as a team leader. "Everyone loves working with you" was the feedback I was receiving.

I wandered over to Diane's area to tell her about my transfer, but she was not at her desk. I asked one of her co-workers when she would be back at her desk and was told she was not working this week due to a family tragedy. "What happened?" I asked. The answer hit me like a ton of bricks. "Her brother and a fellow officer were hit by a truck on his military base and both were killed."

I stood there in shock. I felt like I had been punched in the gut. What a waste of two lives, one of whom I knew and admired so much. I went back to my desk in a daze. And, sure enough, I had gotten an email from Diane telling me that there was going to be a memorial service for Matt the following week. I had to attend.

3

The service was held at a church near EHS. I knew I was most likely to see several former students at that service. I proceeded through the receiving line and hugged Diane as soon as I got to her. Her family was holding up as best as could be expected, but there was such a sadness enveloping all of them. The service was beautiful, with a military honor guard present. Matt was receiving full military honors.

I greeted several former EHS band students outside the church after the rifles were fired by the soldiers. We were all saying that it was nice to see each other again, although not under these circumstances. I was "holding it together" for the most part.

Then Matt's fiancée, Tina, approached me. I recognized her right away. She took my hand and whispered, "Come with me." She led me on a walk over to the high school and to a spot outside the band room. She stopped and said, "This is the exact spot where Matt proposed to me. If it was not for the band, I doubt if I would have ever known him very well."

At that point "I lost it," as did she. We both burst into tears and hugged. How blessed I was to have experienced this moment with her. She wanted to share with me her feelings and memories at a place that was so important to her in her life.

The losing of a former student was an event that I never thought I would have to experience. Someone with incredible leadership skills and potential in life, someone I had taught, had his life senselessly snuffed out. A senseless tragedy. Little did I know that a few years later I would see a similar event acted out on a movie screen. All these feelings would return.

41 - A TRANSITION

THE REWARDING AND SATISFYING TIMES with students, seeing the faces of former students in my mind, all were filling my brain more frequently. The possibility of transitioning back to education was real.

By this time, the Teacher Enhancement Act had passed the Connecticut Legislature. This provided much-needed funding to raise teachers' salaries state-wide. This was done to make it more attractive for people to enter the profession at a time when the school systems did not have the financial means to pay their teachers enough to be competitive with other professions. From a monetary standpoint, this seemed like a good opportunity to transition back.

The Connecticut Music Educators Association, of which I had been a member during the '70s and '80s, was advertising an opening for Executive Secretary–Treasurer. It would be this nonprofit's first paid position. My first thought was that perhaps I would be a good candidate for this job due to my music education and computer background.

I inquired about the position and ultimately was hired. The plan was to set up an office in my basement, and with all the available space, I could actually house the entire CMEA music library. Being the music librarian would also be another facet of the job. This would work out well, since I would be able to be home for my daughter before and after school.

As a result of my hiring, I tendered my resignation at The Hartford. A luncheon was held for me at a local Simsbury restaurant on my last day. What a nice, warm sendoff that was by my colleagues. I knew I would miss the camaraderie and being a part of the team of professionals with whom I had worked. I made some good friends, some of whom I would be in contact with for many years afterwards.

Other areas of my professional musician career would benefit from this new situation for me. Working outside of the music education field had given me the time and energy to pursue a performing career. Many opportunities arose during the years in data processing. Becoming a substitute player at the Goodspeed Opera as well as the Hartford Symphony were musically challenging and exciting. I was certainly quite thankful for these opportunities.

2

The prospect of being involved with all of the Connecticut middle school and high school regional festivals, as well as the All-State festival and the CMEA annual conference, was exciting. I knew many Connecticut music teachers already and would have the opportunity to get to know many others.

Those volunteers on the CMEA Executive Board and the heads of the various state committees in music education were inspiring to get to know. I found these people to be sincerely interested in serving the educators and students in the state. However, there were those whose egos got in the way of their efforts. It was a challenge to work with them. But you had to take the good with the bad.

The job of Executive Secretary–Treasurer was not a full-time job. During my second year in the position, the question arose as to how many hours was "part-time." This began to be a sticking point for me. I was putting in what was increasingly longer hours, including weekends. The CMEA office phone seemed like it never stopped ringing.

I found out, after speaking with others who had worked for nonprofits, that this was not out of the ordinary. The more work you did, the more was expected. I had been called by a gentleman from an out-of-state "nonprofit" watchdog group. I agreed to answer their survey questions. I explained the problems I was having with the workload-versus-salary issue. The survey representative told me that his group was finding this to be the case with most people who worked for nonprofits all over the United States. The organizations' volunteers did not understand that they should not be piling up the work on their employees just because they were being paid.

After much thought, I put in a formal request for a salary increase based on the average number of hours I was working, which was about thirty hours per week, including time on the weekend. I based this number of hours on my original conversation with the then president of CMEA when I was thinking about accepting the job. He related to me that the expectation would be four hours of work per day. Based on those numbers, I thought the salary of $23,000 offered was reasonable for the year. I had other sources of income, such as private lessons and professional performing opportunities, so I felt this part-time job would work. And, after all, I did not have to commute!

However, since I had experienced thirty-hour work weeks, I thought it was reasonable to ask for a raise to $30,000. In my letter to the executive board about what was told to me over the phone by the CMEA president prior to my hire, I explained all of this. The board contacted the former president and he told them that he did not remember telling me that. That was an unfortunate lapse of memory. Those facts I heard from him were the main reason I had accepted the job in the first place.

The executive board ultimately denied my request for an increase. I had no recourse but to start looking elsewhere for employment. And as fate would have it, it was a CMEA event which further guided me back to music education.

42 -
MR. HOLLAND'S OPUS – THE MOVIE

DURING 1995, MY SECOND YEAR working for CMEA, a movie was released called *Mr. Holland's Opus*. The buzz about this movie amongst the world of teaching was strong. Word had it that it was the story about the career of a music teacher. CMEA organized a private showing at a local movie theater for CMEA members only. It was a formal affair. We all dressed for the occasion. There was to be a wine and cheese reception in the lobby afterwards. I thought this event was a great idea and could not wait for the event.

I had no idea that this movie would have such an effect on me. First of all, the opening scenes of the movie take place in 1965, the same year I was a high school junior. I was looking at the screen, seeing the exact same visions I had in my memory of my own high school years. I was floored! From the sets to the costumes, hairstyles, cars, building interior and exteriors, this was exactly the same vibe as Hicksville High School.

The creators of this film had "nailed" the time period. The cast, including Richard Dreyfuss, Olympia Dukakis, Glenne Headley, William Macy, and Jay Thomas, did an amazing job.

After the initial jaw-dropping opening, the movie settled into the story about the career of an instrumental music teacher. The years passed during the story and so did the history of the times. There were so many moments in the story that resonated with me, either as a former student or as a teacher. I was constantly saying to myself, "Been there, done that!"

For example, one memory was the fact that Teacher Glen Holland had a young female student at one point who had a huge crush on him. Holland had to be the adult and handle the situation as a learning experience for the young lady. I certainly could relate to what I was seeing on the screen.

Another was Holland's attending a funeral for a former student who was killed in Vietnam. Having been to a similar funeral seven years earlier, I had a hard time watching that segment. It took all my composure not to break down. I dabbed my eyes with my handkerchief and blew my nose during the whole scene. I thought for a moment I was going to have to get up and leave the theater.

I was reliving parts of my own career, but there was more. The ending of *Mr. Holland's Opus* is about as inspirational a movie ending as I had ever experienced. Holland had lost his job due to budget cuts after a multi-decade career. He had finished packing his belongings on his last day along with the help of his wife and son. As he walked out of the building for the last time, he heard noises coming from the auditorium. He opened the door and saw a packed hall with an orchestra on the stage consisting of his students and alumni as well. The realization hit him that this was all in tribute to him.

Glen's wife and son, who were in on all of this, led him down the aisle to a front-row seat, and as he was walking, he saw so many familiar faces from his career along the way. His wife took the stage and introduced a special guest. The state's governor, Gertrude Lang, came down the aisle with her entourage. She had been a student of Holland thirty years before, during his first years of teaching.

As his student, she struggled to play the clarinet and had been frustrated to the point of wanting to give it up. But Holland's patience and teaching skill inspired her to succeed. As the governor, she stepped up to the podium and gave the following speech:

My apologies for my tardiness. Principal Walters, I'd like you to know, yes, I brought a note from my mother. Mr. Holland had a profound influence on my life, on a lot of lives I know, and yet I get the feeling he considers a great part of his own life misspent. Rumor has it he was always working on this symphony of his and this was going to make him famous, rich . . . probably both. But Mr. Holland isn't rich and he isn't famous, at least not outside of our little town. So, it might be easy for him to think himself a failure. And he would be wrong. Because, I think he has achieved a success far beyond riches and fame. Mr. Holland, look around you. There is not a life in this room that you have not touched. Each one of us is a better person because of you. We are your symphony, Mr. Holland, the melodies of your opus. We are the music of your life.

Holland was then invited up to the stage to conduct the first performance of that symphony he had always worked on, with Governor Lang playing the clarinet in the orchestra. The performance of Holland's symphony concluded the movie. I left the theater moist-eyed. The overwhelming thought in my mind was that I had to get back to teaching again.

Little did I know that in less than two years from that inspirational evening, I would be standing on an auditorium stage in Glenn Holland's shoes.

> *"Anyone who does anything to help a child in his life is a hero to me."*
>
> —FRED ROGERS

43 - PARISH HILL – A ROCKIN' SCHOOL

I AM JOB HUNTING AGAIN. I am going back to music education. I was excited. I missed it. As I scoured the newspapers for job openings, I came across one in Regional District 11, which included the small Eastern Connecticut towns of Chaplin, Hampton, and Scotland. The job specifically was at Parish Hill High School, which contained grades 7 through 12.

I gathered it was a last-minute opening since the school year was to begin in three weeks. I called the number listed in the ad and spoke with an administrator. He invited me out there for an interview. He asked me to bring my resume with me, since time was of the essence.

The ride out to the school was not as long as I thought it would be. It was about a half-hour drive. When I arrived, I found a building which was circular in design, shaped like a large horseshoe. When I stepped inside, I couldn't help but notice the hallways were in a large semicircle from one end of the school to the other. I had been in a number of schools in my lifetime and had never seen anything like this.

I interviewed with a panel of administrators and faculty. I got the impression they were impressed with my experience in education. My resume caught their attention as well. After talking with them and answering their questions, I was asked to fill out a formal application. I was hired!

The job responsibilities were right up my alley. I would have a middle school band—grades 7 and 8—and a high school band. There would be class lessons at both levels. A new wrinkle for me would be two middle school general music classes and a high school guitar class. Fortunately, I owned a guitar and had taken lessons back in the '70s. I was sure I could survive that class, but the middle school general music classes would be totally new for me. I had three weeks to get ready for this new experience.

The job had been advertised as a "nine-tenths" position, which meant I would be responsible to cover nine periods of a ten-period school day. I would be assigned periods 2 through 10, which included all the prerequisite duties and planning periods. Financially that was not too much of a "hit," although I knew in the back of my mind that the work required would be the same as a full-time position.

A couple of days later I met again with the principal, Jan Marino, and I asked him about the recent history of the music program and how things had been going. He was honest with me. "Jim, the reason this job opened so late this summer was due to our former band director not having received tenure. Myself, and others on the staff, were not happy with the general lack of discipline. There were problems and rumors going around. We felt we had to let him go."

I appreciated the honesty and realized I was about to walk into a situation in which I was going to have to "straighten things out." I had done something similar in Bloomfield, which I knew was no picnic. I appreciated the "heads up" from Jan. He sent me to the guidance office to retrieve my class lists. I was curious to see how many band members I would have in each group.

I met my new colleague, whose name was Uma. She was so nice and welcoming. She did the vocal end of both levels. In talking with her I was impressed with her musical knowledge and her overall demeanor. I sensed that the kids probably adored her. She mentioned that the high school band had about forty students during the previous year, so when I went to guidance and saw the band list, it was a reality check.

Seventeen students were signed up. I went back to Uma and she filled me in on "Mr. C," the former band guy. She characterized the band program as a "country club" with very lax discipline. The students did whatever they wanted, including massive fooling around during rehearsals. And she questioned the need for a couch sitting on a high platform above the auditorium stage in the wings. I checked that out and it looked very comfortable and well-used. Its very presence up there made me uncomfortable. I knew it had to go.

Seventeen students signed up for the high school band. The group had lost about half of its members over the summer. Included in those kids were some, I would imagine, who were so frustrated with how things were being run, they just gave up. And then again, others dropped the course when they found out their buddy band director was not coming back.

I again fell back on my experience and planned my high school repertoire for the small group. But until I heard them play, I would not be able to make decisions on what we could play. I did not worry too much about the middle school band. I knew I could make them comfortable with me right off the bat. And, surprisingly, I was enjoying playing the guitar again! I was looking forward to that class.

What to do with the general music classes! Jan had told me what I did with them was totally up to me. I thought back to *Mr. Holland's Opus*. What did Glenn Holland do when his Music Appreciation Classes were tanking? He started to sprinkle in some lessons about the new music genre that was sweeping America during the '60s—Rock and Roll! Perhaps if I gave my classes an introduction to Rock and Roll, who knows what might happen?

I had to admit I was a latecomer to the whole pop music scene. I was a teenager when groups like The Beatles came over to this country. I was so into Mozart and Beethoven during those years that I hardly noticed the genre of Rock and Roll at all. However, as I became exposed to pop music, especially through my students, I became fascinated with the whole rock scene.

My wife and I got tickets to go to Hartford to see a stage production of *Sgt. Pepper's Lonely Hearts Club Band*. I was not particularly excited about sitting through an evening of The Beatles' music. But wouldn't you know it, the production and its music blew me away! I immediately went out and purchased the famous album. I was hooked! Better late than never.

My thoughts at Parish Hill began to formulate. I thought, *Why not take these middle school kids through the history of Rock?* I further received inspiration after watching a public television series called *The History of Rock and Roll.* There had been eight episodes broadcast one summer and I ended up purchasing the entire series on video tape. I watched the series multiple times. The series started in the early '50s and progressed through the early '90s, just as rap and hop-hop were emerging.

I could use these videos in class, although I would have to do some editing for language and sections that were a bit too "adult" for middle schoolers. I had a turntable for my class use, so I sent out the word to the faculty that I could use any Rock LPs they might be able to lend to me for my use in class. I was flabbergasted when the records began to roll in. I had just about every important Rock record at my disposal you could ever want!

The Guidance Department scheduled this class as one of the students' semester-long "specials." As a result, with the two sections per semester, I could reach more kids. I dug into the class preparation like I was a first-year teacher. I was psyched! I was as enthusiastic as I had ever been in the profession. What a way to land on my feet again!

44 -
SMALL SCHOOL – NOT A PROBLEM

TEACHING IN A SMALL SCHOOL meant that you quickly came to know all of the students, whether they were in your classes or not. Likewise, the faculty was easier to get to know as well. I was enjoying this aspect of being at Parish Hill. My fellow teachers were such an interesting group of people. I was realizing that these kids out in rural eastern Connecticut were lucky to have this group of professionals teaching them. I was hoping I could add to that environment.

The year started well. I was scrambling a bit with my high school guitar players. The class had eight kids and one of them was a far better player than I was, while the others were your basic beginners. I recruited my all-star class member to be a class helper and he proved invaluable in that role.

The middle school band was a nice group of kids who needed lots of "TLC." They seemed to respond well to my encouragement and prodding. The high school band was another story. At first, as I anticipated, they were somewhat resistant to "the new guy," but to my surprise, they quickly got on board with what I was doing. I sensed that the kids that had hung with the group really needed some direction and loved the idea that I really wanted them to succeed and learn. "Mr. K" was not "Mr. C."

The Rock and Roll survey classes were going well. The kids seemed to digest the content of the videos eagerly. Surprisingly, many of them had never seen an LP record. Who knew? I incorporated "drop the needle" quizzes, reminiscent of the segments on Dick Clark's old *American Bandstand* TV show. This is where teenage contestants were quizzed on short excerpts of the popular hits of the day. The kids in the class loved doing that.

Guidance told me that there were not enough slots for all the kids wanting to take this class. It was becoming quite popular. I actually had some staff members coming to sit in on classes so they could enjoy the videos and music. It was a trip down memory lane for them.

Hall duty was another story. It was really challenging to keep an eye on a huge circular hallway. One could only see about one-fourth of the hallway at a time. The kids knew this as well. I had been told that the architecture was based on the theory that students felt more comfortable if they were not being constantly observed. Nice theory, but reality got in the way. These architects must have skipped high school!

There was a group of three or four high school guys who decided I was someone they thought they could intimidate. I don't know where they got that idea, but I suspect they didn't think that playing a musical instrument was a manly activity. Their pet name for me was "panty wipe." I would hear that just about every day I entered the male bathroom for my duty check. "Psst . . . here comes panty wipe" would come floating out from inside the boys' bathroom as I walked in. Finally, one day I had heard enough of that. I cornered those guys and said, "Gentlemen, if I hear that phrase directed at me one more time this year, you will be reported to Mister Marino." They were taken aback by that and I thought, *Well, this will be the end of it.*

Not so. A week later I heard it again in the hallway as they passed me. So, I did what I told them I was going to do. I had already apprised Jan about what had been going on. I told Jan and he suspended all four guys for a week. I am sure their parents were none too happy. I never heard from these guys again. Score one for the band director!

Later in the year I actually marched with the high school kids during a local town parade. We had no one to play the bass drum, or should I say, we did, but they had trouble keeping a steady beat. As a result, I let him play the snare drum and I stepped in on bass. It was tiring along the parade route carrying that big drum. But having a steady beat gave the band the confidence we needed. We were small but we had a lot of spirit! The good players in the group were causing their own enthusiasm to rub off on everyone.

A few weeks after the parade, all of a sudden, we had an influx of "new" old band members. Seven kids signed up to rejoin the band. Kids were coming back!

The year finished up with a school production of *The Sound of Music*. Uma prepared the acting and singing. I got to conduct an orchestra of area professionals, which was a treat for me. I was amazed at the talent on stage. Many members of the band and chorus were involved and they did a wonderful job with this challenging show. I had a nice feeling of satisfaction as the school year ended. I was looking forward to the next.

45 -
A STABLE SITUATION, UNTIL IT WASN'T

Year two at Parish Hill began with the fact that a new principal had been hired. My relationship with Jan had been solid and professional. He had been honestly interested in what I was trying to do with the instrumental music program. He had my back. To me, that was a sign of an effective administrator, namely, to deal with parents when there were inquiries or complaints. Part of an administrator's job is to know what is going on in each department and be familiar with each teacher's teaching style. He never hesitated to pass along to me any positive comments he might receive from parents about the music program. Those comments would always make my day.

The 1996–97 school year started with the obligatory teacher "in-service" days. They included normal workshops, meetings, and planning time. I noticed that the stage area where I taught my lessons and band rehearsals had been cleaned up quite a bit over the summer. Even the stage floor had been varnished. Once I got used to the smell, I appreciated the efforts.

We were introduced to our new principal, Mr. John Coparco. He had come from a large city school system in Rhode Island. My thought was how different this school system was going to be for him. He came across as tough but had a great sense of humor, which buoyed the spirits of all of us on the faculty. I got the strong sense that he was the type of person you did not want to cross. I made it a point to go into his office the next day and introduce myself.

As soon as I walked into his office, I knew I had hit the jackpot! Displayed on the wall behind his desk was a New York Rangers hockey jersey. My team . . . my sport! After he saw my jaw drop, he said, "Jim, you like hockey?"

I exclaimed "Absolutely!" I related to him that having grown up on Long Island resulted in my being an avid Rangers fan since I was eight years old. I could see his eyes glinting as he talked about his experiences being a minor league hockey player in the New York Rangers farm system.

He related, "I was going to play for the Rangers until I blew out my knee. I was a tough defenseman who did not fool around on the ice. I played for the Providence Reds in the American Hockey League." I just sat there, transfixed.

The two of us proceeded to talk about hockey for several minutes. We seemed to have hit it off very well. He then asked me a bunch of questions about the music program. He asked me if I had seen the band roster yet. "Yes, I am so pleased that the numbers have increased," I commented. All the eighth graders had signed up from last year as well as fifteen former band members from two years ago.

John's next words were "Jim, I just want you to know that I have spoken with a few parents, who told me how excited they were to have their kids back in the band program again. Sounds like you did a damn good job last year."

At that point, I gave John a brief background about last year. I related to him about how a bunch of students dropped out, probably because the band was not going to continue to be a "country club." I told him also about the percussionist whom I had overheard saying he was going to get me fired. John said, "Jim, I already know who that is. Derrick's father is the chairman of the school board. Other teachers have told me they have heard Derrick say the same words. We are all watching this kid's butt this year. He is not going to get away with that anymore,"

Good, I thought. Looks like I wasn't the only teacher who gave him poor grades in their class. Derrick had received a low grade from me last year and never made it past the first half of the year in band. He had dropped out, but not before he made sure I got the word that my job was on the line.

2

Year two started with a continuation of the same schedule I had from year one. My nine-tenths position was still in effect, but I had to start teaching now during the first period and my day was over after period 9. I thought at first that might work out better, but shortly after the year began, I noticed that I rarely left school earlier. I was staying on to do a bit of planning for the next day. I had also started a science fiction club, which was meeting once a week after school.

It was obvious that here was another school system getting a full day's work from me for less than a full day's pay. Now that John was here, I felt I could make a good case for the position to become full-time.

Both bands got off to a good start, as did guitar class and the rock and roll history class. I had spent time over the summer editing some of the course videos to get rid of the more "adult stuff." You know how rockers could be! I had a tape-editing machine at home, and that came in super handy.

In the meantime, John and I started exchanging neckties a couple of days a week. He had complimented me early on about some of my "music" ties. I had also inquired about where he got those sports-related ties he sometimes wore. One day we decided to swap for the day. That was so much fun knowing that we were able to have fun during a sometimes stressful school day.

I had to admit to myself that Parish Hill was growing on me. It was amazing to me to see that I was enjoying the concept of "less is more." With fewer students I was definitely able to get to know them better. And, there were some very needy kids. It was obvious who the students were who were not from the most financially stable situations. My heart went out to them.

The support staff at Parish Hill were a professionally effective group. I was impressed with the way they went about serving the kids. To address an increasingly evident problem, the administration called an "all-school" assembly where the subject was bullying, race, and homophobia. *The 'panty-wipe crew' was probably at it again*, I thought.

The school assembly was eye-opening, to say the least. Students got up in front of everyone and spoke about their experiences. The reaction of the rest of the school was informative. There was not a sound in the auditorium for the entire hour's program. Some of my band students were speakers, and I learned so much about them that day. They showed honesty, talked about their inner pain, and were courageous. The session was a wake-up call for all of us. It was one of the most positive programs I had ever witnessed in a public school.

3

The holiday concert went off without a hitch for both bands. The chorus, under Uma's direction, performed well. She was so musical and her interpretation of the music was exemplary. There was much optimism around the music department heading into the spring.

Things were rolling along in January until I felt like I had been hit by a freight train. Since I had not been teaching yet for two years at Parish Hill, I did not have tenure. That is always in the back of your mind when you are new in a school system. But because things had been going so well, I had no cause to be insecure about my position. I had no cause to worry about having to "land on my feet" as I had done three times already during my career.

The "gut-punch" came down in a letter from the system's curriculum coordinator. The middle school and high school music department positions were going to be combined into one position for the '97–'98 school year. One person would be doing both vocal and instrumental music. The position cut meant I would no longer have a job. Uma had tenure and seniority.

I went to her later in the day. She was in tears. John grabbed me before I left for the day and told me he was going to lobby the school board on our behalf. "Hang in there, Jim, let's see what happens," he advised.

I was in a slight stupor over the next few weeks. Why would the board of education choose to do this just when the instrumental program was reviving and beginning to flourish again? I woke up in the middle of the night one day with a depressing thought. I knew the chairman of the board was Derrick's father. I could not stop thinking, *No, that couldn't be what was happening here, could it?*

46 -
MY "MR. HOLLAND" MOMENT

I WENT ABOUT MY JOB with as much passion as I could muster. If this had to be my last year with these kids, I was going to do my best. I noticed that John was in a surly mood more often than usual in recent days. I knew he was advocating for us every day. That knowledge gave me some hope.

One evening at home I received a call from George Sanders, an old musician friend of my wife and me. George was a music educator as well as the assistant principal trombone in the Hartford Symphony. During our chat he mentioned, "Hey, I just heard there is now an opening in the Manchester Schools for an elementary instrumental long-term sub."

"Really?" I exclaimed. Manchester was the next town over from where I lived and had a fine reputation as a school system and a solid instrumental music program. George had known about my prospects of being cut from Parish Hill. "Why don't you give them a call and find out what it's all about?" George suggested.

This was interesting news, but my first thought was *Do I want to leave another school system before the end of a school year?* I spent a sleepless night debating this with myself. *No, I don't*, one side argued. But the other side of the issue was *This may be a way to get my foot in the door in Manchester*. The debate continued. *I don't want to leave these kids. I have invested so much energy in teaching them. And yet, I have to think about my career in the long term. Manchester would be a great place to land.*

I called Mary Kalbfliesch the next day. She thanked me for my interest and explained what would be included with the long-term sub position. It was a full-time commitment to cover three elementary schools' instrumental lessons over the last three months of this school year. And, the possibility that I would be hired as a member of the instrumental music staff was strong. I could start as soon as possible.

I received a lot of positive vibes from her, so I made an appointment to meet with her a couple of days later. I took a professional day from Parish Hill. Mary told me they would be able to hire me on Step 5 on the salary scale, which was the equivalent of a fifth-year teacher. I hesitated for a moment, knowing I had many more years of experience under my belt. But then Mary explained that I would be receiving double increments to more quickly move up the pay ladder. That sounded good to me. I signed a letter of commitment. I would begin in two weeks.

2

Now, to tell my friends at Parish Hill. I made an appointment to see John. I had a feeling he knew what I was going to say. "John, I am giving the Board my two weeks' notice today. I am going to take a long-term sub position in Manchester. I feel like I am letting the kids down, but I don't see any other choice for me. Manchester would be a great place for me to land."

John paused for a moment as his eyes looked straight into mine. "F**k 'em" came blasting out of his mouth. His tone of voice was what I would imagine he would use to yell at a hockey referee over a bad call. I felt John's rage, yet I knew he was not directing that at me. He was yelling, in absentia, at the Regional District Eleven school board.

He continued, "Jim, what I am about to tell you does not leave this room. I, myself, am leaving the school system at the end of this school year." I was shocked to hear him say that. He just got here. "No one knows this but a small few," he whispered. I was amazed he would share this information with me, but not surprised, knowing the relationship we had built up. "I have had it with the small-town narrow-mindedness of the board, especially the chairman."

Well, that spoke volumes and it confirmed what my suspicions had been. Derrick's dad had gotten rid of me the only way he could have, by cutting my position. Both John and I wished each other the best as I left his office. Derrick had won.

3

It seemed like the next two weeks passed by like a flash. I had told my students about my decision to leave and again experienced the usual sadness and disappointment from a lot of them. To quote Yogi Berra, it seemed like "déjà vu all over again." I had grown attached to the school, administration, the staff, and the kids. Again, as had happened multiple times before in the past, I had been thinking about how I wouldn't mind teaching here for the rest of my career. This was the fourth time I would be leaving a school system. Here we go again.

My final day at Parish Hill finally arrived. They had cancelled my classes in the afternoon so I could gather all my belongings and pack everything in my car. I had finished packing in my Rock history room, boxing up all the video tapes and records. I left copies of the videos for the person who would be replacing me. That took quite a bit of work over the past several days but I thought I owed that to my students. Just as I finished filling the boxes, the classroom phone rang. It was one of the school secretaries. "Mister Kleiner, could you please report to the auditorium?"

"Sure, be right there" I answered, wondering what was going on.

I walked through the stage side door and the first thing I saw was that the stage was set up with chairs filled with some of my band students. I glanced then at the auditorium, and it was filled with students. It had to be the entire school! They all stood up at once and gave me a standing ovation, which seemed to last forever. I saw John at the side of the stage, encouraging the ovation to continue.

I was in shock. My eyes were tearing up. All I could think of was *Keep it together. This has to be what Mr. Holland felt. What a feeling!* The noise died down and my band president, Russell, proceeded to speak on behalf of the music department. He thanked me for my time as their music teacher and they presented me with two items, both of which I have cherished to this day.

Russell first presented me with a wood-grained plaque. It was musically themed, with a gold medallion mounted in the upper right corner. Diagonally across the plaque was mounted a real conductor's baton. Russell read the inscription:

With Appreciation to: JAMES KLEINER for Leadership, for Inspiration and for Adding a Touch of Beauty to Parish Hill

We Will Miss You!
March 24, 1997

I was stunned. I had never seen such a beautiful plaque as this one. The second item presented to me was a T-shirt, which said in block letters:

WE WILL MISS YOU, BAND AND CHORUS

The T-shirt contained signatures and comments by many band and chorus members. Things expressed included "You helped a lot of people – including me. Thanks for everything and good luck"; "You don't understand how much better you allowed me to play, Thanks"; "Thanks for all the hard work!"; "Thank you for the support and encouragement. We'll miss you."

There were many other wonderful well wishes and signatures, including one from John Coparco. This T-shirt was professionally printed with all of this. Everyone had signed in advance.

I was incredibly touched. I had to pull myself together. I went to the podium and said, "I want to thank all of you from the bottom of my heart. I am so touched by all the kind words and the gifts, which I will cherish forever. Parish Hill is a special place. I will miss all of you and will always remember your kindness. It has been a privilege to teach here."

I was amazed that I was able to get through that. But I did. It really was the "Mr. Holland" moment of my career. It is one that I will carry with me in my heart and memory forever.

> *"What a teacher writes on the blackboard of life can never be erased."*
>
> —UNKNOWN

47 - A SHORTER DRIVE

MY FIRST DAY IN MANCHESTER included a meeting with Mary, the music coordinator, who had hired me weeks before. She summarized my responsibilities as a long-term sub, and the expectations she had for me to finish the school year at each school. "The principals at each school don't expect you to pull off a concert in May," Mary related, "but take stock of the situation at each school and see what you can do."

What she said was exactly what I had been thinking. What I also decided was that we were going to have concerts at all three or none at all. I did not want to show favoritism to any one school. I toured the schools that afternoon. The principals in each case were happy to have instrumental lessons resume.

During one of the discussions, one of the principals filled me in on why the sudden opening had arisen. It had been discovered that the former teacher was having an affair with a former student, who was now of high school age. I was surprised I had not heard about this elsewhere, either in the newspapers or on the local news. Issues concerning teachers seemed to be sensationalized over the years in the press or media. It was obvious in this case things were kept out of the limelight.

It was time to get these students "up and running" again. The three schools were in neighborhoods of differing economic environments. Washington School was in a lower middle class, ethnically diverse neighborhood. Verplanck School was definitely blue collar. And Martin School was situated in a middle to upper class neighborhood, bordering the local country club.

The bottom line was that Manchester was a diverse community

with a wide cross-section of folks. Martin School had a robust elementary instrumental program going, which was evident as I began lessons there. A first for me during my career was that Manchester had a string program. The strings were already under the direction of a staff of string teachers at each level. The Martin string students were covered, as were those at the other schools.

Verplanck also had a good number of students waiting for me. We were able to continue the schedule that had already been in place. The downside was the twenty-minute lessons that existed because of the number of students enrolled. I immediately started to look at the roster to see if we could expand lessons to thirty minutes. Half-hours were not long to begin with, especially for a class of more than two students.

Washington School had only eleven enrolled wind, brass, or percussion students. I was pleased to find a couple of kids who had dropped out earlier in the year. With a bit of prodding, they agreed to join a lesson class again. So, we now had thirteen in the program.

Manchester had a good supply of school-owned instruments available, so I found that to be a positive. But my experience in dealing with minor instrument repairs was going to come in handy, I knew for sure.

I settled in at the three schools over the first few weeks and I made it a point to get to know the fourth and fifth grade teachers. If I was going to be pulling students out of their classes, I wanted to establish some sort of rapport with them as soon as possible.

One morning at Verplanck, I went into a fifth grade class to speak to a couple of my students, not noticing the "Testing, do not disturb" sign posted on the door. As I walked in the door, the teacher, who I found out later was ex-military, physically escorted me right back out the door! I was taken aback by this, but later found out how stringent the rules were against interrupting these standardized tests. I guess I found out the hard way. As it turned out, this teacher, who was a former musician herself, became one of my biggest supporters and allies over the next few years.

As things turned out, the spring concerts seemed possible at all three schools. I can thank the administrations and staff at each school for being quite cooperative with me in terms of my scheduling of extra rehearsals. These kids were going to be able to have a concert experience after all. Parents and relatives were very appreciative of this.

We scheduled the Washington School concert in the afternoon. The principal advised that it was safer to have the concert and other school events during the day. I took her word for that.

Verplanck and Martin hosted evening concerts and they went quite well. We got through to the end of the school year. I was able to visit the third grade classes during the final weeks of the year to recruit for next year's fourth grade beginning instrumental classes.

My experience had paid off. I had seen and done enough in my career to get through this situation and never felt more confident about what I was doing. I felt great support from everyone in the Manchester music department. I liked my colleagues. I felt fortunate to have landed in this town.

48 - TWO FOR THE PRICE OF ONE

OVER THE SUMMER I HAD been notified that due to a current staff member getting priority, I would not be able to have a full-time position in the fall. Furthermore, I was being given three days to cover the same schools. I would have a three-fifths position. This was not ideal, but I was willing to play the long game. I liked being a member of the Manchester Schools' staff. I was not going anywhere.

Out of the blue one day, as I habitually would peruse the want ads of the *Hartford Courant*, I came across a listing in the education section. As I had learned a few years ago, keeping tabs on the want ads could be beneficial. I saw a part-time opening for a fourth grade instrumental music teacher. *Hmm*, I thought, *let me make a phone call.*

As it turned out, it was a beneficial phone call at that! I spoke to the music supervisor of the Lebanon public schools, who sounded anxious to speak to me in person once I told her about my experience. She told me that Lebanon Elementary School was in need of a teacher to start fourth graders in the instrumental program. The position had just opened up.

A few days later I headed out to Lyman Hall High School in Lebanon and met with Alicia Gagnon. She explained that the position would be a two-day-per-week commitment. Guess who had two days free each week? I told her I could do that. I was hired! And on top of that, I could choose the days based on my schedule in Manchester. Lebanon was totally flexible, Alicia told me. As I left the meeting, I pondered the fact that I would be teaching in two separate school systems simultaneously. And they said it couldn't be done!

I spoke to Lebanon El. Principal Bob Borello, and he was also fine with me picking the days I would be there. I could teach there on Tuesdays and Fridays, the days I was not in Manchester. And I was pleasantly surprised to find out that the recruitment of the fourth graders for the instrumental program had already taken place during the previous spring.

A couple of days later I went to visit the school and met with Bob. He showed me my teaching area, which was tight, to say the least. It was an 8' × 10' room, but it did have a desk for me to use. He told me that he would make sure the teachers would be flexible. That made things easier to set up a schedule. I knew immediately after seeing the teaching space that I would not be able to have more than two or three students in each class. Half-hour lessons would work knowing I had about thirty students.

Another interesting year was approaching. I had again landed on my feet. But this time in two places at once!

49 -
A DISAPPOINTING REUNION

AT THE BEGINNING, IT SEEMED like the trick was to think ahead and do my planning for two different environments. This, as it turned out, was not as challenging as I had thought. In fact, the biggest problem at first was heading towards the correct town on the right day. A couple of times that first month, I absentmindedly headed towards Manchester on a Lebanon day and vice versa. I attributed that to just having turned fifty years old. It had to be that, right?

In any case, the routine turned out to be refreshing for me. I had always found benefits to teaching at multiple schools during the school year. Different atmospheres, administrations, colleagues, neighborhoods, parents, and of course their children. I appreciated the fact that the majority of my students were in my classes because they had a high interest in what they were learning. It was my job to keep that interest up and keep them motivated. The older and more experienced I became in the world of music education, the more I valued this feeling.

I also appreciated having the opportunity of teaching beginning players from scratch. There were always those moments when I could see the "lightbulb" go on. The smiles and enthusiasm were priceless. If you are a teacher reading this, you know exactly what I am talking about. We live for those moments. They are what keep us going through the tough times. We love those moments of wonder and discovery.

The fall seemed to go by in a flash. I wasn't minding the extra miles to get to Lebanon. The drive with all the colors was awesome. In December I received an email from Russell, my former band president at Parish Hill. He invited me on behalf of himself and some of my former students to attend their holiday concert. What a nice gesture. I told him I would attend and looked forward to seeing my former Parish Hill kids.

The concert date arrived and I drove out East. It was a familiar drive to Chaplin.

2

I was filled with nostalgia to be back at Parish Hill. I settled into a seat and looked at the stage, which looked like a Hollywood set. Christmas trees, holiday objects, and fake snow (I was surprised at that point they did not have fake snow wafting down from the rafters) on the stage.

The chorus came out first and were dressed in new outfits with seasonal colors. *That clothing must have cost big bucks*, I thought. My former colleague, Uma, was not listed on the program. She obviously did not stay to take the new position.

The new music director, whom I shall call "Mr. X," came on stage in a glitzy tuxedo and proceeded to put on quite a show. The choir was smaller than I had remembered. They sang all holiday music that one could just as easily hear in a supermarket or an elevator. I was yearning for a selection with more musical substance as I had heard Uma do with them during the past couple of years. They proceeded to do their best and received nice applause from Mom, Dad, Grandmom, and Grandpa. I was struck by the lack of harmony. They sang mostly in unison. It reminded me of an elementary choral performance.

The band then came on stage. It was nice to see that most of the students I had for the past two years were still in the group. Again, the band, like the chorus, was "dressed to the nines." The boys were in tuxedos and the ladies in fancy concert dresses. All I could think about was what a financial cost it must have been to outfit the kids in both groups. Where did the money come from? So, they had the money to do this at the expense of cutting a position?

The band played music that was not near the level we had played last year. Two or three grade levels down was my guess. Simplistic and musically unsatisfying was how it struck me. I was seeing the new direction of this music program right in front of my eyes and ears.

This situation seemed to be familiar. A new direction based on someone new, either an educator or, in my experience, a new administrator. The emphasis here at Parish Hill had been changed from musical excellence to fluff and show. I thought I was watching a holiday television spectacle.

The band finished up and it was obvious to me by watching their faces that the music content of their concert was not very satisfying to them. How did I know this? Because I was on the stage with them during their previous year's holiday concert. I saw a marked difference.

The audience was appreciative and I am sure they enjoyed all the accoutrements on the stage. Mr. X seemed to be basking in all the applause a bit too much. Through his body language I was seeing his ego give the impression that this concert had been all about him and not his students. The applause died down and then he began to speak.

His speech went something like this: "Doesn't this stage look amazing? (applause) Thanks to all who contributed their time and support to make this great show. The students look great too, don't you think? (applause) I am so proud we were able to bring up the level of this music department from what it has been in the past. The students here at Parish Hill deserved a better experience in the music program and I gave it to them."

I was shocked and enraged at those words. I had all I could do to not stand up out of my seat and yell at this charlatan. I could see my former band kids exhibiting shocked looks on their faces. This jerk had basically trashed the previous teachers at this school and, in the same breath, the students who were on stage with him. My first thought after the students left the stage was to go backstage and confront this guy and give him a piece of my mind.

I gave myself a few moments to cool down. I was thinking about my former students by that time. I was not going to make a scene and ruin their concert night experience. I ended up waiting in the lobby and spoke with a few parents and their kids. "Great job, guys. It's so great to see you, and I miss you" was my general sentiment. I quickly left the building before I had the chance to confront Mr. X. It would not have been pretty. I had not been back to Parish Hill until recently as I needed a picture of the school for this book.

As a postscript to this sad situation, I heard a few weeks later that Mr. X had done away with the immensely popular middle school Rock history course. He commandeered that room to make it his office. I guess the stage was not good enough for him.

3

As the spring continued, my music room became somewhat of a sanctuary for the Lebanon El. principal. Bob needed a place at times to escape the hustle and bustle of the main office. My room was downstairs and way off the beat and track. He knew where he could hide and take a few deep breaths. He seemed to enjoy listening to the fourth graders play, and I know the kids were thrilled to have him there. Bob paid attention to his music teachers and I appreciated that. Plus, I always knew what was going on in the school. That was cool!

I thought back to my Vernon days. Principal Don Elwood and I at Skinner Road School would shoot baskets together in the gym between some of my classes. I knew that he also needed to get out of his office at times. We had many a laugh together. He was a great human being. Dave Parker, principal at Vernon Middle School, was another person whom I could confide in. I bowled against him in the Vernon teachers' bowling league. He knew how to give it to me and my partner, Jean Slyne, who was the secretary at Skinner. Jean was a sweet person and my favorite secretary of all my career. And, quite a bowler too. She definitely carried our team. By the way, Dave loved it when we both gave it right back to him on the lanes.

Andy Maneggia, another principal I had at VCMS, always had my back. I never saw anyone stay as calm as he did when things got hectic. He was a rock! And of course, my tie-swapping buddy John Caparco. I will never forget his support and encouragement at Parish

Hill. I did not know it at the time, but I was to have several other incredible administrators in Manchester.

4

The spring concert at Lebanon El went very well. I was so proud of those kids. We performed in the gym and it was jam-packed with proud parents listening to their children's first instrumental music concert. We held the concert early in the evening due to the age of the students.

A few weeks before the end of the school year I received word that Lebanon was cutting the fourth grade beginning instrumental music due to budget cuts. Another reality check. I was again the victim of circumstance. I was down in the dumps for a couple of days until I got the news that Manchester could offer me two additional schools to cover, so I would be a full-time staff member. I would have had to leave Lebanon anyway.

I felt satisfied that I started the Lebanon El kids well. I thanked the Lebanon staff at the end-of-the-year faculty luncheon. I received a warm handshake from Bob. He thanked me for what he called "a great year." That was all I needed.

50 - A FULL-TIME TEACHER ONCE AGAIN

IT WAS BACK TO BEING a full-time teacher again. That felt good. I now felt like a significant part of the Manchester music program. I continued to be impressed with the caliber of my colleagues. The music department had a nice mix of experienced teachers and young educators as well. And, there was an abundance of enthusiasm amongst the entire group. I loved that.

It was fun to continue to have the responsibility to recruit new instrumental students from the fourth grade classes at the beginning of the year. Instrumental demonstrations were a significant part of that. Manchester had a tradition of busing all the third grade students to the high school at the end of the year for a demo concert. Each instrument was demonstrated and performances would be given by the high school band and orchestra.

At the beginning of the kids' fourth grade, I would be tasked with visiting all the classrooms for the instrument sign-ups. I would also visit the fifth grade students already in the program and organize the lesson schedule. There were lots of things to do in a short amount of time.

The classroom teachers were usually quite flexible and cooperative with my "invading" their classrooms on a regular basis for a few weeks. I was still on the alert for any "Testing" signs. I certainly did not want to be body-slammed out of a classroom again.

Setting up a schedule for lessons for the elementary music staff was becoming increasingly challenging. Although we were able to "pull out" students from their classes once a week for their lessons, each year there seemed to be more restrictions on when we could do so.

Math was the first class from which we could not pull out kids.

We had to know specifically which was the math instructional time for each teacher. This restriction caused some classes to be heterogenous, which was not ideal. Homogeneous classes were always the goal. This was something we had to live with.

The year progressed and I was pleased with the progress of the students. The performance goal was the Spring Inter-elementary fifth grade concert. All of us elementary teachers would work on the same ensemble music and then we would combine them into a large performing group. Manchester High School auditorium was a perfect venue due to its large stage.

In the meantime, we would schedule each school's band spring concert to take place at their own school. as well. It was an exciting event, especially for the fourth graders, who would have the chance to play in their first concert. It always was much fun for me to see the reaction of the parents and grandparents at these concerts. They were all so proud!

The school year ended, and as things were winding down I was hearing that the Bennet (one of the town's two middle schools) band director was not going to be rehired. Evidently there were problems with discipline as well as the teacher's absenteeism. The gentleman had been part of the ARC (Alternate Route Career) program the State of Connecticut had in force to enable folks to train to be educators after coming from other careers. In this case, it was obvious this person was not cut out to be a teacher.

Here I was, an experienced middle school teacher. Would I be considered to possibly fill that position? No one had contacted me up to this point to see if I was interested. I did not want to get my hopes up, so I just focused on the upcoming summer break.

51 - LEARNING FROM MY STUDENTS

IN THE MEANTIME, I WENT into the following school year with a sense of anticipation and enthusiasm. I was enjoying the experience of teaching such an ethnically diverse group of students. This year I was assigned again to four of the town's elementary schools. Each school in its own neighborhood was unique. I liked the differences. Each school had its own distinctive "feel."

Waddell School was the new building I would have to get to know. It was in a similar neighborhood to Verplank, a solid blue-collar area. Not surprisingly, the school was quite welcoming, as were the parents and students. I was looking back to the other schools as well.

The classes at Washington School were still being held on the stage of the gymnasium. Fortunately, there was a solid hinged stage door that would close off the stage from the gym. And to my delight the door was remarkably soundproof. I also liked the fact that the backstage door opened right into the parking lot. If I forgot something in my car, I could quickly sneak out and retrieve it in short order.

2

Shortly into the school year at Washington, I would have an experience that would have a profound impact on my life. It began one day at the end of a clarinet lesson with two enthusiastic fifth graders, Sasha and Tanisha. As they were packing up their clarinets, Sasha asked me, "Hey, Mister Kleiner, what kind of music do you listen to?"

I answered, "Well, I like to listen to classical music, jazz, Broadway show tunes, and some New Age music as well. What do you ladies listen to?"

Sasha replied, "Oh, I don't think you would know about the music we listen to."

"Hey, ladies, I would love to know what you listen to. Here is a sheet of paper. Write down your favorite singers and groups for me."

They both looked at each other with wry smiles and eagerly began to write. After noticing how much they were enjoying this task, I was looking forward to seeing what they were writing down. I looked at the list and saw a few familiar names, but not many. "Hey, ladies, I love the fact that you have Alicia Keys on the list! I think she is great." The girls looked at each other, aghast that I would know who Alicia Keys was. I took the list and bid them goodbye until next week.

"Have fun with the list, Mister K!" Tanisha exclaimed. I wasn't sure what I had gotten myself into, but I knew I had my work cut out for me. In any case, I knew I had much to learn.

I had seen Alicia Keys on TV earlier in the year and was so impressed I went out and purchased her first album, *Songs in A Minor*. I absolutely loved it. Here was a wonderful pianist, song writer, and lyricist all rolled into one. I had already made a mental note to buy her second album, *The Diary of Alicia Keys*. I thought about that as I looked at the list the girls had made for me, which included Destiny's Child (which included Beyoncé, one of the few people on the list I had heard of), Keyshia Cole, Ciara, Rihanna, Ne-Yo, the group Danity Kane, Mary J. Blige, and John Legend. A who's who of the present day "R and B" music scene.

So, what was I going to do with this list? The thought occurred to me that anyone on a list with Alicia Keys would be worth a listen. Over the next couple of days, I purchased CDs of all those artists. I had a six-CD changer in my car, so I filled it up. That week in particular, it worked out that I had a few rehearsals for a production of the well-known Broadway show *On the Twentieth Century*. Goodspeed Opera House in East Haddam had hired me to play in the pit orchestra. I had some lengthy travel time in the car, to and from the theater. I had ample opportunity to listen!

That week's listening turned out to be a revelation! My brain was flooded with endorphins listening to this music. I could not get over the passion of the lyrics, the harmonies, and the infectious rhythms. I could not stop listening. I was hooked.

Sasha and Tanisha's lesson was to roll around the next week. I had made sure I had the CDs in the car with me just in case. Tanisha could not wait to ask me, "Hey, Mister K, did you listen to the people on the list?"

"Yes, I did," I answered.

"I bought a CD of each person and group."

"No, you didn't," Sasha said incredulously.

I responded, "Just wait a moment, ladies, and let me go out to my car and get the CDs," as I quickly opened the backstage door. I brought them in and spread them out on my desk. The girls glanced at each other with a surprised look on their faces.

"I can't believe you did this!" Sasha exclaimed.

I said, "I listened to them all week and I really enjoyed hearing these people's music. They are amazing!" I then reeled off some of my favorite tracks and the girls' jaws dropped. I went ahead and played a couple of tracks on the sound system for my now amazed students. "No One Will Do" by Mary J. Blige, "Don't Stop the Music" by Rhianna, "I Found Myself" by Ciara, "Survivor" by Destiny's Child, "Single Ladies" by Beyonce, "Shoulda Let You Go" by Keyshia Cole, and "Fallin'" by Alicia Keys. It was my special treat for them. We could dispense with playing clarinet this week. They had added a wonderful new musical experience for me. The girls left the stage with huge smiles on their faces after class. I had one as well.

It did not take long for the word to get around Washington School about what had happened. I kept my new CDs with me during my lesson days and between lessons I would often play a track. Kids would stick their heads in the stage door to listen. I noticed an uptick in practicing over the next few months from several kids. This was a bonus. I didn't know if there was any correlation between the practicing and the R and B music coming out of my room. But I wasn't going to argue with the result.

I had learned much about a new musical genre because of my students. I had learned from them. And, the best thing of all was that it became known around Washington School that Mr. Kleiner was "cool."

> *"When I was a kid, I'd practice Chopin on piano – and I love Chopin! He's my dawg! Then I'd go out on the stoop and blast the radio."*
>
> —ALICIA KEYS

52 -
STAYING PUT

THE SUMMER BREAK WAS A good time to visit my brother-in-law out in California. Our family ended up enjoying the beautiful city of San Diego, including a day trip to Mexico among other exciting events. One afternoon while I was sunbathing out at the beach, my cell phone rang and at the other end of the line was Dr. Alan Beitman, superintendent of the Manchester Public Schools. Alan had been the long-time principal of Manchester's Illing Middle School and had recently taken the job of superintendent.

He began the conversation by saying, "Jim, this is Alan Beitman. I wanted to let you know that as of yesterday, the position of band director at Illing is now vacant. Would you be interested in interviewing for the position?"

I thought for about two seconds and replied, "Yes, sir, I would!"

"Okay, good, We are in the process of setting up an interview committee and it looks like the interviews will be in a couple of weeks."

"Alan, I am in California right now on vacation, but I will be back East by the week of interviews. Thanks for notifying me. I really appreciate that."

"No problem, Jim. I will let you know when your interview is scheduled. In the meantime, enjoy yourself out there on the West coast."

A couple of weeks later, we returned and I took the interview over at Illing. The interview committee consisted of some of the school administration, as well as the new coordinator of music, Donna Rusack. Included also were members of the Manchester music faculty. I had met them all during the past year and a half. And, I already knew Donna as she had taken the coordinator position earlier during the previous year. I felt good about the interview. There were many familiar faces.

During the interview, the committee asked me the expected questions about my musical philosophy, and my experience in teaching lessons, band, and jazz band. All were things I had done multiple times during my career. The group also seemed to like the fact that I was a working professional musician as well. One of them commented on the challenges of balancing two careers. I certainly agreed with that point. That was one of my goals from the beginning. Perform and teach. As they say, I was "having my cake and eating it too."

I felt really good about the interview. I knew in the back of my mind that I had gotten every job in music education for which I had interviewed. So, why not this one?

Maybe I was too cocky. I did not get the position. Evidently the committee felt someone else was a stronger candidate. My string of successful interviews had come to an end.

The Fall of 1998 approached. I was looking forward to a year of teaching elementary instrumental music at four schools where I felt quite comfortable. I loved the fact my feet were firmly planted in the Manchester schools!

53 -
AN ODD DECISION

I VISITED MY SCHOOLS DURING August and began to prepare my teaching spaces for the opening of school the next month. During those times, school was still starting after Labor Day. School-owned instruments needed to be tested to determine whether repairs were needed. I would usually not look forward to that because it was a long, painstaking process. However, I would then realize that I should feel lucky to have so many instruments to offer the kids.

There were always several teachers in the buildings during these summer days. I don't think the general public realizes how much extra time teachers give to prepare before and after the school years. I had learned very quickly that teaching was not an 8-to-3 job. Oh no, it was much more. We did what we needed to do to be ready. This dedication comes with the job. Every teacher knows this.

I was working on some school instruments one afternoon when I got a visit from Donna. She took me into the faculty room and we partook of the coffee available. I thought we were going to just "shoot the breeze." But that was not the reason she had sought me out on that day.

"Jim, the band job at Bennet Middle School just opened up," she explained. I was shocked! Both middle school jobs opening up over the same summer? She continued, "I wanted to know if you would like to interview." I told her I would have to think it over and she said that was fine.

Over the next couple of days my mind was playing the "pros and cons" game. I was excited about covering my elementary schools again and had done quite a bit of preparatory work already. And yet, the thought of taking another middle school position was tempting.

Tony Susi, who was leaving to take a job in a neighboring town's high school, was a superior music educator. Who could resist that situation? I agreed to interview.

2

The interview was between me, the school principal, and the chorus teacher who also served as the team leader for the Bennet music department. I thought the participants in the interview would include others. Where were other members of the music department? Where was Donna? I put these thoughts aside and did my best. I felt quite good about this interview, as I had for the previous interview earlier in the summer. But I did feel a bit uncomfortable because I was not questioned with much depth.

During the following days I continued my elementary preparations. I was hoping to hear something soon from Bennet so I might have the time to get things organized over there if I did get the job. Then, Donna came to visit me and was not a happy camper. "You did not get the job," she moaned. "I questioned the principal and asked him very bluntly about whether or not he had seen your resume."

I had never seen Donna so upset. I already knew she was upset that she had not been included in the interview. After all, she was the Bennet string specialist as well as music coordinator. Something smelled bad about this whole situation to me. I am sure Donna felt the same.

As it turned out, the new hire was a young man right out of the Connecticut Department of Education's ARC program. The situation became quite clear. The powers to be at Bennet ended up hiring an ARC candidate instead of an experienced middle school band director. Both Donna and I agreed. "Lots of luck with that!" The saving grace was that this person was coming into a stable situation. But, as it turned out, that stability vanished very quickly.

54 -
ANOTHER LEAP OF FAITH

THE SCHOOL YEAR CAME AND went. I was enjoying the educational atmosphere in all my schools. The kids were as enthusiastic as I had experienced in my career. My performing career was also busy and rewarding. I was enjoying my professional life to the max.

Over that summer the administration had decided to replace the ARC graduate that had spent the year at Bennet. I had never met the gentleman during the year. I expected another invitation to interview but I was not aware of any interviews having been scheduled. Subsequently I heard that a second ARC candidate was to be hired for the fall.

I had heard horror stories about what had been going on over at Bennet in the band program. No wonder this guy had been let go. But it seemed not to make any sense to go again with another ARC candidate in lieu of someone with experience.

We met Dave at the music faculty meeting prior to the school opening. He seemed like a nice enough guy, having been a flight instructor who always had music as a hobby. He decided he needed a career change. Good for him. I did have much respect for those people coming out of the ARC program. It certainly takes a certain amount of bravery to undergo a career change. I knew that from my own experience. We all wished Dave well and offered assistance if he ever needed it.

The fall went smoothly for me, especially with having a few years of experience in Manchester under my belt. Having overall teaching experience is one thing. But having been in a specific school situation over multiple years can be quite helpful. Familiarity is an asset.

In the meantime, I began to hear stories about how things were going at Bennet. At our November faculty meeting, Dave was not looking good. Somehow, he looked as though he had aged a few years during the past couple of months. In December, just out of curiosity, I attended the BMS holiday concert. I was shocked!

Dave's seventh and eighth grade band played selections from their band method book. They were short unison selections which lasted about a minute each. They did finally play a simple band arrangement at the end of the concert consisting of Christmas carols. This program, and its execution, said volumes. It was obvious this concert was thrown together at the last minute.

I did not find this level of performance with the orchestra. Donna did her usual solid job with her students. What was going on behind the scenes with the BMS bands?

As it turned out, I found out soon enough. A few days after the concert, Donna came to see me after school. "Dave is going to be leaving the BMS job. He is quite unhappy and told me he doesn't want to continue in the position," Donna exclaimed with an exasperated tone. "I have been asked to inquire if you would consider taking the BMS job starting in January."

My immediate reply was "Really? Why would I consider taking that job? I have already been turned down for a middle school job here."

I was not happy, but I was not trying to take things out on Donna. This whole situation was certainly not of her making. I know she understood my reaction and probably expected as much. Her next words were "Let's go take a walk."

We walked the school grounds and had a heart-to-heart. I had a huge amount of respect for Donna, not only as a musician but also as a person. She was a total team player and an effective leader. She was "up-front" to me about the Bennet situation. Dave had not been able to keep the necessary decorum with some of his students and that was not all his fault. Donna explained that he had received little support from the school administration in trying to deal with the problems that had their origin in the previous year.

The reality was that the previous ARC hire had no control at all in the classroom. Donna was in the building every day, so she knew. Ultimately, the guy was calling in sick every other day. Dave had walked into a mess. Donna had little input into his hiring to be able to warn him.

We must have walked for about a half-hour before ending up back inside the school. My mind was again balancing the pros and cons. However, something was different this time. My juices were flowing. Could I pass up another chance at righting a situation I knew my experience would give me the chance to do? I was no stranger to coming into a new situation and establishing myself.

I had some stable situations, some more so than others. Sykes, VCMS, Bloomfield JHS, Ellington HS, Parish Hill, Lebanon El., Manchester elementary schools. This was quite a list. *Could I do this again? Do I want to do this again?*

I could not resist. "I will do it," I told Donna before she left. She had a total look of relief. She was excited. "I will do this for the good of the department and for you," I exclaimed. She smiled from ear to ear. I did too. I was ready to take the leap again.

55 -
STANDING MY GROUND

AFTER I HAD THE CHANCE to run a rehearsal with some students from the BMS band the deal was sealed. I was impressed with the fact that the lesson was attended by the BMS school administrators, including Dr. Beitman. The school principal was not there, which I thought was odd. Donna told me later that the group in attendance liked the work I had done with the kids and that my experience was evident. That made me feel good. I was in a state of optimism and anxious to get started.

The music department at BMS was located in the Cheney Building, a three-story structure which sat across the street from the main school complex. BMS was the old Manchester High School and was built in 1915. There were four buildings which were arranged in a rectangular formation with a large area of open space in the middle. I loved the old trees there. That open space was known as the "Quad."

All of the fine arts classes were housed in the Cheney Building. The music department was on the third floor. The only way there was up a huge flight of steps through the front door. Definitely old architecture, to say the least. The band room was large and spacious but contained four large poles to help support the ceiling. There were also three practice rooms with windows to the outside. A large instrument storage area was off the opposite side of the band room. That area also included the music library and the band director's desk.

My first visit to the space came a few days before school reopened in January. I was disappointed in what I saw. The place looked like a disaster area. The instrument storage area reminded me of a war zone. The old metal lockers were strewn with old pieces of equipment, and there was an odor of rotten food in the air. I found a few old lunch bags to be the culprit and came across an old bottle of coke which contained congealed liquid! God knows how long all of this stuff had been lying around.

The same day I found out that the school had just hired a new principal. In the middle of a school year? I met Kathy about an hour later. She walked into the band room and introduced herself. She was small in stature, but I could tell she was a "no nonsense" type of person. She took one look around my teaching area and said, "I want this all cleaned up before classes begin."

So much for a good first impression.

Kathy continued her tour around the Cheney Building as my cleanup efforts had new motivation. Shortly after this, Keith Berry, the Manchester High School band director, walked in. I told him about Kathy's edict and he immediately came to my rescue. He told me that he would be back tomorrow with a crew of kids from his band. And, sure enough, they all showed up the next day and we all "sand blasted" the entire area. Keith sprung for pizza as an extra incentive for the helpers. They were a "godsend."

The reality facing me now was that this was not going to be an easy gig. It was obvious to me I was going to have to lay down the law from the get-go. I knew, as I had done in the past, I was going to have to strike a fine balance between doing that and at the same time not alienating everyone. Easier said than done. I hoped my Bloomfield Junior High experience would be a benefit. My strategy was set.

2

I turned my attention to my teaching schedule. I had three separate bands, one each for the sixth, seventh, and eighth grades. That was the good news. I liked the idea of working with individual grades. The bad news was two-fold. The first issue was that I would be seeing the students in small heterogeneous classes. These classes would meet with me five times over a two-week period. This was not ideal, but I could work with it.

The second fact was that each band would have only one combined rehearsal per month. How was I going to balance teaching basic instrumental fundamentals in the small classes and not avoid having to work on band music for the majority of the time? I kept an open mind and would adapt as the rest of the year progressed. This would be a new experience for someone who was used to multiple full band rehearsals per week during my first decade of teaching. There was no way around it. I was going to have to learn and adapt.

Classes started and I felt a certain calmness. I had forgotten how much I enjoyed teaching kids twelve, thirteen, and fourteen years old. I remembered how there was never a dull moment. Watching kids grow in so many ways during those early teen years gave me a sense of wonderment. Helping guide these youngsters was a passion of mine from day one of my career. As the saying goes, "This is why we teach."

After a week or two, I was able to determine who the "players" were in each group. It was obvious who the kids were who gave Dave the most trouble. Several were in the percussion section. I had a meeting with them early on and asked them why there were several mallets and pieces of other auxiliary percussion lying on the roof of the building next to Cheney. Eventually they sheepishly admitted they had tossed them over there. I told them in no uncertain terms that was a no-no.

I came on strong. I told them that I was not going to replace those mallets. Once I had the maintenance staff retrieve those items from the roof, if this type of foolishness occurred again, they would all be meeting with the school administration.

I had to submit a work request to the maintenance department and it took a couple of weeks for them to remove our stuff from the roof. In the meantime, I did not allow any mallets or drumsticks in the room, including any of the kids' own equipment. They had to use their hands and fingers to play all the drums. Maybe this way they might better appreciate the value of these implements and the fact they are not projectiles. Their hands and fingers took a beating. That made the desired impression. When the auxiliary equipment, mallets, and drumsticks reappeared in the band room, from that day on I never saw anything lying on the roof across the street.

As I got to know the rest of my students, I realized that the problem group were the eighth graders. They had been through the previous year and a half and were just continuing the fun. I laid down the law with them. My classes and rehearsals were much more structured and work intensive. They started to adapt, slowly but surely. I liked what I was seeing. They had been working harder than they had in a long time in the band room. My thoughts at that point were that I wanted to show them that hard work has its benefits and rewards. I came up with a plan.

56 -
STICKING OUR NECKS OUT

THE EIGHTH GRADE BAND'S CHALLENGE would be the Great East Festival. This event consisted of an adjudication, followed by the rest of the day at the Six Flags New England in Agawam, Massachusetts. They needed something to motivate them. I presented this plan to the band at our January combined rehearsal. I impressed on them the importance of being adjudicated by experienced professionals. They seemed interested.

And then I gave them the "bad news." I told them, "Ladies and gentlemen, we will be evaluated by two judges on all aspects of your performance. This will be a great learning experience for all of us. But the *bad* news is that after we play, they are going to force us to go to Six Flags New England for the rest of the day. We have to take the bad with the good."

I could see in an instant their faces go from dread to joy. They were all in! The school administration thought it was a great idea as well. Kathy said she would chip in for the bus transportation if we had a quick fundraiser as well. Subsequently, we arranged to have a candy sale in February. I submitted the paperwork and we were on our way.

One immediate benefit was an improvement in decorum in both the class groups and large rehearsals. This meant I could relax a bit and get off their case more often. I would be able to "loosen up." This worked to an extent, but I was still having problems with my solo trumpet player. He was a talented player. In the rest of the kids' eyes, he was an influencer, but he did not always handle this leadership role in a positive way. If Ron did not feel like being a leader during a particular class he seemed to go out of his way to be a disrupter. The latter was more often the case.

My lead trombone, Ted, was a different type of leader. He was talented as well, a quiet kid, who led with his solid musicianship and great rehearsal decorum. His mom was on the BMS faculty and was a great supporter of the arts. I mentioned to her more than once how much I appreciated her son being in the band.

I had the "Ron" faction and the "Ted" faction coexisting. I worked hard at getting the "Ron" faction under control in the small classes, and that seemed to be helping. But I knew this was going to be a slow process. I knew this was where Dave and the other previous teacher from the ARC program had a disadvantage from the very start. It had been hard for them, without any experience in dealing with this age group, to play the long game. That takes experience. Chipping away at bad work habits and attitudes took time. Who knew that any better than me?

I had been spoiled in some ways with my first band way back all those many years ago. That group at Sykes ninth grade school was a gem. Of course, it was a different time as well. After being out of education during most of the 80s and 90s, I was noticing a huge difference in the students and parents after I returned. The work ethic in the average kid was not generally the same. They seemed to be spread in more directions in their lives. Parental involvement with their kids in school had increased. Although not in all cases, but it seemed that when a student had more problems in my classes, it was usually because their parents would be "hovering" over everything they or their teachers were doing. This phenomenon had become known as "helicopter parenting."

Ron and Ted were a case in point. I had multiple phone calls with Ron's mother about problems he was having in instrumental music. She was always stressing the fact to me that he was taking private lessons and should be getting better grades. I was always explaining to her that performance was not the entire grade. Namely, his decorum in class and rehearsals was not exemplary.

The third quarter report card grades came out and the following week in March, I received a phone call from a father whose son, who was a member of the percussion section, had received a low grade. His dad was none too happy with me and let me know in no uncertain terms. We agreed that I should call him every few weeks to give him an update on how things were going. I probably should have been more communicative with him about his son. Lesson learned. After teaching for so many years, I was still learning.

We rehearsed right up until the Great East trip. I managed to have an extra eighth grade band rehearsal a week before the trip. I was grateful to Kathy and the faculty for letting me do this. However, in reality, there were so many musical issues that needed attention, but there was just not enough rehearsal time. I had to prioritize things like ensemble, intonation, balance, and blend. Not everything was anywhere near where I would have liked.

The trip date finally arrived. We bused to a middle school not far from the amusement park and performed our selections for the adjudicators. One of the judges was Bill Sittard, a well-known and highly respected Massachusetts high school band director. As it turned out, he had some very good suggestions in his remarks. I was aware that he and the other judge really knew what they were talking about. The reality set in when I saw the judges' rating. We received a bronze medal, the lowest of the possible ratings.

We were presented the judges' rating sheets and a plaque in a ceremony at the park. We had lucked out as far as the weather was concerned. It was a mild day in May, and there was no rain in sight. The kids were super excited and were dismissed out in the park for the afternoon. They did have to check back with their assigned chaperones at two designated times during the afternoon. I saw nothing but smiles on their faces during those check-ins. That was to be expected, I guess, but it made me feel like all of the work with the BMS eighth grade band had been worth it.

The adjudication trip had accomplished what I hoped it would.

It was the highlight of the year. On the trip home on the bus, at one point, a student yelled, "Kleiner, Kleiner, hip, hip, hooray!" The rest of the kids joined in. I finally had to stand up and take a bow. At that point, I knew. I had "arrived" at Bennet Middle School.

"You don't actually lose . . .. You learn."

—TANITOLUWA ADEWUMI, NINE-YEAR-OLD CHESS CHAMPION

57 -
TWICE AS MUCH IN HALF THE TIME

IN LOOKING AT THE ADJUDICATOR'S sheets in the weeks that followed the trip, I had a much clearer vision of how to instruct my bands during the upcoming school year. The comment from the Great East judges that had the most effect on me was the one made by Bill Sittard. In the paperwork we had submitted to the judges, we had to list the amount of rehearsal time we had per week. Bill's comment was "With the rehearsal schedule you have, I don't know how you were able to get the band to play as good as it did." I took that as a sincere compliment.

I had mentioned my band rehearsal schedule to a few of my colleagues in other school systems. One of them exclaimed, "You have got to be kidding!" Others laughed, and so forth. One combined rehearsal per month was certainly out of the ordinary in Connecticut school instrumental programs.

Bennet and Illing had previously been junior high schools with grades 7 through 9. When the schools went to a middle school model, the schools then housed grades 6 through 8. In addition, they went to a small instrumental class schedule. No more pullouts of students from their academic classes, as we did in the elementary schools. The more I thought about this, the more it began to make sense why Manchester lost both of its highly acclaimed middle school band directors within the span of two years. The "middle school model," at least in Manchester, was failing its students in the instrumental music program.

As I previously mentioned, while I was out of the profession, the state of Connecticut Teacher Enhancement Act had boosted the salaries of teachers. I have no doubt this attracted and retained good teachers. While this program had the intended effect, it also brought increased scrutiny to the teaching profession.

A certain segment of the population was opposed to this legislation. Their rationale was "Why should teachers get a raise in salary? After all, they only work 180 days a year." In addition, other state residents and legislators demanded increased accountability for us. We now had to have CEUs (Continuing Education Units) each year. This requirement meant attendance at teacher training sessions on various educational issues. Along with this, more standardized testing of students was added.

Inevitably, with more scrutiny came school schedule changes. Students would no longer be taken out of any academic classes for music or anything else. Our new music coordinator in Manchester, our colleague Keith from MHS, made a great comment at a department meeting one day. He said, "We are now being asked to do twice as much in half the time."

2

Year one at BMS ended with a Spring Concert with all the bands performing. The seventh grade band was encouraged, I am sure, by the prospect of going to the Great East Festival next year. The sixth grade band showed promise. Those students who had not shown great practice habits were encouraged to use the summer months to catch up. Manchester had a summer band lesson program, so I tried to steer as many students into that as I could.

BMS had a tradition of awarding the John Philip Sousa band award to the most deserving eighth grader. I was familiar with this award from my days at Rockville High School. The student's name would be engraved on a plaque hung in the band room. And a trophy was awarded to them as well. This was quite an honor for a young musician.

My trumpet section leader Ron thought he was going to receive this honor. However, I felt it should go to Ted, for his quiet leadership and excellence on the trombone. After the award was given to Ted at the concert, his mom came to me and thanked me for giving it to her son. She had tears in her eyes. On the other hand, Ron came to me after school one day. He expressed disappointment at not receiving the award and wanted to know why he did not receive it. I explained to him why and advised him to be more of a leader at MHS. I told him that someone of his talent should be a leader in every way. He seemed to accept what I was saying. He had the look in his eyes like he had learned a life lesson.

"I like a teacher who gives you something to take home to think about besides homework."

—LILY TOMLIN AS EDITH ANN

58 - THE EVOLUTION AT BMS

THINGS AT BMS EVOLVED UNEVENLY as the next few years progressed. On the one hand, the students became used to my way of doing things. This was good. That being said, I continued to struggle with the schedule as it was. Monthly combined band rehearsals and essentially piecemeal groupings of instruments in the band classes. I was never able to convince the guidance department to give me some latitude to combine kids playing like instruments together. Students were scheduled by academic teams, and whatever combinations of instruments resulted, so be it.

Despite this schedule, however, there were good things happening. I had total freedom to create my own curriculum and grading system. I created a "BMS Band Handbook" that was given to the students at the beginning of each school year. It explained the expectations and requirements for my band students. Also included were the student's practice requirements outside of school. I wanted the parents to know all of this right up front.

2

During my second year at BMS, per my request, a large whiteboard was installed on the wall. We had ditched the blackboard and chalk. Now I could use erasable black markers with whiteboard erasers and cleaner. No more chalky mess on my hands and clothing. But now my hands had black marker spots instead. Oh well, they were teacher battle scars. No problem!

My tactics with new students had evolved. Since my Vernon days I had trained my band kids that when I stepped on the podium, that was their visual signal to stop talking and start paying attention. I learned that if you stood with feet apart and crossed your arms in front of you, the image you would project would be one of seriousness and strength.

As the sixth graders entered my room on the first day with me, I would stand like that. That seemed to work well. The kids quietly sat down and they had an "Uh-oh, this guy means business" look on their face. So far, mission accomplished. And, my acting skills this far in my career had made me Oscar-worthy.

After welcoming one and all, I would say, "Ladies and gentlemen, we are now going to go over my rules for band classes and rehearsals. I have one thousand rules, so it may take a while to go over them all." I loved to then look over the class to see whose eyes had rolled back in their heads. As I walked over to the whiteboard I could usually see and hear some nervous glances and titters. I would then write the following on the board:

"RULE #1
When you see Mr. Kleiner step up on the conductor's podium, you stop talking or playing. From that point on you listen!"

I could literally read their minds at that point. *We have nine hundred ninety-nine rules to go, yikes!* they were thinking. "Ladies and gentlemen, does everyone understand rule number one?" I would firmly say. Some would nod, while others were paralyzed and could not move. "Okay, on to rule number two," I would drone. You could hear a pin drop in the room. I then carefully and deliberately wrote this:

"RULE #2
SEE RULE #1
RULE #3
SEE RULE #1
...
RULE #1000
SEE RULE #1"

It would feel like time had stopped as I would turn back to face the class. Slowly, but surely, those folks who were on the ball and not half asleep would begin to exhibit a slight upward curve of their mouth. And then the phenomenon would spread to everyone. They got it!

Inevitably I could feel the whole band room exhale. "Yes, folks, you now understand that there is only one rule in my band. That's rule number one. And, to complete the rule, when I step off the podium, you may relax and chat." What I didn't tell them was that I was often stepping off the podium to get a quick sip of my coffee. My cup was always close by.

My seventh and eighth graders had already heard this spiel and there was only an occasional reminder that was necessary with them. All my students knew that I would be tough when it came to doing our work, but at the same time, they knew I had a sense of humor and cared. When I stepped off the podium, I transformed from Mr. Hyde back to Doctor Jekyll.

3

Another activity during that first class, with all the grades, was to have them fill out an index card with their name, instrument, instrument make, and serial number. The serial numbers were the final entry on to the cards when they first brought their instruments to school. Many of the younger kids did not know about the numbers or where they were located. All of this was worth the time spent in case any one of them would leave their instrument somewhere in the school or on the bus.

The new sixth graders this particular year went through both the "rule" indoctrination and the index card task with no problem. This group included a trumpet player named Scott, whom I had started on his instrument a couple of years prior at the Verplank Elementary School. I remembered him as being very enthusiastic, always prepared at his lessons, and having a natural buzz.

As I listened to each kid play in class over the first few weeks, I realized that Scott was playing his trumpet as good or better than most of my seventh and eighth graders. He could play up to a high G above the staff. Musically, he was outstanding for his age. When time came during the year for the opportunity for middle school players to audition for the Eastern Region CMEA Middle School Festival, I enrolled Scott along with other interested students, all from the upper grades.

As I helped these kids prepare for this audition over the next few months, Scott and the others were working diligently. Some of them, like Scott, had been taking private lessons outside of school, so I knew they were getting extra help. That was always beneficial when it came to these auditions.

In the meantime, the sixth grade band was progressing quite well. I was pleased. I liked working with them. They were more like sponges when it came to learning new things. This feeling I had with them would influence me a few years "down the pike."

And then the word came down from CMEA. Two of my eighth graders, one seventh grader, and a rare sixth grader passed the audition. Of course, it was Scott. His score was off the charts. He had the highest trumpet score for the entire eastern region! This was among all the middle schools in Eastern Connecticut. He had scored higher than all the upper classmen. He had made first chair trumpet in the Orchestra!

When the festival music arrived from CMEA for student preparation prior to the February rehearsals and concert, I noticed one of the orchestra trumpet parts for Scott was an arrangement of Wagner's overture to the opera *Rienzi*. My heart almost stopped! I felt like I needed some oxygen. Having been familiar with this work, I knew that the overture begins with a solo trumpet note. And on top of that, I soon learned that the orchestra was playing first on the program and *Rienzi* was the first selection. The solo was a single extended note, starting softly with a long, gradual crescendo. And it would be played twice during the first several measures. Scott was going to play the first note of the entire concert all by himself.

The festival finally rolled around, and as I would have expected, Scott was doing a great job during the orchestra rehearsals. His age didn't seem to factor into the equation. He was consistent in his playing and the orchestra conductor was quite pleased.

At the performance, there was an air of excitement and expectation. I decided to go backstage and get a good view of the orchestra from there. I noticed that Scott was very diligent during the tuning note and I was proud of him for that. He "got it" that tuning was very important.

The conductor walked onstage and turned to the audience to loud applause. At the same time, Scott just happened to look over off stage to where I was standing. He saw me just as the conductor was turning back towards the group. So, what was Scott doing? He was waving to me with an excited and joyful look on his face. All I could think of was that I had distracted him.

My entire life flashed across my eyes. My heart was pounding. In what seemed like a split second, Scott turned back to face the podium just as the conductor put his arms up and then came down with the downbeat. Scott brought the trumpet up to his lips in what seemed like a millisecond and played a perfectly soft B natural and then made an awesome crescendo. My pulse once again started as if I had received an electric shock. My student had nailed it!

59 -
SCENES FROM THE THIRD FLOOR

I LIKED HAVING PRACTICE ROOMS. However, some of the neighbors that lived next to our building would complain about the musical sounds emanating out of the practice room windows and "disturbing" their peace and quiet during the school day. Principal Kathy relayed their complaints to me as someone had been continuously calling the school about this "problem."

I wrestled with this but in the end would not give in to putting any restrictions on practicing and my instruction in those rooms. Certainly, with a non-air-conditioned space during the warmer weather, the windows had to stay open.

I did have an old air conditioner in the band room. There were actually two of them, but one did not work. For the months of September, October, April, May, and June, I would have the AC on most of the day, just to keep things bearable. Often, I would bring a change of clothes to put on after lunch. I hated the feel of soaking-wet clothes.

2

One morning I entered the band room to see the chairs set up in a different formation. The band chairs and stands were fanned out from the corner of the room in front of my desk. This setup had eliminated the room's support-poles' as a sight line issue. Why hadn't I thought of this? Who did this, a "band-room angel"?

A few minutes later our young custodian, Jeff, walked in and said, "How do you like this setup? I was a trumpet player in high school and this is the way we used to set up, catty-corner."

"Jeff, I love this setup!" I blurted out. "I owe you a bottle of scotch."

This was the beginning of a nice relationship with Jeff. We had many long discussions about music in subsequent years. On top of that, he was always eager to help out if I needed equipment moved around, especially on concert nights when we were performing in the gym across the street. I started taking Jeff with us on our Great East trips as a chaperone. He had been hanging around the band room all during his band years and now he felt comfortable doing that again. I could relate to that. Jeff was a "band rat," just like me!

3

As the years passed, I was becoming more concerned about the building itself. It was really showing its age. After all, it was built in the 1920s. At one point there were concerns about break-ins from the surrounding neighborhood. As a result, when the evening custodians' shift began, they would sometimes lock the building's front door. I would return from a faculty meeting across the street and be locked out. I complained about this and nothing was done.

Jeff heard about the situation and a few days later he slipped me a front-door key. "Don't say anything about this; I could get in trouble," he advised. I really appreciated the gesture. It also enabled me to get in the building on Saturdays, which I took advantage of frequently. So much for working only 180 days. This wasn't the first time a custodian had given me a key to the building. It felt like the 1970s in Vernon all over again!

Inevitably, the issue that the administration was fearing actually happened. There was a weekend break-in at the Cheney building. I was called to the main office on Monday morning and apprised of the situation. Several school instruments, including a bunch of violins, were missing, along with a few computers. There were several student-owned instruments missing as well. I knew I had always taken down serial numbers on my index cards for a reason. This was it. I turned over the index cards to Kathy and she was grateful.

After a few weeks the Manchester police solved the case. The local music stores helped, as attempts were made to sell some of the stolen instruments to them. The police quickly zeroed in on the people involved with that and found all the instruments and equipment inside a home down the block. Two high school kids were responsible.

I was called down to the police station to identify the instruments and was an instant celebrity for having kept my index cards! I also received a call from the chairwoman of the School Board, thanking me for helping to retrieve her daughter's saxophone. Good karma was coming my way and I was enjoying it!

4

I wish I could say I enjoyed BMS concert nights. But that was never the case. Yes, we had to perform in the gym, which in itself was not ideal, but the fact that the gym was across the street made things worse. When we had the seventh and eighth grade concerts, there was not enough room to sit the bands, chorus, and orchestra in the gym when they were not performing. I had to enlist faculty to watch one of the bands in Cheney and then walk them over when it was their time to play. All the groups were shuttled back and forth like this. It was a logistical nightmare. It made for unnecessarily long evenings as well. And on top of that, temperature and weather conditions were always a concern.

One year, our spring concert landed on a very hot and humid evening. The seventh grade groups had finished and the eighth grade band was ushered over. There was actually enough room that evening to seat the seventh graders in the gym bleachers. All of us in the gym were soaked in sweat due to the lack of AC. There was an unusually annoying level of talking in the gym while the eighth graders were playing, noise from the audience and students alike.

The seventh graders were naturally excited about their performance. I could see our faculty helpers reminding them to be quiet and respect their fellow peers who were performing. As a staff, we had always tried to stress this to our students throughout the year.

As the noise level was growing, it was beginning to get hard for the eighth grade band to concentrate. It was brutally hot. You could see and hear the audience fidgeting. I felt myself losing patience. I finally felt I had to say something.

After our first selection and prior to announcing our next piece, I spoke to the audience. "Ladies and gentlemen, we all know it is extremely hot in this building tonight. The noise level in here is much too loud. I would encourage you to settle down and let us finish the program and we can all get out of this heat. Thank you." I was not a "happy camper" and neither were my teacher colleagues. We finished up amidst a much calmer atmosphere. It was a relief to get out of that gym. It was like leaving a sweatbox.

The next day I got called into Kathy's office. She told me that some parents had complained about my words at the concert. I told her I did not think what I said was disrespectful to anyone, especially considering all the noise that was coming out of the audience all evening. I felt I had to say something. The concert had been videotaped and Kathy asked for the copy so she could look at it. I forwarded it to her and I never heard about it again. I think she understood what her staff had gone through, on a hot and humid evening, to try to ensure a meaningful experience for their students.

I understand how some adults that night might have been upset at what I had said. However, I thought it was obvious that I was mostly speaking to my seventh graders at that time. Or at least I thought it was. This would not be the only time my words at a concert would be misconstrued. More on that later.

5

I always felt quite fortunate to be able to continue my professional music career at the same time I was able to live my dream of teaching kids. There came a time I had been hired to play at the casino venues, namely, Foxwoods and Mohegan Sun. Visiting performers would sometimes require an orchestra to back them up. One of these experiences for me was at Mohegan and involved me playing clarinet for the singer Anne Murray. She had several hit songs in the '90s. I loved playing these gigs because I would have the opportunity to concertize with some fine musicians from Connecticut, New York City, and Boston.

Mohegan Sun would always feed the musicians in between the afternoon rehearsal and evening concert. It was during this meal break that I got to chat with Anne Murray and she told me she was a former teacher! I thought that was really cool. She was such a nice person with all of us. The concert that night in the arena went quite well. I had a couple of solos and as we all had pick-up mikes attached to our instruments, I could hear my sounds filling up the arena. And seeing myself play on the big screens blew my mind!

A few days later I was sitting at my desk at BMS in between classes. Into the band room came one of my flute players, Rose, who seemed so excited. She had a huge smile on her face. She breathlessly said, "Mister Kleiner, my grandma took me to a concert at the casino and I saw you on the big screen!"

I chuckled and said, "Yes, Rose, that was me. Did you like the concert?"

"I loved it. And you sounded great!"

Well, this was a moment in my career I have never forgotten. Red-haired, freckled-faced Rose couldn't wait to tell me she had seen and heard me play. I had rarely seen a student so excited. She was a quiet type normally, so I loved seeing this side of her personality. This kind of connection with a student was incredibly special.

6

With so many great things going on at BMS during the early 2000s, the occasional frustrations were much easier to brush off. These events seemed disconcerting at the time, but later I would usually have a good laugh when thinking about them. They were the type of occurrences that happen to any teacher during their time in the profession. They were learning experiences which in the long run made them valuable.

A good example of this happened during a critical combined band rehearsal prior to an impending concert. I was cognizant at this point in my rehearsal plan to keep things moving and follow my "fix-it" list. I was always trying to keep things positive to mitigate any feelings of anxiety I might have, or my students might have for that matter.

If we got lucky during these final rehearsals, we could actually run a piece without any stops. Time constraints sometimes got in the way of that, unfortunately. So that was foremost in my mind at this particular combined rehearsal. All of a sudden, the fire alarm went off. My first thought was a four-letter word that I fortunately kept to myself. A fire alarm in the middle of one of these rehearsals was my worst nightmare. I could feel my blood pressure rising but tried to remain calm, knowing in the back of my mind this might not be a drill. I was thinking, *This better not be a drill. The office has to know I am in the middle of a combined rehearsal.*

The band knew the routine, as we put down our instruments and filed out the back door of the room, down the stairs out to School Street. After a few minutes, I saw Scott, one of our assistant principals, coming down the sidewalk to see how things were going. Scott had a funny look on his face. I guess he could read my facial expression. I whispered to him, "Scott, we were in the middle of a combined rehearsal. We have a concert next week. This was not a good time."

He whispered back, "I am so sorry, Jim; we totally forgot you were rehearsing." His apologetic tone made me feel somewhat better.

"Scott, you owe me one," I added with a bit of a chuckle.

I really could not get angry at this man. He had been a great friend to me during the years since I joined the BMS staff. Better yet, he was an insane NY Yankees fan, just like me. In fact, he was more of a baseball nut than I was. The past couple of summers he would take time to visit a few major league ball parks with his son. His goal was to eventually visit them all. That was on my bucket list too.

By the time we returned to the band room, the period was essentially over. I told the kids to pack up and prepare for dismissal.

The next day Scott called me into his office and again apologized for the timing of the drill.

"Don't worry about it, Scott, we will survive," I told him.

Just then, Matt, our other assistant principal, walked in. Scott said to him, "Hey, Matt, don't ever cross this guy."

Matt countered with "Well, what do you expect from a Yankee fan?"

Matt was a huge Red Sox fan. Later that year, during the baseball playoffs between Boston and New York, whichever team lost a playoff game to the other, either Scott or Matt would wear the winning team's jersey around the school all day. That must have been torture for both of them. But the whole staff and school loved it!

7

It took a couple of years of experimenting with my jazz band setup until I arrived at something that worked well. The electronics presented the challenge. There were not enough electrical outlets in the right places for us to plug in the keyboard and guitar amps. It was an old building. I decided to purchase my own heavy-duty extension cords and power strip. An "out of pocket" teaching expense. This finally solved the issue. We were in a formation that made rehearsal sense.

One day I walked into the band room in the morning and saw that the extension cords and power strip were nowhere to be found. Just then I saw a large fellow with my electrics in hand, looking like he was about to go down the steps and out of the building.

"Excuse me, sir," I said, "those are my cords and strip that I use with my jazz band."

He answered, rather arrogantly, "Sorry, extension cords and strips are not allowed in this building due to the fire codes." I had seen this gentleman walking around the school at times and realized he was the Town of Manchester fire warden.

"Well, sir, those cords and strip are my personal property so I would like to have them back."

"I am depositing these in the principal's office," he intoned.

By this time, I was getting hot under the collar. "Is that really necessary? I am on the faculty of this school and so would appreciate not being treated like a student!" My voice was showing my emotion.

"Sorry, man, these are the rules," he droned as he ambled down the stairs.

I bit my tongue and let him go. Later in the day I went to Kathy's office and told her what had occurred that morning. She gave me a look as if her mind was thinking, *Oh, him again!* I took from her disgusted look that she was up to her neck in faculty complaints about him. This was the same town official who was always threatening to shut down concerts during an actual performance if things were not right on, and in front of, the stage.

Kathy said, "Look, Jim, he is still in the building. I will get these back to you tomorrow. He always insists upon following the fire code. Just get these out for rehearsals and put them away and out of sight."

Good compromise, I thought. This would cause more work for me before and after rehearsals. Whatever!

8

My course was called "special." Of course, all of us on the faculty who taught the disciplines of Music, Art, Physical Education, or Home Economics, believed that, being slightly prejudiced, of course. Because none of us had morning homeroom, we were instead assigned to the rest of the school duties. Included in that list, of course, was cafeteria duty.

From a logistics standpoint, this duty was more challenging at BMS than at any other school I worked at during my career. First of all, the cafeterias were located in the Franklin Building, the huge edifice at the front of the school facing Main Street. It was literally a full block away from the Cheney Building, where I was coming from. I managed to time the walk at one point and it took about three minutes, walking briskly on clean pavement, to get between locations. The alternate route was through the school buildings, up and down stairs and the elevator. This took longer and was unpredictable due to the hallway traffic.

Having a class prior to this duty, none of us teachers could get there at the beginning of the period, so either Scott or Matt would go down ahead of time and keep law and order until we arrived.

The "battlefield" plan on site was to have two of us in each of the two small cafeterias. On this particular day, I arrived with my colleague Ann, as she had travelled from the art department. We were both a few minutes late, as was usual. Scott was covering our space that day. He handed over the monitoring duties and proceeded back upstairs to the office.

I noticed right away that the room was particularly quiet. Something did not quite seem right. After all the kids were seated and started their meals, Ann and I suddenly found out what was "coming down." I saw a kid at the other end of the room stand up. He yelled, "FOOD FIGHT!" In a few seconds, food was flying around the room. I felt something warm hit the back of my neck. It had the unmistakable feel of mashed potato.

At the same time, I had to duck as a piece of food was flying at my face. As you can imagine, the noise level went from pianissimo to fortissimo (for all you musicians out there). "All right, folks, knock it off!" I said in my best "teacher voice." But no, they weren't going to listen to me. Not on this day.

What the masterminds behind this dastardly event did not think about was the fact this cafeteria was directly beneath the main office. As a result, both Scott and Matt were in the room shortly after the noise level had gone off the charts. The thought hit me that they both slid down a pole, like in a firehouse. Is their "cafeteria pole" hidden out of sight somewhere? The only other explanation was that they slid down the stairway banister.

In any case, as soon as they appeared the damper was closed on these festivities. By this time Ann and I were able to locate the leaders of this event. There were four or five guilty parties. We gave their names over to the proper authorities and their punishment was to clean up the room while their cohorts watched. This included a mop and water bucket, enthusiastically donated by the custodial staff.

The general edict was that if each table was not perfectly clean by the end of the period, that table would spend the next few days in "in-school suspension." The students thought that this would be the end of things, but no, not quite. For the next two weeks, Scott would be in the room during this lunch period, which would now be a "silent lunch." No talking whatsoever. This was a fate worse than death for a young teen.

The word got around about what had happened. Ann and I became part of Bennet folklore. We had survived an all-out cafeteria food fight and lived to tell the tale. That was worth getting hit in the neck with mashed potatoes for sure!

9

Another necessary duty was for the faculty to monitor outside the school building before and after school. Each morning I was assigned to stand on the corner of Main and School streets, to monitor the walkers. At first, that seemed like a pleasant duty, weather permitting of course. And at least during the fall and spring, even more so. But once I got out there, I realized why this duty was not for the faint of heart. Mainly this was so because there was no crossing guard at this spot, a major intersection with a traffic light.

Students would know the difference between a red and a green light. And so would the drivers. Sure, this would be true in a perfect world. But the reality was a different story. The kids would at times cross before the red light had changed and some drivers would try to outrun a traffic light. The driving on Main Street was poor at best. After a week of this duty, I was a nervous wreck. What a way to start each school day.

I mentioned this situation to Scott after a few days of this and he came out to watch. He thanked me for the input. But nothing changed. We had a couple of close calls as usual over the next couple of weeks. Then one day, a "gentlemanly" motorist stopped on School Street near where I was standing and proceeded to ball me out for not keeping the kids from crossing in the middle of the road. "Why don't you do your job and stop those kids from crossing in the wrong place!" he yelled at me.

I yelled back, "Well, if people like yourself would drive slower, things would be safer! We need a crossing guard out here too."

The guy quickly answered, "Go to hell!"

Well, I thought, *that was a productive conversation.*

I had reached the end of my rope. I went to see Scott later that day and asked him to assign me to a different morning duty. I related to him what had happened that morning and I knew he was well aware of my concerns for the past few weeks. My final words to Scott were "Scott, this is the last day I am going to stand on that corner. You need a crossing guard at that spot."

The next day there was a crossing guard at the corner of School and Main streets. My morning duty was now monitoring the Quad as the bus students arrived. Thanks, Scott, we were now even!

10

On the second floor of the Barnard Building was the teacher's lounge. I liked eating my lunch over there instead of the small lounge we had in Cheney. I thought it was good to get out of my area and mingle with the other staff. It always served me well, no matter what school system. Even though it involved putting on my coat, in season, and venturing out in all kinds of weather, cutting off a few minutes of my lunch time, I still did it. I usually got into great conversations with my colleagues, sometimes forgetting the time and having to rush back to get ready for my next class.

On one particular day, I got to the faculty lounge and noticed that I was the only one there. I thought that was odd, but it then dawned on me that the seventh grade was on a field trip and that explained the dearth of other bodies in the room. I put my lunch bag down and went to the sink to wash my hands. I turned on the water and was immediately sprayed with a shower of liquid. I realized I was a victim of the "tape down the sprayer handle" trick.

Before I could disengage the sprayer handle, my face, hair, and shirt were dripping wet. At least there wasn't anyone else in the room to see me. I was not a happy camper at that moment. *I thought I worked with adults* was an immediate thought. I hurried back across the street to the band room. I was soaked. I grabbed an old towel and did the best I could to dry myself off.

It was warm in the band room and that was helping my clothes to dry, but I still looked like I had just gotten out of the shower as my class walked in. I got some weird looks and eventually had to explain to my curious students. I made light of it to my kids, but I was not happy about being the victim of this prank.

At the end of the school day, I wrote a note in large letters on a sheet of white lined paper. I went over to the lounge before I left for the day and taped the note over the sink. The note read, "No thanks for the unexpected shower you gave me today. The mess caused a disruption of my lunch time and forced me to answer some uncomfortable questions from my students in my next class. Please come over to the Cheney Building when you get a chance and we can discuss the whole event."

I signed the note and left it at the end of the day because this joke smelled of the custodial staff. Of course, the next day the note was gone. I had heard "through the grapevine" that Kathy had hauled in the head of the custodial staff and chewed him out. *Okay*, I thought, *justice done.*

11

During the late '90s and beyond, the internet was becoming more of a factor in everyone's lives, including mine. I had noticed the benefits of my daughter's ability to receive extra help from her high school calculus teacher online. Not only through email but also the Messenger feature gave students a way of asking questions and receiving help.

I was surprised one evening, while I was online, to receive a "hi" from one of my sixth grade band students. It was a quiet and shy trombone player named Sara. My initial thought was *Okay, here is a kid who would probably not have the courage to ask a question during band but felt more comfortable to message me here.* She was able to do this because I had written my email address on the whiteboard for this very reason. They could contact me with questions outside of school hours.

She started to ask a question about her trombone slide being sticky but was interrupted by her "sister" who was annoying her. I was not sure at that point what to say and was immediately taken aback by her next message. It said, "My sister just said my boobs were too large."

I paused momentarily and then responded, "Sara, let's not go there. Bring your slide to me before school and I will check it out."

I signed off and sat for a few moments trying to process what had just happened. Then I recalled meeting Sara's father about a month ago at the parents' night. He was a Manchester police detective and impressed me as being a nice guy. But something was still not right. I started to wonder if I had been chatting online with him rather than his daughter. Had he been trying to find out what kind of an adult I was? Did it make him suspicious that I would give my email address to my students?

I had other reasons at the time thinking that this had been an attempt to entrap me. Shortly after taking the BMS job, I was told in no uncertain terms that I was not to have any students with me alone after school. Sure, the building was not part of the main campus but across the street. And yes, I was a middle-aged male teacher. But to eliminate my ability to give a student extra help really had rubbed me the wrong way. I had made my feelings known to the powers that be about this.

Eventually I changed my email address and my experiment with giving students extra help was over. For the rest of my career, I was never alone with a student after school hours. I did not like the trend in society that was taking place. This was totally frustrating. The thought crossed my mind that perhaps I should have stayed working in the private sector.

60 -
MARCHING DOWN MAIN STREET

I KNEW THAT WHEN I took the job at Bennet Middle School, there would be a marching band commitment for the town Memorial Day parade. I had heard the Manchester parade was a long one. That was fine with me. Knowing we would have to rehearse long and hard for this parade, we might as well get our money's worth.

The first parade was only a few months after I took over in January 2000. BMS had uniforms. They were basically blue with a white "B" on the front. Pants and tops made of wool. Definitely old school.

The tradition was for the seventh and eighth graders to do the marching. We diligently assigned uniforms to each student after a few days of "try-ons." Of course, this activity took away teaching and learning during these times, but it was necessary nonetheless. I was assisted by a few parents, and fortunately they had much more patience with the process than I could muster. One mom even volunteered to mend some of the old uniforms. The uniform sizes were another problem. There were no ninth graders in the band anymore, so there were larger sizes that needed to be modified, or discarded all together.

Members of the Manchester High School marching band came down to Bennet to help at a few of our rehearsals. We rehearsed on School St., back and forth in front of Cheney. The police would put up barriers to block off an area of about 100 yards. It honestly was not a bad marching environment.

The seventh graders didn't have marching experience, at least not with their instruments. They would struggle a while but eventually got the hang of marching and playing simultaneously.

I impressed on the drum line the responsibility they had and was happy to see they took it seriously. They worked hard. We used the traditional BMS street beat and the line included snares, bass drums, tri-toms, and bells.

The Bennet banner was impressive and there was no shortage of volunteers to carry it. I was pleased to be able to have the help of an experienced town member to come in and work with our flag line. His help was invaluable. All of this preparation was worth the fact that more people town-wide would see the marching band in this parade than any other band activities during the school year.

The Memorial Day parade came, finally, and it was a brutally hot day. The humidity was gross and the temperature was in the upper eighties by step-off. The parade was large and we were the final musical group. We had decided ahead of time to take bottled water in a wagon. One of the parents volunteered to pull the water wagon along the parade route with us. Good thing we did this.

As the march progressed, the heat was starting to get to all of us. It was inevitable that one of our tri-tom players, who was at the end of the percussion line, veered off during a segment of the street beat. He crossed over the sidewalk and began to march up the front lawn of one of the homes along the route.

The adults marching along with us knew immediately what was going on. Our student had become faint but was marching on while fighting consciousness. He was doing okay with that, but he had lost the ability to recognize where he was going. One of the volunteers marching with us grabbed a bottle of water and ran after our stray marcher. I watched as he grabbed the young fellow before the kid fell down on top of his drums. Another man who was sitting on his lawn helped by grabbing the drums and taking them off the kid's shoulders. Our chaperone yelled to me, "I have him, keep going."

With that disaster averted, we continued on, minus one tri-tom player, and finished the parade. Once we returned to the school, the kids took off the uniforms, most of which were soaked with sweat. The band downed the rest of the water we had available, as well as flocked to the water fountain in our hallway. Our tri-tom victim had turned out fine after spending some time in the shade and getting hydrated under the supervision of the adults.

Having had that experience with a hot day marching in Manchester, I decided right then and there that we would never again wear those heavy woolen uniforms. It was time for a change.

61 - TIME FOR CHANGES

WITH THE MARCHING BAND UNIFORM dilemma on my mind, an opportunity suddenly presented itself. I received a call from the owner of a tux rental store on Main Street. He had about eighty tuxedos that he was planning on discontinuing and wondered if we might be interested in them for use by the band. The thought struck me that he may have noticed that our uniforms were quite shabby as he watched us march by his store during last year's Memorial Day parade. I was intrigued. At the end of our conversation, I agreed to stop off at his store on my way home from school the following day.

The tuxes turned out to be dark grey and included pants, jackets, vests, and bow ties. There were a myriad of sizes, and my thought was whether or not they would fit seventh and eighth graders. The store owner assured me that they were easily modified and offered to fit the clothing to my specific band members if I could get their sizes to him. *Wow*, I thought, *what an offer!*

I thought things over for the next few days and then decided to take him up on the offer after getting the go-ahead from Kathy. She volunteered to provide the $1,000. he was asking. It was a done deal.

The same parents who had helped us during the parade, along with a few others, volunteered to help measure my students. If we hustled, we might be able to get the bands into the tuxes by the holiday concert. A mom by the name of Vera took over as the main person to coordinate all of this activity and I was very grateful to her for doing this.

Many hours were put in by this team of people, resulting in our being ready to wear the clothes at the concert. As the concert approached, I was watching the weather reports like a hawk. Knowing that we had to shuttle the kids from Cheney across the street to the gym was concerning. There was a risk of having the tuxes get wet.

As it turned out, the extra effort to get the kids into the tuxes prior to the concert was more than I had bargained for. But the thought of seeing the band dressed up in formal attire for an indoor concert told me it would be worth it. Fortunately, the weather gods smiled on us that evening. And the reaction to the band's new look was positive. The tux jackets were a new experience for the females, for sure. But they didn't seem to mind. If they did, I did not hear about it. The guys seemed to like the look.

The Memorial Day parade followed a few months later. I decided to ditch the jackets and only wear the white shirts or blouses with open collar, along with the vests. More casual but more practical for the anticipated heat. That worked well. We had quite a few positive comments from the parents and townspeople along the parade route. The first chapter of the new uniforms had gone well. Not so well for chapter two.

2

During the following summer I made it a point to go into BMS to get a head start on two issues. The first issue was the music library. It was housed on the side of the storage area that got the most exposure to the sun. The heat and humidity in that room had rendered most of the music unusable. The sheets of paper were crumbling. There should have been a heavy-duty humidifier running in that space for most of the year.

Without the ninth grade and sufficient rehearsal time, using this music was impractical, regardless of the condition. I was relying on music for the bands to play that I had used in other middle school situations. The result of these factors was that I made preparations to discard most of the music that summer. Some arrangements I could salvage and those were shipped up to MHS.

The second issue I was dealing with that summer was that the tuxes were a mess. Most of my parental help had dissipated due to their kids going on to the high school. I was faced with refitting most of the remaining band kids due to their growing over the summer. All the tux parts were now out of size order and in some cases dirty and all needed dry cleaning. But I tried to remain calm, knowing that this was a normal situation for any set of band uniforms and I had dealt with this sort of thing multiple times in the past.

When the students arrived in the fall, I tried to have an organized fitting day. It did not go well. It seemed like we had a good number of smaller seventh graders than the year before and it was difficult to find sizes that fit. The tuxes generally were too big. It got to the point where I was spending too much rehearsal time dealing with uniform issues as concert time approached. There was just not enough time.

We got through the holiday concert and looked quite disheveled in our tuxes. We had not had the benefit of a mass professional fitting as we had the year before. Dealing with the tuxes had become an unanticipated burden. We had solved our uniform problems and yet created more problems. And these problems were just as bad, if not worse.

One day after school I had a visitor. It was Vera, the parent who had been such a great help and advocate for the tuxes the year before. It was nice to see her. She seemed disturbed about something and then told me she was not happy with what she saw at the holiday concert. I wondered why she had been there in the first place, since her kids were now in ninth grade.

She was blunt, as usual. "The tuxes looked terrible on the band members!" she intoned. "They were wrinkled and ill-fitting. How could you let that happen?" I paused for a moment, my thoughts being *How about the music? Did you listen at all?* I had thought the concert was quite strong musically. I tried to explain to her about the problems the tuxes had given us this year so far. She wouldn't hear it.

I was getting "chewed out" by a parent. Not the first time that had happened to me, but by this time I was in no mood. "Vera, you need to back off!" I exclaimed. She left my room in a huff. My final words were repeated to me by Kathy the next day when she called me into her office. "You told her to 'back off' and that probably was not the right thing to say."

"Kathy, I am a teaching professional and I don't like being lectured by a parent as if I was a student," I replied.

Kathy agreed with me. "I get it, Jim, I get it."

That incident with Vera ended the tux era at BMS. I decided to go the T-shirt route for the marching band. I went to a local vendor and we designed BMS band T-shirts. I displayed an example to the band and they were quite enthusiastic. We wore them for the parade and they were a great hit. Except, of course, with Vera.

As I marched by her along the parade route, she yelled at me with a weird look on her face. All I heard was "MISTER KLEINER . . .." I did not hear what she yelled next as the drum roll started for our march. Guess that was a good thing.

It had again been a hot day. The T-shirts looked great along with the dark slacks. We had a new uniform which would work during an 80-degree day. The shirts proudly said, "Bennet Middle School Band." I was confident I had done the right thing.

62 -
HOLDING IT TOGETHER

THE SIXTH-GRADE BAND STUDENTS WERE a feisty bunch during my second BMS year. It took a few months to get them settled down, which was unusual. But this group had a few more "players" than usual. By that I mean there were kids who, for whatever reason, felt they needed to be the center of attention during my classes. There was always one or two each year in all the grades. I had my ways of dealing with them, including using a designated "hot seat" during class rehearsals.

The "hot seat" tradition involved my moving a chair and music stand to the front of the band, right next to my podium. I made it known to one and all that if there was anyone who was disrupting the class on a continuous basis, they would be required to come up and sit in this chair. My rationale to them was that if they felt it was okay to be a distracting force in the class, then it was only fair that they sat in the front so all of us could hear them play their part from a more prominent place.

I am certain these "players" thought the attention was going to be great. But, inevitably, when they got up front and realized that everyone was hearing their every note, their comfort level dipped drastically. The system worked like a charm most of the time. When their period in the seat had concluded, these folks rarely made a reappearance.

Unexpectedly, one day a band member actually volunteered to sit in the "hot seat." This student was a diligent and competent performer during class. She just wanted to display her expertise to one and all. My thought was *Why not?* Let her set an example for the rest to emulate. During that class period she did not disappoint.

Others took note and over the next few weeks, more of them took her place.

The "hot seat" had evolved from being a place you did not want to be to a place you did! It had become a badge of honor to be invited to play there. Who knew!

2

One young man who had been a repeat occupant of the original "hot seat" during the first couple of months of his sixth grade band membership was my bass clarinet player Charles. He was a precocious young man with a constant need of attention. I worked with him as I would any other kid with those bad habits. However, Charles was a tough nut to crack. He was a constant test of my patience. I had pulled him aside after band class to discuss his behavior more than once. Each time he would turn on the charm and promise to mind his manners from then on. But, alas, things did not improve.

One day, after a particularly musically frustrating class for all of us, the students were lining up for dismissal. These kids had to put on their coats prior to heading down the stairs and leaving the building to cross the street on that cold December day. I heard a commotion, turned around, and saw Charles take the coat of another kid and throw it out into the hallway. He and a few others thought this was funny. But the student whose coat had gone flying was not laughing. It looked to me like a case of bullying. At that point I had had just about enough of Charles' antics.

"Charles, over here please. We need to have a chat," I intoned. He put on his best "I didn't hear you" act, which was popular with some sixth graders. "Over here, let's go!" I said as I raised my voice. No reaction again. I finally felt I needed to show him and the rest that I meant business. I went over and with my arm, guided Charles into the doorway of the music library room. He had a startled look on his face. I put my face closer to his and said, "Charles, we have been through this before. You seem to have a real problem listening to adults. I saw what you did with Ronald's coat and you owe him an apology." I could see Charles' eyes and knew he was processing what I was saying. I continued, "You are a smart kid, my friend, but you don't always act like it. I don't ever want to see you do something like that again or there will be consequences in the main office for you."

Charles' teacher had just arrived to accompany her students across the street. She had heard the tail end of my lecture to her student and was not happy. As they left, my sense was that Charles was not used to being called out for doing bad stuff. *Maybe his actions reflect the kind of discipline, or lack thereof, that he receives at home*, I thought.

3

Two days later I found a note in my faculty mailbox. I was requested to report to the assistant superintendent's office at 3:00 pm the following day. That next day I received a note from Kathy. The note contained the fact that the parents of Charles were in school yesterday with a complaint about my actions with their son. They claimed I had physically and verbally abused him at the end of class. *Wow, really? You have got to be kidding!* I thought. I waited for Kathy to return to the office so I could talk to her about this, but she was not in the building.

The next morning, I received word from the Bennet MEA (Manchester Education Association) building representative that I would be joined at the meeting by the Connecticut Education Association Uniserv Representative Bob Silver. I recognized Bob's name from the CEA literature. I again went up to see Kathy after lunch, but she was in a meeting.

That afternoon after school, I found myself sitting in the school system administration building. I was not in a great state of mind. For starters, I had not been given any chance to explain to anyone what had happened a few days before until Bob arrived. Finally, someone could hear my side of the story. After my explanation to him he said, "Jim, I hear what you are saying but, unfortunately, since you do not have tenure yet here in Manchester, there is nothing

I can do for you other than be a witness to the meeting." I had not been in Manchester for the two years needed for a previously tenured teacher to be able to receive tenure.

Dr. Martha Lyons was the assistant superintendent with whom I was to be meeting. After a short wait, Bob and I got called into her office. She opened with "Mister Kleiner, we are having this meeting because of an incident on Monday in which a student of yours, Charles Dixon, has accused you of physically and verbally abusing him. His parents have filed a complaint and are quite upset at what happened to their son. They have told me the story." I was waiting for my chance to explain my version of what had transpired. That chance never came. Dr. Lyons continued, "We really can't have teachers like you teaching our students here in Manchester."

By this time, I was biting my tongue almost all the way through. I could feel myself an inch away from losing my cool. Bob noticed this and he grabbed my arm as I was ready to blow my top. His experience in these matters really "saved my bacon." All I could see in my mind was the face of my daughter, Janet, who was a freshman at the University of New Hampshire. *I can't lose my job right now, she has just started college* ran through my mind.

Dr. Lyons' voice broke my daydream. "We have a letter of resignation here which you are to sign. If problems like this continue during the rest of the school year, this letter will go into effect at the end of June. Your subsequent actions will dictate how this will play out. If all goes well, this letter will be discarded."

My first instinct was to refuse to sign that letter and leave her office. I looked at Bob and he nodded to me. His nod said, "sign it." I knew the year had been going very well up to that point and my gut told me the rest of the year would be a "slam dunk." I signed the letter.

Bob and I left the office and I thanked him for being there with me. His advice was to play the "long game" and continue to do what you do in the classroom. He had seen this tactic used by administrators all over Connecticut. I followed his advice. I let things go and vowed to continue the good year I had been having. I would continue to do my job to the best of my ability. I have no doubt that Bob, along with the MEA representative, had engineered this compromise with the administration. Without that, I could have been forced to resign or fired on the spot.

My career had been put in jeopardy by a self-centered student, enabling parents, and poor administration. This was not the decade of the 1970s anymore. I do not believe this scenario would have taken place back then. Things had changed on so many levels for educators. I was not going to end up being a statistic.

4

The rest of the year went just as I had imagined. Concerts, a parade, and another trip to the Great East Festival. And, by golly, the eighth grade band received a silver medal this time. We were moving up in the world. And, of course, my MVP trumpet player, Scott, led the way in the seventh grade band. I never heard about "the letter" so I guess "no news was good news."

Kathy and I never spoke about the entire incident until the following fall. One day she called me into her office and closed the door. Her first words were "Jim, I want to apologize for how I handled that incident you had with the sixth grader last year. I am very sorry you went through all of that." I was surprised and humbled hearing her words. She continued, "Jim, Charles' parents recently came in again and asked me to apologize to you for them. Their son ended up the year enjoying band. They realized that things probably had not happened the way their son described. Apologies are in order from all of us. The resignation letter has been discarded and there will be no mention of it in your personnel file."

I thanked Kathy and walked out of her office as if in a dream. I had thought the entire matter had been dropped and forgotten. Evidently not. My questions about the Manchester administration had vanished. I had faith in all of them once more. My respect for

Kathy went through the roof and never wavered again.

I met Charles' parents at the parent open house several weeks later. They were lovely people and very complimentary towards me. I was floored. How does that saying go? "All's well that ends well." I had held it together with Bob Silver's help. It had been the right thing to do. Another lesson learned. More lessons to come.

63 - TWO DRUMMERS

I WAS PARTICULARLY EXCITED ABOUT a new class which I had been given the opportunity to develop. The class was called World Drumming. There was a high interest in drumming among the Manchester middle schoolers. My thought was that perhaps this class might be a good outlet for kids who were not in the band program. I convinced the administration to invest in a couple of African djembe drums to supplement the Latin percussion we already had. During the first semester we had eleven students in the class, including a severely autistic student. Keith was a large kid. He was accompanied to class with his full-time aide, whom I already knew. Sue and I often ate lunch together along with other staff in the teachers' lounge in the school building across the street.

Another member of the class was Robbie, who I had already known when he was a trumpet student of mine at the Verplank school. Robbie did not stick with the trumpet very long as a fifth grader. In speaking with his guidance counselor at the time, I learned that he was going through a rough time at home. I did not ask for details but I felt sorry for him having to go through home problems. But here in my class he was back involved with music again, this time as a drummer.

I quickly found out all Robbie wanted to do was play the drum set. He had learned a basic rock beat somewhere and was ecstatic when he could play the set in the band room. His schedule included having a study hall during my planning period and asked if he could come over across the street to my room and practice. I said to him, "Sure, Robbie, but I have to limit your practice time to twenty minutes since I do have some planning to do as well."

One thing that Robbie did not do was play softly. I began to bring in earplugs and would use them during his practice sessions. I did not mind, though, because I could see in his face the joy he was experiencing. He had found his element and I was not about to restrict his creativity. I could see that his interest in his rock beat was beginning to carry over to the other percussion instruments. I showed him the proper technique for playing many of the other auxiliary instruments and his eyes would light up. I told him about the percussion class at Manchester High School and recommended that he sign up for that. A couple of years later I found out that he had taken my advice.

Keith turned out to be a revelation. Sue had remarked to me after he had been in a couple of classes that he really would get excited when he knew it was World Drumming time. He wasn't very verbal, but she could see his enthusiasm on the way to class. We quickly discovered that Keith loved to play the hand drums. If we demonstrated to him a speed of beat, he would model that and hit the drum. He was like a human metronome! He could hold a steady beat for an extended time. He was always right on the money.

Keith was not the first autistic student I had during my career, nor would he be the last. Everyone, including me, marveled at the way he could keep that steady beat. He could participate in the class on that level. He was a definite asset to the class.

World Drumming class had turned out to be a great class and lots of fun for all. Except, I must admit, when the kids started asking me to write on the whiteboard music staff. They wanted to know what the beat looked like in notation. I was happy to do so. They were learning notation! However, later in the semester, it became a "careful what you wish for" experience for me. Their beats became so complex that I had problems writing them down. Half the time they had me stumped!

64 -
A DAY LIKE NONE OTHER

IT WAS A SUNNY SEPTEMBER day, quite mild for that time of year. It was the type of day that made you glad you lived in New England. The colors were still on the trees and the leaves were just starting to fall. Days like that always brought me peace of mind.

The day began with a jazz band rehearsal before school. Those rehearsals would never fail to wake me up. I am a morning person anyway. Just give me a good cup of coffee along with some jazz and I am good to go.

By that time in my life, it was as if I had rediscovered jazz. Jazz was no longer a style of music I taught in school based on my experiences in high school jazz ensemble at Hicksville High School and my love of Dave Brubeck. I had long since become immersed in all types of jazz and it was my go-to choice for a lot of my music listening. Trinity College in Hartford broadcast a morning jazz radio show. Every morning when I first arrived in the band room, I would turn on that show. It got me moving.

I had a sixth grade class first period and then had my planning period. I was looking over some scores when my colleague Laura Ridarelli, who was the string teacher, walked into the band room. "Jim, did you hear about the World Trade Center?"

I said, "No, what happened?"

"Two planes hit the Twin Towers and they are on fire and damaged really bad!" she answered. "I just saw the incident on the TV in the faculty lounge." I looked at my clock and it was about 10:30.

"Oh, my god," I exclaimed. I thought about running across the street to the Barnard Building to check the TV. However, my next class was starting in ten minutes. Little did Laura and I know that by this time, both towers had collapsed.

And then came the announcement over the PA system. It was Scott who said, "We are now in a lockdown situation. All students and staff are to remain in their rooms. There will be no passing of classes at the bell." Laura and I looked at each other with worry on our faces as she hurried back to the orchestra room. My heart was beating much faster than it had been five minutes ago.

I sat at my desk for the next hour and a half, pushing some papers around while listening to the radio. National Public Radio was covering the events and I could not believe what I was hearing. In the meantime, the lockdown continued. I began to hear the sounds of sirens moving through Manchester in the distance.

What I did not know was the scene of confusion going on at the BMS Main Office. As I found out later that day, some parents had rushed to the school to pull their kids out. No one knew whether these events in New York, Washington, and Pennsylvania were only the beginning of other terrorist attacks. I could understand how those parents felt. However, during a lockdown, no one is allowed in or out of the school buildings. That is the whole point of a lockdown.

I found out later on that the sirens I heard were of the town of Manchester police heading towards all the schools. They had been called by school administrators. Some parents had become unruly. They had to be calmed down and assured that their kids were safe.

In the meantime, the lockdown was taking forever. There had been no students in the Cheney Building the whole time. It was quiet, almost too quiet. My mind was racing, trying to envision in my mind the World Trade Center buildings collapsed in rubble. Around noon the announcement came that the students would be dismissed according to our half-day schedule. The lockdown had been lifted and all of us faculty were to report to the quadrangle for coverage of the student dismissal. I grabbed my coat and walked across School Street.

The first thing I noticed was that there were very few cars on the road, except for some cars of parents parked in front of the school.

They were being cleared by police since the buses were starting to arrive. By 12:45 all the students had departed, whether they were walkers or bus riders. Some also went home with their parents.

I finally made it to the faculty lounge and to my horror began to see the images of the fateful morning. Other staff members were there as well. All of us were trying to hold it together. It reminded me of watching pictures of the *Challenger* disaster several years earlier with some of my colleagues at The Hartford. There was not a peep in the room. Dead silence. Tears as well.

I drove home and we watched all the horrible pictures all afternoon and for days to come. It had been a day like none other.

65 -
GOODBYE TO CHENEY

THE NEXT FEW YEARS AT BMS were good ones. Aside from my frustrations with the lack of full band rehearsal time, many things evolved on a positive note. Our concerts had eventually migrated over to the MHS auditorium. The hall was large with a huge stage. What a difference from playing in the BMS gym! An acoustic shell had been installed on the stage and that improved the acoustics significantly.

Although performing away from BMS involved rehearsing at MHS before each concert, including bus trips and equipment moves, the overall musical e xperience was much better for all concerned. We could also feature the band, orchestra, and jazz ensemble on the same program. There were plenty of seats for the audience. All in all, this was a "win-win" for everyone.

The MHS music department was a great help. They provided a stage crew, ran the lights, and set up the sound system. We had easily accessible warmup areas behind the stage where all the high school rehearsal rooms were located.

The only glitch was the scheduling of the concerts, especially for the December holiday concert. Since the auditorium also housed events and performances by town groups, the school groups often did not have much choice as to our concert dates. The two middle schools, as well as a few of the elementary schools, and of course, MHS, were all vying for dates.

At BMS we agreed to take the early date, which was during the first week of December. Someone had to be first, so we at Bennet agreed to "stick our neck out." Why not? It meant we had to really hustle to get our groups ready, but on the other hand, we got the concert over with and could relax for the rest of the month without the performance looming.

2

I would be remiss not to mention that I attribute our success at BMS, in part, to the fine background my students were getting in the fourth and fifth grades. Our elementary teachers were doing a solid job. I could tell this by the way the sixth grade band was playing.

In the meantime, during the 2004–2005 school year, the town of Manchester School Board and Town Council were debating over building a new school. There were racial equity issues at the elementary school level. And, there were infrastructure issues as well. BMS was showing its age. Built in 1915, the building needed upgrading in many areas. The town initially was talking about building a new high school. That sounded exciting to me. The present high school could then be used as a middle school, thus eliminating the need for two middle schools. Illing could still be used and BMS could be knocked down or used for some other town purpose.

Several sites around Manchester were proposed for the new high school, but I was dismayed that in each case there was blowback from the neighborhood involved. "Not in my backyard," or "NIMBY," as the syndrome was known as, seemed to be the general rule. *Really? Why would you not want a brand-new high school in your neighborhood?* I pondered. I really did not understand that thinking. But, alas, that was the reality.

Another factor in the equation was that the Manchester Historical Society did not want the town to abandon the BMS building. Their feeling was that there was too much history at that site, including the fact that it had been the original MHS. It had also survived a fire in the early 1920s while Elizabeth Bennet had been the principal. The story goes that she had a great part in getting all the students evacuated from the building that day. She had been one of the town heroes.

Eventually the decision was made. Bennet Middle School would be renovated and become the building to house all of the town's sixth graders. All of the seventh and eighth grade would be housed at Illing.

There would be no new high school. I was disappointed. It seemed to me that Manchester was making a mistake by trying to update the BMS building. But the decision came down. It was a done deal.

The plan was to take two years for the renovation. In the meantime, the town's sixth graders would be housed in their neighborhood elementary schools. I was assigned to teach grades 4 through 6 at Keeney Street School, Verplank School, and Washington School. It would be back to starting fourth graders again. It had been five years since I had done that, but I had missed it. Having fifth and sixth graders again sounded good to me also.

The BMS faculty's final task was a huge one. We had to pack up everything so it could be moved while the renovation was in progress. We had to label where we wanted the specific equipment and instruments to go. We had been told that the Cheney Building would not be part of the renovations or be in use at the new school.

The new sixth grade school would be called Bennet Academy. All of us on the music staff planned on what we needed for the upcoming year and decided what would be stored until the new school opened. It was a large task, but we were the best people to do it.

66 -
IT DOESN'T GET ANY BETTER

THE PLANNING COMMITTEE FOR THE Bennet Academy included the BMS music department concerning what kind of facility we would need for the sixth grade program. We knew from recent history there would be seventy to one hundred band members arriving from the eight elementary schools.

Space would be an issue for all of the music department.

We saw the plans at the first meeting with the architects. The music department was to be housed on the basement floor of the Barnard Building, which was located directly across the street from the Cheney Building. This meant there would be no more need for having my students cross the street in all kinds of weather to get to a band rehearsal.

I consulted the handbook of music facilities put out by the Wenger Corporation, whose business was music equipment. I had prepared myself for that first meeting. First glance at the plans for the band area revealed plans for a rehearsal space that was wide but not very deep. That space was the combined space of four classrooms in the old BMS configuration. This new space was not ideal, but once I saw the space for instrument and equipment storage, I was sold. In addition, the fact that the music department was located on its own floor and separate from other classrooms was a plus.

I was convinced that the construction planners knew what they were doing. One of them said, "And by the way, you will be getting all new equipment for the facility, especially new stands and chairs." My thought immediately was *This feels like Christmas!* There was a feeling of excitement from all of us music teachers as we left that meeting. I was beginning to become a "convert." This building renovation was, perhaps, more of a good idea than I originally thought.

2

Arrangements had been made for some MHS band kids to come over to BMS and speak to my eighth graders about the MHS marching band. When they arrived that day, I was surprised to see "drum-set" Robbie amongst that group. I had been wondering how he had been doing up at MHS. I had heard he joined the marching band and I was thrilled to hear that. Little did I know that he had become one of the leaders of the MHS drum line.

"Hey, Mister K, how's it going?" Robbie exclaimed as he came into the band room. I went over to him and shook his hand.

"Great to hear about all the good things you are doing up at MHS!" I said. I introduced him and the other high school kids to my eighth graders. And who stepped up to speak for the MHS group? Robbie.

He was the designated speaker, proceeding to give the "pep talk" about the marching band. As he concluded the presentation, he pointed to me as I stood in the back of the room. His words at that moment were "I want you guys to listen to this man. He knows what he is doing."

I was humbled by those words. I thought back to all the times in the past I had given up a quiet room so that this young man would be able to do what he loved—play the drum set.

As the MHS students left the room, I had tears in my eyes and a lump in my throat. I had seen a success story right in front of my eyes. There was this enthusiastic kid who was on the right road in life. The drums were helping him along the way. For a teacher, it doesn't get any better.

67 - PACKING UP

I COULD NOT START THE process of packing and labeling most of my equipment to be stored or moved from the Cheney Building until after the Memorial Day parade. This took a bit of planning, but I thought I was keeping up with events and in good shape.

The music department's plan for the parade was to combine the two middle school bands into one marching unit, with each school wearing their T-shirts. We had two combined rehearsals, one at Illing and then the other at Bennet. I loved the size of the group! Over one hundred marchers, including the banners and flags squads.

The day of the parade was spectacular. Warm and dry, with the sun bathing everything. I got the sense that the people along the parade route loved seeing both schools together. We got a huge reception, filled with cheers and applause, continuously down the parade route. I figured that this would be the last parade I would be involved in since I was assuming I would inherit the sixth grade band program. After all, I was on this site for the past several years. I "knew the territory."

I was happy and content with the prospect of teaching at a sixth grade school. It had been twenty-four years of teaching instrumental music in six different school systems up to this last month of the 2005–06 school year. I felt like I had my feet squarely on the ground in my career. No more did I have to worry about landing on my feet, or so I hoped.

2

With the parade having been a huge success, I began the packing process. I had to label each piece of equipment signifying its destination. My understanding was that I could send some pieces of percussion equipment to temporary locations for the two years of the renovation, as well as other stuff, including the drum set, the band tuxes, and the many trophies and plaques won by the band over the years. I took the opportunity to sort the music library by difficulty. I sent some arrangements up to MHS, as well as Illing. I kept the music I knew could be used for the sixth grade. I ended up working during a couple of Saturdays due to the fact I had a key (thanks again, Jeff!).

During the last few days of the school year, we had a number of faculty meetings and ended with a barbeque in the quad. We all said our goodbyes and left to enjoy our summer.

3

I took the opportunity to visit Keeney Street, Verplanck, and Washington schools during July. One day while I was at Keeney, organizing the music room, a guy with a familiar face walked in. It was none other than my Yankee buddy Scott! "Jim, guess what, I am the new principal here," Scott said with a huge smile.

I smiled as well, "Hey, Scott, that is great news. Go Yankees!" We both laughed and shook hands. I told him that I was really happy with the room I had been assigned to teach my lessons. It was right at the front of the school, with wall-to-wall windows looking out over the front circular school driveway. The room was spacious and bright. What a great place it was going to be to make music with young musicians. I was totally psyched!

I went to Verplanck the next day and met Sandy, who was the new general music teacher. She seemed enthusiastic and had a great personality, two prerequisites, I thought, for an effective general music teacher. Sandy showed me to my teaching space, which was a small room in a hallway near the main office. I had taught in small areas before. This space was much larger than the room at Lebanon Elementary, so I felt it would work out fine. The band was going to be rehearsing on the stage, so I knew that was an alternate place I might be able to use if I had a large class.

The school itself was a large building, which reminded me of my old elementary school in Hicksville, Fork Lane School. Verplanck looked and felt like the same place, and I understood why when I saw that this Manchester Elementary School was built in the early 1950s, right around the same time as Fork Lane. The architecture was virtually identical.

Having a positive outlook on teaching in my first two schools was somewhat dampened shortly after my visit to Washington School. I had taught in this building before and thought the stage of the gym was a great place to teach. I went in to talk to Trisha, the principal, to introduce myself. She was cordial but seemed quite busy, but I thought it was nice of her to take time to see me. She asked me if I would be willing to use the boys' locker room to teach my lessons since the gym stage was now being used for all of the general music classes.

I was skeptical having had the experience of teaching in a school locker room in the past. I knew that the locker room was used on Saturdays for the town recreation program and something about that worried me. I looked at the room and was not impressed. I bumped into Don, Washington's physical education teacher, and told him why I was there. "Jim, you don't want to teach here anytime," he warned me. "After the weekend this room is a mess, it smells of rotten food, and it's too close to the bathroom facilities. The area is not cleaned well. From a sanitary standpoint alone you do not want your students in there."

Don knew what he was talking about. This was part of his teaching area. And once he mentioned it, the dirt and smell were evident to me. I went back to Trisha to tell her I could not teach in that area. I gave her the reasons. School began and my lessons were being taught in a hallway foyer. But Trisha assured me this was only temporary. And it was.

After a couple of weeks, I was given the room upstairs that was used as a game room for the after-school program. Teaching among pool tables and foosball machines was better than smelling rotten food and the bathroom.

3

The work had begun on Bennet. I passed by the school every once in a while to see the progress being made during the following two years. It was hard to tell what was going on. It was a typical construction site. I thought it was interesting that all the buildings, at least on the outside, were getting a significant face-lift. School Street was blocked off from traffic for obvious reasons. The street was full of construction equipment and building materials. Somehow, I did not imagine things were going to be done on such an extensive scale.

I peeked into the quad one day and saw that all the old trees had been removed. That was a shock. I saw that the rumor that they would construct second-floor walkways to connect the four buildings was true. Those had begun to appear. What a different look it all was! I wasn't thinking about the interiors of the buildings at that point. I would have to wait for over a year to experience that, but I would find out it would be worth the wait.

More good news that summer was the word that our BMS school principal had been appointed Superintendent of Schools. Kathy had been a strong advocate of Bennet Academy, so as I was watching this school building transform, Manchester's school administration was transforming as well. Congratulations, Kathy!

68 - THE BRIDGE YEARS AT THE ELEMENTARY SCHOOLS

I DON'T KNOW WHAT I was thinking. I had anticipated that the next two years would be a relaxing and laid-back period in my teaching career. However, as soon as the school year began, I realized that I had been totally wrong. My teaching schedule was the opposite of relaxing.

I realized this reality during the first faculty meetings at my three schools. I learned that the elementary schools would be on a six-day rotation, indicated by days A through F. I knew this type of arrangement would be problematic. How would I keep track of this, not to mention the kids? I knew their teachers would help them with this but who was going to help me?

I took one look at my plan book and realized this was not going to be as confusing as I thought. I always used a plan book right from day one in my career. Here it was going to be my savior. Using paper was comforting, but so much of a teacher's information was now online.

Lo and behold, Keith was able to procure laptops for all the music staff. I chose a Mac, since I had a Macintosh at home. Having a way to communicate being at multiple schools was a huge advantage. I no longer had to "wait in line" to use a school-based computer. After all of this good news, I didn't think that working with days A through F would be a problem.

My schedule was organized so I would be teaching two consecutive days at each of my three schools. Verplank was my A and B days, Keeney St. was days C and D, and Washington was my teaching assignment on days E and F. Okay so far. But I then realized I would be dealing with three grades, three or four teachers per grade, times three! Nine separate grades, anywhere from nine to twelve teachers and all their students.

Okay, I can do this, I thought. *I have taught elementary music before, no problem.* I was glad I had all of my elementary instrumental experience. Otherwise, I might have been in a panic. The biggest worry I had was that each school's day had a different start and end time. I'd better make sure my alarm clock at home was reliable. I had been known to forget to set my alarm at times. I'd better clean this up.

2

The first three weeks were filled with classroom recruiting in the fourth grade and meeting and scheduling the fifth and sixth graders. It was a good time to make connections with the teachers and office staff. The secretaries invariably would know all the "ins and outs" of the school, whereas the custodians knew the "hows and wheres."

One of my strategies during my career was not to bother the principals with everyday issues. They had enough on their plates. I would only go to them if I felt it was absolutely necessary. As I have mentioned before in this book, I have had the good fortune to have worked under many great administrators. I consider myself lucky.

Scott, being the head of Keeney, was someone who I was looking forward to working with again. We had been through the "wars" at the middle school and lived to tell the tale. And, a die-hard Yankee fan to boot. It could not get any better than that.

Washington's principal, Trisha, seemed to have a lot on her plate most of the time. It was often challenging to get into her office to see her. As a result, I relied on the rest of the staff for help at that school.

Verplanck's principal, Mary Luce, came off as being very old-school. She was at the age that I assumed she would be likely to retire during the next few years. She ran a very tight ship with both the staff and students. However, as I got to know her, I realized that she had a soft spot for the arts. Any principal who had classical music played over the PA system as staff and students entered the building each morning had to appreciate what I was doing.

Mary also called a school gathering each morning in the gym to start the school day. It consisted of five to ten minutes of announcements and special presentations by students. The school audience was not allowed to speak during these meetings. Their job was to listen. What a concept! Instead of clapping in the appropriate places, everyone had to raise both hands and turn them from side to side. Silent applause. I was really impressed to see how much the kids bought into all of that.

During that fall, I had been hired to play a production of *The Pirates of Penzance* at the Goodspeed Opera. The show would consist of eight performances per week during the three-month run. I had performed at Goodspeed for many shows in the past, but usually as a sub. That entailed playing one or two shows a week, usually on Friday nights or weekends. But, for Penzance, I was the main Reed III player. As a result, I was required to play the first two weeks of the show, including the two Wednesday matinees.

How was I going to play those performances without leaving for the theater at about 12:30? I cleared this with Scott and Trisha to combine a few classes on those days so I could leave early. However, I was a bit concerned about Mary's reaction to this request, her being of the old school. I went in to see her one day to ask her about getting released early for those Wednesday afternoons. This was important. I knew that I was going to have to play some other matinees along the way as well.

I was nervous, for sure. "Mary, I have been hired by the Goodspeed Opera to play *The Pirates of Penzance*," I said.

She smiled and had an excited expression. "That's wonderful!" she exclaimed.

"But this means for the first few weeks of the show, I am required by contract to play the Wednesday matinees, which start at two. I would need to leave the school by twelve-thirty." Silence followed. *Uh oh, here it comes*, I thought.

Mary broke the silence with the following words, "Jim, I want to tell you that it is quite an honor for this school to have a professional musician such as yourself on our faculty. We are thrilled to have you here. Of course, by all means, leave when you have to on those days. Just make sure everybody gets their lesson in."

I exhaled. "Mary, thank you, I appreciate your kind words and your permission to do this."

I was so gratified after that meeting. I had experienced a few difficult and discouraging meetings with administrators in my career, but this one went a long way to balance those out. I basked in the good karma of the moment. Here was an administrator who "got it." This school was lucky to have Mary. I was going to enjoy teaching at Verplanck.

3

During a break in classes one day at Verplanck, the physical education teacher, Barb, introduced me to a college student who was working with her as a student aide. I was amazed at the fact that I had to reach up quite a lot to shake her hand. She was definitely six-foot something. She introduced herself as Brittany from UCONN. I had the strange feeling that I had seen her somewhere before. I knew that face.

"Nice to meet you, Brittany. How are you liking being at Verplanck?" I asked.

"The kids and everyone have been great so far," she exclaimed.

"I teach instrumental music here on E and F days," I said.

"Oh, that's cool. I used to play trombone in my younger days. I don't get the chance to play much anymore with all the basketball stuff at UCONN."

My immediate thought was *My goodness, now I know where I have seen her!* I said, "I recognize you, Brittany, you are a member of the UCONN women's team, right?"

"Yes, some of us on the team are involved in the UCONN Outreach program. I was assigned here to Verplanck."

I wanted to stay longer and pick Brittany Hunter's brain about coach Geno Auriemma and the rest of the team, since I never missed a game on TV. I was a huge fan of UCONN basketball, both the men's and women's teams. But, after a glance at my watch, it dawned on me I had to scurry to lunch if I was to have enough time to eat. "Brittany, I guess I will see you around. Feel free to stop in and listen to a lesson anytime."

"I will, don't worry."

I looked up her stats online later that day. She was 6 feet 4 inches. I was right on! Only 8 inches taller than me.

4

In the meantime, the lessons at Verplanck moved along smoothly during the fall. One day we were told at a morning faculty meeting that Kathy, our new superintendent, was going to be touring the building that day. Since I was in a small room off the beaten track, I did not think I would be seeing her. However, in the middle of the morning, I got a great surprise. Kathy walked into my room.

She smiled at me and said, "Good morning, Mister Kleiner, how are you?"

"Hi, Doctor Ouelette, nice to see you," I replied, then turned to my students. "Ladies and gentlemen, do you know who this lady is? This is Doctor Ouelette, the Manchester Superintendent of Schools."

Kathy replied at that point, "I heard you people as I was out in the hallway, and I wanted to tell you I thought you sounded great!"

"I agree, Doctor Ouelette, this saxophone class has been working very hard this year." My students smiled.

"Keep up the good work everyone," she added. "Nice to see you, Mister Kleiner."

"Same here, Doctor Ouelette."

As I was leaving the building at the end of the day, Principal Mary came up to me and said, "Did Kathy find you today?"

"Yes, she paid a nice visit to me and my sixth grade saxophone class this morning."

"Good, because I want you to know she specifically asked me where you were so she could pay you a visit. She spoke very highly of you, just so you know."

Hearing about Kathy's compliments that day was a real highlight of my entire career. She and I had been through some "interesting" times together at BMS. For the rest of the day, I was on cloud nine.

5

A few weeks later, I got wind of an impending Verplanck field trip. I had been asked to be a chaperone. The sixth grade, as part of the UCONN Outreach program, had been invited to spend a day on the UCONN campus. This sounded like it would be a wonderful opportunity for these kids to experience what a college campus was like.

The day arrived and I got on one of the school buses along with the four sixth grade classes and their teachers for the trip to Storrs. When we arrived, we were dropped off at Gampel Pavilion, the huge basketball arena. I had only been to this facility once in the past, when the Connecticut All-State concert had been held there.

As we entered the arena, we were told to take seats in the first few rows right at courtside. After a welcome by a UCONN official, out walked four college-age ladies. I recognized each one of them! To say I was excited would be an understatement. The group consisted of the assistant basketball coach, Jamelle Elliot, followed by members of the UCONN women's basketball team, Brittany Hunter, Tina Charles, and Maya Moore. How cool was this!

Each one spoke to the group about the value of sportsmanship, hard work and persistence, all great attributes for the kids to emulate. At the conclusion of the speeches, they opened up the floor for questions. One of my band students asked the student athletes if any of them played a musical instrument. To my delight, each one answered in the affirmative. Trombone, saxophone, piano—each athlete was also a musician! What a great example of all-around young women.

At that point I noticed two very tall young men in the shadows, and one of the ladies asked them to come over and say hello. They turned out to be Craig Austrie and Hasheem Thabeet, two members of the UCONN men's basketball team. The kids gasped at the size of the 7-foot-3-inch Thabeet, as did I. He was carrying a basketball and proceeded to go over to one of the hoops and dunk. Everyone cheered, especially me.

For the next hour, the UCONN students ran a series of games on the court and all the kids participated. No wonder they had asked all of us to wear sneakers that day. I even took a few shots myself, although I was kind of embarrassed to shoot a basketball in front of Maya Moore.

After the basketball festivities, we took the college student shuttle bus over to one of the school cafeterias. The kids got to eat with the college kids on their own turf. The teachers and chaperones helped the kids with their trays and food selection from the buffet-style setup. Some of the kids had never eaten from a cafeteria buffet before and needed some pointers. Our kids sat down amongst the college kids as they ate.

When we arrived back at Verplanck that afternoon, all were tired but happy. What a day! I made it a point to see if Mary was in her office. She was, so I stuck my head in the door and told her, "Mary, that field trip was awesome! The Verplanck kids were great."

She turned to me and said, "Yep," and winked.

As I drove home that afternoon, I knew that this day was another "payback" day for me. Despite the tough times and experiences in the past, there were so many more of these inspirational career days happening to me. I had no doubt at this point that I had made the right decision about a decade ago to venture back into public school education.

6

Over on the other side of town, I had a super enthusiastic group of young band students at the Keeney Street School. Anyone who has directed a school band knows that it is invaluable to have several outstanding musicians in the group. These kids will inevitably pull up the rest of the group. It never fails.

The band was not large, consisting of about thirty members, but what we lacked in size we made up for in having at least one strong player in each section. As a result, we worked on and performed quite challenging music. One of the pieces we experienced was the "Prehistoric Suite," which consisted of four contrasting sections, each named after a particular dinosaur. Of course, the final movement, "T-Rex," was their favorite. I had done this piece in the past with seventh and eighth graders. The Keeney band was up to the task with this group of kids.

I had been talking to my colleague, Mary Walsh, about the Goodspeed show I was playing. As I described the production of Pirates, she asked, "Do they have school groups attend?"

"Yes, at some matinee performances there are school groups in attendance."

Mary asked me for the Goodspeed phone number and a few days later she came to me with the news that she had arranged for our Keeney sixth grade classes to go see a matinee performance. I was excited! Those kids were going to see a fun production of a Gilbert and Sullivan operetta and they would get to hear a great pit orchestra, including me!

At Goodspeed, I asked the cast if they would be willing to meet our students after the performance for a meet and greet, with a question-and-answer session. I was gratified that so many in the cast were happy to participate, especially the actor who played the male lead role. "Meet and talk with your students? Absolutely, count me in!" he replied. I was so excited and was counting the days.

When the day of the sixth grade trip came, I had left Keeney early, as I always did on Wednesdays. I arrived at the theater, assembled my clarinet and bass clarinet, and began my warmup. After the house was opened up and the audience began to file in, I didn't see the Keeney group. But, after about a half hour, I saw Mary W. filing in with the students and chaperones. They filled up most of the center and one of the side balconies.

I waved to the group. Most of them had a great view of the pit.

They could see all the instruments and musicians quite clearly due to the compact size of the theater. I had better be on my toes. They were sure to give me a "review" after the show.

As usual, the performance was top-notch. Goodspeed, as a major regional theater in the Northeast, had won a Tony Award a few years prior. After the show had finished, a Goodspeed representative ushered the Keeney group downstairs into the orchestra level and sat the kids front and center. As that representative gave the students some background about the theater and the production, several cast members wandered out and sat on some chairs provided for them.

It was cute to see the reaction of the kids as they were recognizing the various actors and actresses. And, when the lead actor, the Johnny Depp lookalike with his long black hair, mustache, and goatee, came out, the girls especially were so excited. Each cast member introduced themselves and they all took questions from the kids. I felt especially gratified that many of the cast members mentioned the pit orchestra as being such an integral part of the show. For a musician, that was always nice to hear.

This day was another incredible highlight for me. Seeing my own students among the Keeney group having such a great experience at the show and meeting the cast, I again was reminded of why I became a teacher.

7

During the summer of 2007, I took the opportunity from time to time to check on the Bennet Academy renovation. I could see progress each time. The construction team had done a complete facelift on the exterior of all four buildings. I was impressed. They reminded me of buildings on an Ivy League campus. I wondered what was going on inside, however. It was still about ten months before I would find out.

In the meantime, I was anticipating the upcoming school year, looking forward to the challenges and joys of another year in my career. I could not wait for the first day of school. My wife always thought I was a bit weird because I would feel this way once August rolled around each summer. I was anxious to get started.

I visited Keeney to check on my room about a week before the teachers' meetings during the last week of August. I thought I might say hi to Scott before I checked my room. I walked into the main office and asked the secretary if Scott was available. She looked at the other two secretaries, who both had uncomfortable looks on their faces. I was taken aback by that. "Is he here?" I asked.

"No," one of them said.

"Okay, I will try to see him another time." I walked over to my room. I had a funny feeling from the reaction of the secretaries that something was not right. No sooner did that thought cross my mind than I was surprised to see my room had totally changed.

There was no music equipment or anything else related to music in the room. It hit me like a ton of bricks. This must not be a music room any longer. Just then, the custodian walked in and told me that the music room was now off the other end of the cafeteria. He pointed me to where that was. I walked across the cafeteria floor to the other end and saw the room. It was a smallish room with no windows. All the music equipment was there. I had two immediate thoughts: *Where was I going to rehearse the band and why hadn't someone given me a heads-up about the room change?*

I was sure that Scott would have contacted me about the room change. Something was not right.

Somewhat perplexed, I proceeded over to Verplank to check on things over there. All looked in order in the music area, so I stopped at the main office to say hi to Mary Luce. The secretary said, "Oh, you didn't know? Mary was just appointed as the principal at Keeney. They are in the process of hiring a new principal here at Verplanck."

"Thanks for the news," I said as I walked out of the office in a state of total surprise. *What happened to Scott?* I wondered.

That evening I called one of the fifth grade teachers who was a good friend of mine at Keeney, and she filled me in on what had happened. Evidently, Scott and the school social worker had been caught in a compromising position by a parent visiting the school. This had led to Scott being let go from the administrative staff in Manchester. As I asked other people about this, no one knew any of the details, not that it was my or anyone else's business.

I was so depressed about this. Scott and I had been through so much together over the past several years and I valued him as an administrator and a friend. School systems for the most part don't want these types of situations to become public information. I felt for him and for the social worker. They made a mistake and lost their jobs. I had once been on the precipice of losing my career and knew what they felt. I was certainly not going to judge anyone or anything.

8

The next week we had our school meetings. I found out that the decision had been made to make my former Keeney room into a special education room. It was going to house the school systems' behaviorally challenged elementary students. Dealing with emotionally challenged kids is not something I would be able to do. I do have much patience, but not the level needed for that job.

The room change ended up not being too much of a problem. I was able to rehearse the band in the cafeteria in the mornings. We also had space in the corner to store music stands and my snare and bass drums.

Lessons were going well as school started, but every so often I would hear loud voices travelling the length of the cafeteria. They were coming out of the special ed. room. And what I heard at times was quite disturbing. I was hearing every swear word in the book. Things flared up on a regular basis. I was then beginning to realize what the special ed. teachers had to deal with. I was cringing at the thought of a parent walking into the building and hearing four letter words being screamed at the top of a ten-year-old's lungs.

There was one particular boy who seemed to be out of control frequently. He obviously had big-time emotional issues. One day during a planning period, as I sat in my room with the door closed,

I suddenly heard some choice swear words and then a big crash. I rushed to the door and opened it in time to see this boy dump a large cafeteria table that had been set up for lunch. Plates, silverware, and whatever else had been on that table were all over the floor.

The kid was out of control. He proceeded to say the "F" word and dump the next table over as well. The next thing in his line of sight was my percussion equipment. No one was getting near this kid, but I knew I was not going to let him destroy my drums. I walked out and stood in front of the drums with my arms folded and a stern look on my face. Would I have to physically restrain this kid from doing harm to my equipment?

I grabbed a pair of drumsticks and played a drum roll. The boy looked quizzically and stopped in his tracks. This distracted him enough so that when Principal Mary and a large gentleman intervened, he had calmed down. I was glad I could do my part to help the situation. I got a lot of brownie points that day from Mary and the social work staff. And my percussion equipment survived!

Two weeks later I got my old room back! Good karma had come my way. Mary decided that the room in the front of the school building was no place for what some called the "room with rubber walls." The special ed. room was moved to the back of the building, about as far away from the rest of the school as was possible. Once again, people walking into Keeney could hear music!

My respect for the special education teachers who did their professional best to give these needy kids an education had continued to grow. I knew in my heart these kids had a much better chance at living a productive life with the help of these dedicated teachers.

That spring, Keeney had its annual field day, which was a tradition at all the elementary schools. I loved the fact that the arts teachers were enlisted to run and monitor all the competitive events for the kids. Grades 4, 5, and 6 would take part, so I knew a lot of these kids right off the bat. Relay races of all sorts were the order of the day. It was fun for me to play a different role than I was used to.

We stressed fairness and sportsmanship. And the "at risk" students were included in this event as well. I didn't notice any difference between the behavior of those kids and the others. It looked to me like progress was being made with them. That was sure encouraging.

9

Washington School turned out to be a relaxing environment for me during these bridge years to Bennet Academy. The kids, although small in number, were super enthusiastic and I enjoyed them. Some had private lessons, which was an advantage for them. I liked to bring my instruments on those days there and play along. They loved that.

The highlight of the two years there was when we played our spring concert at Cheney Hall. They loved being on that stage, and the parents and relatives loved the venue. I played along with the small group and filled in some of the gaps in instrumentation we had. The lessons in the recreation area had worked out fine. I give Principal Trisha credit for coming up with that space for our lessons.

As the year was coming to an end, I was getting more and more excited about September 2008. Teaching sixth graders the past couple of years had proven quite satisfying for me. I loved the age group. They still had that raw enthusiasm for what I was teaching them. I had experienced over the years that you could excite that age group more easily than the average eighth grader. I loved inspiring and molding an eleven-year-old. And, of course, most importantly, they would laugh at my jokes!

69 - THE ACADEMY BECKONS

I HAD LEARNED MUCH THROUGH experience over the past several years since I followed a path back to education. I had mellowed in some ways. And, I had felt confident that my philosophy of stressing the positive with my students was the best one. This is not to say that I never "told it like it was," but I had learned that ending every class on a positive note was the best way to go.

I knew that I was now in the era of "don't damage their self-esteem." I had seen that philosophy stressed in everything from education to parenting. I was not convinced. I could see every day the negative aspects of this belief in the way some of my students viewed the world. And I saw this in the way parents were behaving as well.

No longer were parents calling me directly if they felt their child was having a conflict in my class. They were going to the administration first. I hated hearing about problems from my principal or vice principal instead of the parents. It was as though the teacher was now out of the loop. Having been stung by that experience at BMS, I was very concerned. I had also known a couple of other colleagues to go through a similar experience. However, this was the reality now in education, and my colleagues and I had to learn how to deal with it.

I was excited about what was coming next for me, despite these misgivings about my chosen field. Teaching at the sixth grade level was something I could see myself doing for the rest of my career. Sure, I would never again be conducting music by Vincent Persichetti or Vaclav Nelhybel. But there were many talented composers for band out there now producing better and better music for young players. I was part of the professional music scene in Connecticut as well. I had so much to look forward to. Until one day, Keith came to visit.

2

I thought Keith's visit was just a routine "how are things going?" chat. But it was more than that. He got straight to the point. "Jim, I wanted to let you know that Frank (the Illing instrumental teacher) is not happy at Illing and is interested in the Bennet Academy job. I am asking you to help out our department by considering taking the Illing job starting in September. You have lots of middle school experience and would fit in very nicely over there." My head was spinning. "Keith, I was really looking forward to taking over the sixth grade position. I already know the incoming sixth graders from three schools."

We discussed this plan for several minutes. In the meantime, my thoughts were becoming more amenable with this new prospect. I owed much to Keith, who had been a great help to me over the past few years since he took over the position of music department coordinator. I had so much respect for the job he was doing at Manchester High School. I had seen my former students flourish under his program. And then, the words came out. "Okay, Keith, I will do it." I tried to sound enthusiastic even though I was far from it.

My excitement at being on the ground floor at Bennet Academy had vanished. Over the next few weeks, I tried to get excited about teaching middle school again. I did have much experience to fall back on. Oh well, time to land on my feet once again.

As I was driving home during the last week of school, I had to stop at the local XtraMart for a few things, including to fill up my gas tank. As I went into the store, my cell phone rang. It was Keith calling. "Jim, Frank just resigned. He has taken a job in South Windsor at the middle school there. So, we have to hire someone new. I am giving you an option. Bennet Academy or Illing?"

It took a millisecond for me to respond. "Bennet Academy," I answered.

"Okay, you got it!" he answered. I didn't have to "land on my feet" again after all. I was getting too old for that!

70 -
THE NEW BENNET ACADEMY

IT WAS A HOT DAY as we gathered outside the front entrance to the newly renovated school. I already loved the new sign high on the front of the Franklin Building, saying "Bennet Academy" in large silver, metallic letters.

We walked in and our tour began. The thing that hit me immediately was that the stairway up to the main office was not where it used to be. *How do you move a front stairway?* I pondered. That was the moment I realized that they really did renovate the interior as well as the exterior of these buildings. The new principal, Dave Welch, was acting as our guide.

"Look different so far?" he said. He then explained that the construction crew had stripped the entire interior of the building back to its studs and started over. Three floors worth! No wonder the construction site was always filled with debris.

As we walked up the front stairs and approached the second-floor office, we noticed something quite startling. Everything was brand new. And I mean, everything! We were each given a floor map and I was glad about that, seeing that the first stairwell we used was not there in the old building. Hopefully, these maps would help us from getting lost. At this point, Dave let us walk around at our own pace.

Of course, the music department teachers made a beeline towards the Barnard Building, which was in the rear of the quadrangle of buildings. The Barnard Building was in the back and the Franklin in the front. B for back, F for front. Easy for someone my age to remember.

We followed the map through the Cone building, which housed the library on the second floor above the first-floor gym. The Cone building's second floor hallway connected the Franklin and Barnard buildings. We made our way down the staircase to the half-basement first floor of the Barnard. I had the architect's sketch of the music floor in my mind as I walked towards the rehearsal room. I gawked at the beautiful woodworking all over the hallway and on the doors.

I looked in the instrument-storage room. It contained classy wooden storage bins for instruments. There were racks to store the larger stringed instruments as well. Finally, as I entered the rehearsal room, I felt something strange. Cool air! The building had central air-conditioning. Finally, for the first time in my teaching career I would be teaching in an air-conditioned space.

The rehearsal room was just as I had pictured it—not too deep but wide. At the end of the room on my right was my desk. It had a new desktop computer on it. I had been told that the desktop was wired into a sound system for the room, with speakers in the ceiling and a video projector suspended from the ceiling as well. I would be able to show videos from the desktop to be seen on the large screen, which I could pull down from the ceiling. Brand-new stands and Wenger chairs were on their respective series of storage racks. I thought I had died and gone to heaven!

Nowhere to be found, however, were some of the things I had labelled to be moved over from the Cheney Building. My percussion equipment was found in a storage room next to the instrument-storage room. So far, so good. But I was missing some major items. My drum set was not there. My two African djembe drums were missing. The tuxes we had used for uniforms were gone, along with all the trophies that had been awarded to BMS over the years from various festivals over the previous years. All were gone. Perhaps they had been sent to the wrong place. I made a mental note to pursue this situation later.

The entire faculty gathered after lunch, but not after most of us had wandered down to one of the various restaurants on Main Street. Fed and happy, there was quite a buzz as we sat at the library tables. Then Dave began the meeting. He introduced the architect and head builder of the project. Kathy was there as well. She had been a main force in convincing the town to house all of the sixth graders in one building. One by one, we gave each of these people a standing ovation for the incredible job done. I was never so happy to have been so wrong about this renovation. Shame on me, and welcome, Bennet Academy!

71 -
GETTING THE KINKS OUT

AS WITH ANY NEW TEACHING space, it took time during that first 2008–09 school year to get used to the schedule, the environment, the faculty and staff, and the administration. We had a veteran administration and that proved to be an advantage. Dave was amenable to most things the music department requested, including pushing through an increase in the stipend I was receiving for doing jazz ensemble and other school events, including concerts. That was greatly appreciated. Having his appreciation for the arts was certainly helpful. He "got it."

At one of our early staff meetings the discussion was about how we all should approach this new sixth grade school. Was it an elementary school or a middle school? I put my two cents in and said it was, in reality, a "melementary" school. Dave loved that phrase. I heard him use that term often during the school year.

At first, I was not thrilled about the morning duty the "special teachers" (art, music, phys. ed., family-consumer science) had to do. We were asked to be in the courtyard (weather permitting) and then gym to greet and monitor the arriving students. The kids would sit on the gym floor by team, and at a certain time, one teacher from that team would come down to the gym and walk them back upstairs to their rooms.

After a while, I found this duty to be an advantage. I was able to get to know all the students in the school. And, I could chat with any band members if I needed to right then and there before the school day started. It was definitely loud in the gym, so I often had a pair of earplugs with me. Problem solved!

One day a week I would hold a jazz ensemble rehearsal before school. This group was voluntary and from year to year I did not know how big the group would end up being, or what instrumentation the group would have. I used a jazz method series specifically including parts for every instrument, including flutes and clarinets. My belief was that at this level, all students should have the opportunity to learn and experience jazz, not just the traditional brass, saxes, and rhythm instruments. I loved the way that worked out. After all, we didn't need to look like Duke Ellington's jazz band. The kids were only in the sixth grade and were at the very beginnings of exploring the jazz idiom.

I was fortunate each year to have students who played keyboard and drum set. All of them were taking private lessons already prior to coming to Bennet. I looked forward to our 7:00 am jazz rehearsals. What a way to start the day!

The only glitch was that I had a very heavy piano amp which was really hard to move around. It must have weighed 50 pounds or more! I would do my best to move it when needed from the instrument storage area to the band room. Eventually I just stuck it in the corner near my desk to keep it available.

That spring I had my normal yearly checkup with my physician. I was lying on the exam table at one point, and as I got up my doctor said, "Oh, you have a hernia."

"I do?" I answered incredulously.

"Yes, you do. Watch your stomach area as you sit up," she added. So, I did and I saw a pronounced bulge emanate from my stomach area. I could not believe it. I had never noticed that.

"Does it hurt?" she asked.

"No, it does not hurt at all. I did not know it was there." The doctor gave me the name of a specialist to visit and have it checked out.

I went to the specialist the next week and he said that I had a ventral hernia, which meant I had a weakened area in my stomach wall. He asked me if I had been doing any heavy lifting. I knew immediately I had. The piano amp! The doctor advised me that there was a surgical procedure that could repair the hernia, but the recovery was usually painful. Since it was not bothering me, he advised me to just leave it be. I took his advice. I still have this condition to this day, but it has yet to bother me.

The next day I was discussing this with my colleagues at school. The workman's comp subject came up more than once, but I was not predisposed to go that route. Too much paperwork and angst trying to prove it was the amp's fault. I let things drop.

A week later I arrived at school, walked into my room, and saw the piano amp at the opposite end of the band room. I immediately wondered, *Who moved that?* I walked over to it and saw that it was resting on a square of two-by-fours with thick rubber casters. Someone had made this monstrosity portable.

During lunch that day I found out who the "culprit" was. It was our custodian, Maggie. She came into the lunch area and said, "Did you find my present? I heard about what happened to you trying to move that amp around, so I made a cart for it to ride on."

I said, "Maggie, I can't tell you how much I appreciate what you did. Thank you so much! That was so thoughtful of you."

"I know you work hard with your students, and I wanted to make things easier so you can move that amp anywhere around the school." And she was right. After that, I could move the amp anywhere.

Maggie was cut out of the same cloth as my BMS custodian Jeff. How could I have been so lucky to have custodians like this working with me? Maggie ended up working on our floor at the academy the following year as well. After that, she was gone and I never found out why. Nobody seemed to know. I knew that I would surely miss her.

Settling into the new building did not take long at all. Even the problems with the AC causing our air temp to be really cool at times did not bother me. It was always better to wear an extra layer than to have that BMS Cheney Building feeling of having to change my clothes after lunch.

I was happy at Bennet Academy. I knew I had made the right

decision to spend the latter part of my teaching career there. It was a comfortable and professionally satisfying environment. This was a good feeling, although I did not know at the time that there would be a few more bumps on the road.

72 -
THE NUMBERS GAME

THERE WAS A TREND IN instrumental music education that had become increasingly bothersome to me. Were the numbers of students you had in your program evidence of your success? Well, in my mind, yes and no. On paper, each fall I would receive the numbers of fifth graders that had played instruments in all of the eight elementary schools. Of course, now they were all coming to Bennet Academy, so I could see from the lists how many students to expect and what my instrumentation would be. At that point, I could plan on what music to use during the upcoming year based on the instrumentation.

Each year I would receive this list and then discover during the first week of classes that I did not have the expected number but instead one that was much lower. After the first year when my expected number went from one hundred to sixty-five, I knew what to expect. There were several reasons for this. Families would move out of town, kids would drop out of the program due to lack of interest, or some would end up attending private or parochial schools. The situation was certainly not a reflection on the elementary instrumental teachers who had prepared these kids.

The usual abundance of percussion students further exacerbated the problem. I was always searching for music with many percussion parts so these students would have enough to play. One problem I faced back in Bennet Middle School days came to mind as I was reflecting on all of this.

2

Back during one year at BMS, I had been notified by one of my many percussionists that he was not going to be able to attend the spring concert. As a result, I did not assign him a part for the concert. Instead, I would have him double one of the other parts during our rehearsals. The night of the concert I was in my usual tizzy trying to remember a thousand things. We were at MHS by that time and there were so many things to keep track of, even though it was a great venue.

That concert night we had our usual group of multiple players back in the percussion section. I was keeping my focus on multiple things and did not notice that this young man who had told me he was not going to be with us had actually showed up. I did not notice he was there. And he, being the nice, polite kid he was, just stood in the back of the band. He had nothing to play the entire night.

I actually did not realize this had happened to him until a couple of days after the concert, when I received a note from the boy's father. The note said that he had been humiliated watching his son just stand there and not participate. I immediately called this man and explained to him that his son had told me he was not going to be at the concert. The dad sheepishly explained that his son had subsequently told him about all of that. The man apologized to me for the note. All was forgiven and forgotten. I had thought I had seen everything at a concert, but this was a new one.

3

The numbers game began to take a toll on concert performances. One Bennet Academy concert was a prime example of this. I had programmed what I thought was a great arrangement that I thought fit well with the holiday. The piece was called "Bells," and it had ten different percussion parts. This was perfect for my large percussion section. It was not an easy piece, but everyone worked really hard on it, especially the percussionists. There was a growing sense of pride that I could see with the group as we readied that piece during the rehearsals.

The concert night arrived, and I was in the high school band room warming up and tuning the band. I sent the percussionists out to the stage to make sure their instruments and equipment were all ready to go.

As a department, we had the concert night at MHS down to a science. The orchestra would perform first, then the curtains would be closed and the chorus would perform on risers in the pit. While the curtains were closed, the high school stage crew would quietly reset the chairs and stands to the band setup.

While this was going on, a few of my percussionists came to me after the tuning and told me that four of our eleven percussionists had not shown up. My first thought was *OMG, what are we going to do?* This meant that four separate parts were not going to be covered.

My mind was racing. Should I pull the piece off the program here at the last minute? As I thought about it, I just could not do that. Too many had worked too hard on this piece. "Bells" would stay! I could see the other percussionists in a huddle and later I found out they were deciding who was going to cover the parts of the missing players. We performed our first piece and it went quite well. Then it was time for "Bells."

It was such an effective and lovely original piece that I was encouraged at how well it had begun. And then, the "silences" began. Whole measures, due to the missing players, were totally silent. It began to throw the instrumentalists off. Entrances were ragged and I struggled to keep things together. My valiant percussionists were running around like the old silent movie crew "The Keystone Cops" trying to cover everything. At one point someone dropped a drumstick, then the suspended cymbal went crashing to the floor.

It was excruciating, but we got through it finally and I don't think that Grandma in the audience probably knew the difference. But the sad part was that we all did.

This was a problem that had come to the point that something had to be done to cut down on the number of kids starting on the drums. That spring at one of our music department meetings, the band folks stayed behind to deal with this issue. We made the decision that no percussionists would start in the fourth or fifth grades. Sixth grade would be the time that a student would be able to concentrate on percussion. The requirement for those students would be one or two years of playing another instrument. The elementary bands would have band members fill in on drums for their pieces.

The new policy worked. It seemed drastic at first but turned out to solve the numbers game. There would hopefully not be any more "Bells" disasters in the future. And with myself being a closet percussionist anyway, I looked forward to giving my sixth graders their first experience banging on those drums.

73 -
A TOUGH CROWD

I WAS PARTICULARLY LOOKING FORWARD to the Winter Concert in 2012. Our choral director, Mike Dunning, had asked me to accompany the chorus by playing the violin obbligato to a piece they were going to perform called "Winter Dreams." I arranged the violin part for clarinet and the rehearsals had gone very well. It was a beautiful work and I appreciated being part of it. I always enjoyed playing one of my instruments in front of my students and their parents and family members. It certainly did not hurt to show them all that I was, in fact, a musician as well as an educator.

The MHS auditorium had 1,100 seats and was notable for its good acoustics. After experiencing the Rockville High School auditorium back in the '70s, I looked at this upgrade as "payback." (By this time, over thirty years later, the RHS auditorium had been completely renovated and had become a state-of-the-art facility. Way to go, Town of Vernon!) The MHS venue also featured a Wenger acoustic shell and soundboards suspended from the stage ceiling. We actually did not have to rehearse on the stage prior to a concert anymore since the acoustics were so good.

The Bennet performing groups were large. But my colleagues and I knew that there would be a certain percentage of kids that would not participate on concert night. Some of their parents worked evenings and required them to babysit. Other parents did not have the transportation to bring their kids to the concert. I can remember, on more than one occasion, picking up a student and giving them a ride to the concert, with the school's and parents' permission.

We had rehearsed the logistics for the evening. After each group performed, they would be guided by the faculty chaperones to the reserved seats in the front section. That night there were a couple of hundred seats reserved for them. The high school stage crew was all ready to set up and clear stands and chairs. Everything was all set.

The orchestra, under Linda Browning, on stage first on the program, followed by the chorus in the orchestra pit. "Winter Dreams" went without a hitch. I had a blast playing with the group. I had such a nice, warm feeling after while I was putting away my clarinet back in the band room. The chorus kids were excited after the performance, as I had been. As they were seated in their reserved seats, you could feel that excitement. They were glad they were done.

The band settled into their seats on the stage and the percussion section was making sure all was ready in their section. I noticed a particularly high noise level amongst the student performers sitting in the audience. I was confident that would be dealt with by the teacher chaperones. It was traditionally a problem at past concerts to have to settle down the students who had just performed. As a staff, we consistently focused on preparing them for this piece of concert etiquette. They were encouraged to be good listeners after being good performers.

I gave the signal to the stage crew member to open the curtain, despite my concern about the noise level. As the curtain opened, I was aghast to hear some students literally screaming at the top of their lungs! Some of my band members jumped in their seats. I did not see anyone in authority trying to quell the noise. The screaming continued for about thirty seconds until I had no choice but to go out onstage. As I walked out, I debated what to do.

I had two choices. I could start the band's first piece during the noise, or I could take the microphone and say something. I decided on the latter, because I did not want my band members to be distracted while they were trying to play, and I wanted the audience to be able to hear the music. As I went up to the mike, the noise continued.

To preface what happened next, I must explain that the people in the recording booth were not expecting me to speak at that point. And, when turned on, the mikes would operate with a slight delay.

They were new and of high quality, but that was always an annoyance.

Naturally, I forgot that, and when I started to speak, my voice was not being picked up. I had to raise my voice volume to my "teacher voice." All teachers know how to do this. We use our diaphragm to push out our words with a more forceful tone. I was looking at and speaking to the chorus members in the front. I said the words, "This is not . . ." before I stopped, knowing that my words were not being heard. So, I amped up my voice and said, "This is not necessary, folks," in my teacher voice.

Unfortunately, the mike kicked in just then and it sounded like I was yelling. That certainly did the trick. Things were hushed down, but not in the way I had intended. My mistake at that point was not saying more about why it was important for the students to be good listeners, but when the boos started, I forgot about that.

The boos were coming from adults, not students. I could not believe what I was hearing at first. My mind was racing. *Booing? You have got to be kidding!* And after the initial barrage, the boos got louder and more frequent. I stood with my back to the audience for about ten seconds before deciding to leave the stage and let things calm down. Perhaps some adults in the audience thought I was speaking to them? How could that be? It was obvious I was speaking to the students in the front rows.

When I got off stage, I thought things would settle down, but they did not right away. I was not going out on stage with boos and catcalls raining down. I could see my band was getting quite confused, and some had worried looks on their faces. All I could think about was how this was going to affect their performance. After a few minutes, our principal came backstage and advised me that I should go out and continue the concert because it was getting late. I bit my tongue almost all the way through. I held back from asking him why he had not gone on stage to settle things down.

Joe was our new principal. In his defense, later, I tried to look at things from his perspective. Most likely the last thing he wanted to do was get up and bring to task the students and adults in his new role as our new administrator. If I was in his shoes, I would have felt that way. As he and I were backstage discussing all of this, I could hear our general music teacher, Martha Sandefer,, speaking to the audience. She was trying to calm things down. Whatever she said worked and things returned to the ambiance of a normal school concert.

Over the next half-hour, I was floored at how well my band played. I was never so proud of a group of sixth graders as I was of those kids that night. I felt like they were giving me 150 percent at that moment. They were not the most talented band I had ever had at Bennet Academy, but they played their hearts out. The applause for them was loud and sincere. Things had ended on a positive note.

Back in the band room I was gathering my things and making sure that my students had all of their belongings before they departed to meet their families in the lobby. Two sets of parents stopped by to see me, both of whom commended me on how I handled the situation with the students in the audience. I felt gratified by that and went home, satisfied that the concert had been a success.

The next morning at school I found out that some people did not think so.

74 - AN EDUCATOR'S LEARNING NEVER ENDS

I ARRIVED AT SCHOOL THE next morning with the usual post-concert glow. I loved that feeling. The concert was done and there was a sense of satisfaction, knowing my students had a positive learning experience. Another step on their road of experiencing the joys of music. At this point I looked forward to chatting with the band at our next meeting. My usual questions included those about the performance itself and the music. At this point I was open to hearing their opinions about the music they played. I would never discuss the music much while in rehearsal. I would tell them at that point that they could express their opinions once we had performed the piece. So, this was the time for that.

The music department seemed awfully quiet that morning. My music teacher colleagues didn't seem to be around. When I found them, I expected the normal post-concert discussion from them. Nothing. They did not come in to even say good morning. That seemed strange and unusual. I proceeded at that point to unpack my percussion, which had been shipped back early that morning from the high school.

The music staff was excused from morning gym duty on these days after concerts so we could get our act together before our first class. Without the usual chit-chat from my colleagues, I was making faster progress than normal. Then, in walked Joe.

I was surprised at first. It was unusual for an administrator to traverse all the way to the opposite end of the school to visit us. *Something must be up*, I thought.

Joe said, "Good morning, I just wanted to talk with you about the concert last night."

"It was a good one, wasn't it? I was so proud of the way my kids played," I replied. There was no comment from him about that.

"I have had two separate parents in my office this morning before school. They were both upset at how you acted at the concert."

"In what way, Joe?"

"They did not like the way you spoke to the audience before the band played"

"But, Joe, I was not about to have the band start to play until the chorus students settled down. I was waiting for someone to quiet down the kids, and when no one did, I felt it necessary to calm them down myself."

"The parents I spoke to this morning did not like the way you did it."

"Joe, I raised my voice because the microphone was not on and as soon as I did that, the mike kicked in and it sounded super loud. I don't think I had any other choice. Were these parents this morning among those adults who started to boo?"

"Jim, that was unfortunate."

"It really was. I have never had that happen at a school concert during my entire career!"

Joe's answer was "Jim, you seem a bit defensive this morning."

"Joe, I had two sets of parents come backstage afterwards to compliment me for having said something."

"Again, it's not what you said, but how you said it," Joe reiterated. "I have to get back upstairs before the buses arrive. Come see me later on today and we will discuss this more."

Joe left and I sat there stunned. Before I went up to the office to check my mailbox, I passed by my colleagues, who continued to give me somewhat of a silent treatment. As I walked through the hallway, I came upon Peter, our school security person. He told me, "I just want to let you know how upset some parents were after the concert. I took the brunt of some of their anger as they left the building."

"Peter, you must be kidding!" I exclaimed.

"Some said you ruined the concert." I could not believe I heard Peter say that.

I got through my morning lessons and surprisingly, there was no mention of last night's concert from the kids. I expected to be talking about that with every class, but since they did not mention anything, I did not bring it up. I had meetings with both sections of the band tomorrow, so that was when we would address this, with everyone there.

I made it up to Joe's office after lunch, during my free period. As I entered his office, I again thought about asking him why he did not intervene to calm down the reaction of some of the people last night. But I again gave him the benefit of the doubt. He was brand new at the school and this was his first concert. And, I really appreciated the fact that he was there. Having a school principal at a school concert was a rarity, in my experience.

I told Joe that I thought the faculty chaperones could have done a better job. After a few minutes, the discussion ended with Joe asking me if I would be willing to write a letter to all school parents in which I would apologize for my actions. I agreed to do that, because I thought it would be an opportunity to explain to them why it was necessary to say something at that time. The letter would be on the school letterhead and mailed to every parent. I thought this was fair.

Okay, so what to say? I told Joe I would have it done by Thursday of that week, so it could be mailed out on Friday. My first couple of drafts turned out to be a bit sarcastic and I decided that was not the way to go. I would be humble and apologetic, although I was so tempted to inject some sarcastic humor in as well. However, I had to look at the bigger picture. I was so proud of my students. The rest of this school year should be all about them. As a result, after a couple of more rewrites, I submitted the letter to Joe's secretary. He later got back to me that he thought it was well written.

The letter read:

James Kleiner

Dear Parents,

I have been getting some great feedback from students and parents alike about our Winter concert performances this past Wednesday. You have much to be proud of as a parent of a student in orchestra, chorus and band. Their hard work and dedication were evident in what you heard musically that night. I consider it a privilege to have been part of that performance, both as a guest performer with the chorus and in front of my band as its' conductor.

The purpose of this letter is to provide an opportunity for me to let me express my regrets for my reaction to the students' behavior prior to the band portion of the program. Let me be clear that in no way was I speaking to the parents or guests in the audience when I spoke. I understand now that my tone was too harsh, and for that I am sorry. I do feel that the reaction from the students in the audience when the curtain was raised was not appropriate for a formal concert in a public school. I can assure you that kind of vocalization in lieu of applause is not what we encourage here at Bennet Academy.

To think that the situation prior to the band's performance did in any way detract from the overall concert experience for you is bothersome to me and for that I am deeply sorry. To assist us in the music department, I would ask you that you review with your children which type of musical venue it is appropriate to vocalize.

In the future, I will be much more sensitive to your feelings as an audience and will not let my actions ruin the evening for you. For myself, an experience like this just shows me that as an educator, one can always learn from mistakes, even after 30 years of teaching.

> *Thank you again for encouraging your child to be a part of a music performing group here at Bennet Academy.*
>
> *Sincerely,*
> *James Kleiner*
> *Bennet Academy Music Department*

The letter went out the next day and by that time I was not hearing anything more from anyone about the incident, other than nice comments about how the groups performed. I knew the letter had arrived when during the next week one of my students said to me, "Oh, Mister Kleiner, my mother really liked your letter!" That comment made my day.

My colleagues were once again being collegial and all was well again in the world of the music department. My realization about all of this was that all of us have to "eat crow" at some points during our career.

I was gratified that the Manchester music staff made it a point to intensify its discussions about our responsibility to educate our students and parents about proper concert etiquette. A formal statement was drafted and distributed to all the parents of music students throughout Manchester. I was glad I agreed to write the letter. It was a learning experience for us all.

75 - THE UNTHINKABLE

I HAD SET A PRECEDENT back during the Bennet Middle School days of showing my sixth graders a movie, which took up a few class periods at the end of the school year. It was a good opportunity to take advantage of the post-concert days with some activity that would enhance my students' love of music. I invariably chose *Mr. Holland's Opus*.

We took the time to discuss the plot developments in detail as we went along. Included in our discussions would be societal changes they would see during the thirty years that passed by in the story. The kids would get a kick out of seeing what things were like in schools during the '60s. I could give them quite a narrative about that since I lived it. That activity was already in my plan book for June.

But it was now a week to the day after our Winter Concert. I was driving home from school. I turned on the radio and turned to WTIC, the Hartford area AM station, and came upon the ongoing special coverage. There had been a school shooting here in Connecticut that morning. No one at Bennet Academy mentioned it, and since I had not ventured out of my area, this was the first I had heard about it.

There had been a shooting at Sandy Hook elementary school in Newtown. I had been to Newtown High School in the past for a CMEA-sponsored music event, so I was familiar with the area. It was located about 30 miles west of Manchester, between Waterbury and Danbury. The commentators were quite somber as I started to listen to the broadcast.

Then I heard the words that left me stunned. Twenty-six people had been killed by a lone gunman inside the school. Six adult staff members and twenty children between the ages of six and seven years old.

Hearing that news felt like someone had punched me in the gut. My eyes teared up and I began sobbing, uncontrollably. I thought it wise to pull off to the side of the road. I actually began to feel like I was going to vomit. I turned on my flashers and was doubled over for a minute or so until I got control of my emotions. This was a fairly busy road and I needed to get moving for safety reasons. I composed myself and continued home.

When I arrived home, I turned on the TV and every network was covering this tragedy. This was every educator's nightmare come true. Sandy Hook Elementary was not the first school shooting by any means. But the facts that it occurred in my home state and involved teachers, administrators, staff members, and first graders really hit me hard. It hit everyone hard.

For the next few weeks this event was at the center of the news. Going back to school the next day seemed strange. School security was now a pressing issue in schools across the country again. It became harder to access all the school buildings in Manchester. Never again would I be able to enter a school without proving who I was, either by voice, video camera, or ID card.

I thought back to the times in Vernon when I was given the key to the building at VCMS so I could work some Saturdays. The world of education had been going through the normal evolution of progress over the years since then, but school shootings were an unwelcome part of that. The stress began to take a toll on me.

Although the 2012–13 school year went well, as the year came to a close, for the first time in my teaching career I began to think about retirement.

76 -
THE LIGHT AT THE END OF THE TUNNEL

THE YEARS IMMEDIATELY FOLLOWING THE 2012–13 school year were satisfying for me. I felt comfortable in what I was teaching my student and they were responding quite well. I had been seeing the progress of the previous years' kids as they moved on to Illing and MHS. It was gratifying to see their successes as they grew older. Not too many teachers have this opportunity.

Music teachers, as well as Art and Physical Ed. teachers, have a unique advantage over classroom teachers in that respect. They have aural and visual proof of their former students' progress from year to year in their particular disciplines. I tried, whenever possible, to attend the Illing and MHS concerts to see this for myself.

One of these years I was asked to participate in a special event at MHS. The high school music parents' group was going to surprise the MHS band director, Keith, to mark a significant teaching career anniversary. I was asked if I would be willing to play in the alumni/faculty band, which would play in his honor after a high school band concert. I jumped at the chance and attended a "secret" rehearsal the evening before the concert.

It was great to see a bunch of former students in that group. The reminiscing was nonstop. Since the high school band was also in on the surprise, they had rehearsed in secret as well. I knew this would be a real treat for me since all those kids were my former students.

The night of the concert, as the MHS band was onstage, the alumni and faculty assembled in the band room and took their places in the stage wings as the band's final number was completed. Keith came offstage during the applause and the look on his face was priceless as he saw all of us standing there with our instruments. He immediately realized what was coming down and was super surprised.

Assistant Band Director Marco went out and addressed the audience about the celebration as we all took our places amongst the high school players. Keith was ushered out to the podium to sincere applause. He took his baton, talked with us for a moment, and then we began to play.

I was getting a real kick out of sitting in the clarinet section next to all my former students. Once they got over the nervousness of sitting next to me, they obviously enjoyed themselves. We played and it was a great moment. What teacher other than an instrumental music teacher could have an experience like this? Not only for Keith, but for me as well. To conduct and perform alongside kids you had taught in the past was an inspiration. This was another moment for me in which I knew I had picked the right profession.

2

That summer of 2014, I had been involved with my normal professional music performances. Foremost in my mind, however, was the question of retirement. When will it be the right time to "hang it up" as a music educator? I had always envisioned wanting to retire only when I felt I had accomplished everything I had wanted, starting on that first day as a new teacher in Vernon, some forty-five years ago.

Discussions on this subject, of course, included Cheryll. She had retired from her teaching career during this past school year and was loving the freedom. I knew I was getting ready for the same. We decided I would teach two more years. I would retire at the end of the 2015–16 school year. There was now a "light at the end of the tunnel."

77 -
A NEW PLAN EMERGES

DURING THE PREVIOUS SEVERAL YEARS, I had been a member of the Adjunct faculty at the Hartt School Community Division. That position developed after I had been a co-conductor and instructor as part of the Community Division's New Horizons Band program.

The New Horizons program was a national effort to give people fifty-five and older a chance to receive instrumental music class instruction as well as play in a concert band. Dr. Willet had been conducting the group since its founding. He invited me and my Hartt colleague, Ertan Sener, to take over as co-conductors.

As I got involved in this project, I quickly saw the value of giving these senior citizens another chance to continue or get back into playing music. I could see this meant the world to them. Some of these people had not played their instruments for decades. You could see the joy it brought to them these many years later.

I was the clarinet instructor and had a class of about ten people. They absorbed what I was teaching like sponges. Their appreciation was obvious. It proved the old axiom that it's never too late to learn. They played so well and the band was great! We played a few concerts each year, both at Hartt and out in the community.

This association with New Horizons eventually led to me teaching lessons to youngsters of school age as part of the Community Division. I also coached instrumental ensembles as well. What a thrill to be an Adjunct faculty member at the Hartt School, my alma mater!

2

I enjoyed teaching all my students there, but one young lady always brought me joy. Her name was Molly. By the time I had taught her for a few years, she was finishing up her eighth grade school year.

Molly was one of those kids who was such a hard worker. She had an incredible work ethic and progressed nicely because of that fact. One day in early spring, Molly's mom informed me that she would not be taking lessons the following year at Hartt. She would be attending the Loomis Chaffee prep school this coming fall. I was so disappointed to hear that. I hated to lose her as a student.

One day after her lesson, her mom told me that Loomis Chaffee was looking for a woodwind teacher for the next school year. Loomis had an established program of bringing in instrumental music teachers to give lessons to their students. Molly's mom gave me the contact number of the Loomis music department chair in case I might be interested. I was intrigued.

As I drove home from Hartt that day, my mind was spinning. This teaching situation sounded so attractive. It was "right up my alley." Of course, I would not be able to take a position like this if I was still teaching full-time in Manchester. Cheryll and I realized that this was something I should explore further.

The next day I spoke to Sue Chrzanowski, the Loomis music department chair. She seemed interested and it was obvious that Molly's mom had mentioned me to Sue already. We set up a time to have an interview. I drove over to Loomis on a nice April day after taking a personal day. Loomis Chaffee School was about a 9-mile drive for me, crossing the Connecticut River. Windsor was a town I was familiar as Cheryll had taught there in her first year of teaching way back when I was at Hartt pursuing my master's degree.

I walked into the music building on the Loomis campus and met Sue. The campus was beautiful, being set on the shore of the Farmington River. It reminded me of a college setting, with old ornate buildings alongside a modern building like Hubbard music building. Sue showed me around and I was impressed with the facilities. Numerous practice rooms of various sizes, a large and spacious rehearsal room, and an auditorium and stage that reminded me of the Lincoln Center in New York City.

We sat down and discussed my background and teaching experience. She then offered me the position. I accepted. Talk about landing on one's feet! I felt as though I had died and gone to heaven!

I had made the choice to retire from public school teaching a year ahead of the master plan. I had two months left.

3

I drafted a letter of retirement and dropped it off at the Manchester Superintendent of School's office early the next week. I also made appointments with Joe as well as Hassan, our assistant principal. They both seemed honestly excited for me, and a bit jealous too. I let my colleagues in the music department know, as well as others on the faculty. All were encouraging and excited for me. That made me feel so good. I knew I was going to miss this place. The seventeen years in Manchester were basically the second half of my teaching career.

This situation of my leaving was such a departure from the times I had left other school systems during my career. This time I was leaving, not because I was "shown the door," not because I had been caught up in a "reduction in force," not because of a career change, or not because my position had been "cut." I would be going out on my own terms. Just one final concert to conduct and my career would be over.

78 -
THE FINAL CONCERT

THE NIGHT WAS JUNE 9TH, 2015. It would be my last concert as a public-school teacher. As I drove to Manchester High School that evening, I thought about that familiar feeling of excitement and nervous energy I always felt on concert nights. I was trying to calculate in my mind how many years it had been since that first concert at the Sykes ninth grade school in Vernon back in 1971. Forty-four years ago! It was hard to believe. And yet, here it was. Those fourteen- and fifteen-year-old students back then were now in their fifties!

As I pulled up to the school, I shifted my focus to the task at hand. And, as usual, thanks to the MHS stage crew, things went like clockwork. I was very excited about the music my band was playing this evening, and I knew the kids were too. We were going to be playing a piece entitled "Stampede," by Brian Balmages, as our first piece. I had done several works by Balmages during my career in Manchester. He was a creative composer whose music always painted an effective aural picture of unique subjects or events. His music spoke to me, which was one of the prerequisites for music I was going to use with my groups.

"Stampede" was a musical description of a horse or cattle stampede, and from day one, the piece just mesmerized my kids. They loved it. The other selection on our program was entitled "Drive," by Mark Williams. It contained all the elements of music I loved, effective melodic lines, rhythmic excitement, and wonderful harmonies. The band loved this piece as well.

The jazz ensemble was also on the program. As small as it was in number (only nine players), it made up for in enthusiasm. They had become true "jazzers." Any group that would get out of bed early enough to attend a 7:00 am rehearsal had to be dedicated. They were.

I loved the fact that the concert band's instrumentation had been improving since we made percussion a nonstarter until grade 6. I had a more balanced group. This year's band even had four horns! In fact, these kids were each playing on a brand-new instrument. Keith had surprised me and them by providing these instruments early in the school year.

The horn players were so excited, and I will always remember their reaction. They came down for a lesson and I had the new horns in their cases off to the side by my desk. They gradually noticed them and one of them said, "Mister Kleiner, where did you get the horns?"

I answered, "Gee, I don't know. In fact I didn't even know what they were." Of course, that did not faze them as they were used to my pulling their leg as I often did.

"Could we see one?" one of the kids asked. I opened up one of the cases and let them see the brand-new shiny horn.

"Would you like to try them? I asked them.

"Yes, please!" they blurted out. I gave each one of them one to try. You could see in their eyes how excited they were. Finally, I could not hold the surprise from them anymore. I told them they were their new school instruments. They were amazed. As they left the lesson that day, I remembered the joy in their voices. These are the times teachers live for.

The horn section sounded great on concert night, as did everyone else. This concert was as exciting for me as the first one back in Vernon. As we took our bows, I had to fight back tears. I announced to the audience that I had decided to retire from teaching. I made it a point to tell them how much I had enjoyed teaching their children this year. I felt the audiences' love as they gave me warm applause.

As I left MHS that night and drove home, I first thought about writing this memoir. I had always enjoyed writing. And there were certainly lots to remember throughout my career. I thank you, the reader, for letting me share with you the "ups and the downs" of my life's vocation. Although there were several hard "landings" throughout these many years, my final landing was a soft one. It was one of gratitude and respect for all those who helped me along the way. And most of all, for those students who taught me so many important lessons and let me learn from them.

> *"Every life is a destination unknown, a journey of tragedies and triumphs, that ultimately allows us to discover not only our world, but more importantly, ourselves."*
>
> —*THE OUTER LIMITS*, SEASON 4, EPISODE 8, "RITE OF PASSAGE"

79 - REFLECTIONS

I HAVE THOUGHT ABOUT THIS concept of learning for most of my life. I learned during my teaching career that I was experiencing more than just the teaching of my students. I was learning as much as I was teaching. There was not much that I had learned in my college education courses that gave me a clue about this phenomenon. I was getting as much out of teaching as I was putting into it.

I student taught in the town of Cheektowaga, New York, a suburb of Buffalo. The school system had a reputation of having a superb music program. My roommate Frank and I were both assigned to have our student teaching experience at Maryvale High School. We would be experiencing all levels, elementary instrumental, junior high school, and high school.

Our cooperating teachers were Joe Riordan and Bill Weicker at the high school, Bill McElroy at the junior high, and Stan Bratt and Scot Smith at the elementary schools. Stan and Scot were ex-classmates of ours, having graduated from Fredonia a couple of years before our senior years. These educators were at the top of their field. They included us in their monthly department meetings, which, by tradition, were held in one of their homes. There was always a social gathering after the meetings, and the fact that they included Frank and I made us feel right at home.

Having the experiences of class lessons, one-on-one instruction, and band rehearsals were invaluable. Things went so well that during one whole week in May, the high school Wind Ensemble went on a Western New York tour, and Frank and I were entrusted with running the lessons and band rehearsals for the younger students who were part of the concert band.

I was initially looking forward to being a chaperone on the tour. But the school administration had given permission for us both to run the high school program in the upper classmen's absence. As it turned out, this was much more of an incredible experience for us. We were in charge of things and it felt for a week like I had my first teaching job. That extra responsibility was just what we needed. It was a wake-up call.

We survived the week and it felt satisfying to get all of the positive feedback from the students. I was on my way to a life-long passion for teaching. And I was learning so much as well.

If you have read this memoir and are thinking about a career in music education, or are presently involved in your career, here are some suggestions from my experiences:

ATTEND PROFESSIONAL CONFERENCES

I found throughout my career that each time I attended a state, regional, or national education conference, I came away with new ideas and inspiration. They were like a "shot in the arm."

ATTEND CONCERTS OF PROFESSIONAL GROUPS AND OTHER MUSICIANS

These were invaluable opportunities to hear live music. I loved the opportunity to listen to former students continue their participation in making music. The visiting orchestra series at the Bushnell Memorial concert hall in Hartford was always inspiring. I would also try to attend the Hartford Symphony concerts during the '70s, not knowing at the time that during the '80s and beyond I would be able to perform with them numerous times over the subsequent decades. My music education also included influences by my own students, exposing me to classic rock and eventually to jazz and R and B. My eclectic music preferences evolved from so many unlikely sources.

WATCH OTHERS TEACH AND CONDUCT
I tried to do this whenever I could. I found I could learn from other professionals. I would try to incorporate the things I liked into my own "bag of tricks." I particularly benefitted from seeing so many conductors work in rehearsals at music conferences. Those people were appearing there for a reason.

JOIN PROFESSIONAL ORGANIZATIONS
From the Music Educators National Conference, now known as NAfME, the national association for music education, to my state organization, the Connecticut Music Educators Association, and to the ICA, the International Clarinet Association, I have been inspired to learn and become better.

PERSONAL MUSINGS

- Don't worry about things too far in advance. Most situations turn out to be less stressful than you imagined. "Don't sweat the small stuff."
- Learn from your mistakes.
- Don't be afraid of change, for change is inevitable. You most likely will "land on your feet."

SOME THOUGHTS ON TEACHING
Establish a disciplined routine right off the bat.

- After the first concert you can "loosen things up."
- Be calm at the final rehearsals.
- Use humor whenever appropriate.
- Admit when you make a mistake.
- Don't be afraid to laugh at yourself.
- End each lesson with a positive comment.
- Use music that you like and are excited about.

- Keep parents informed.
- Don't bother administrators if you can take care of the problem yourself.
- Offer extra help to kids who need it.
- Be flexible with scheduling.
- Get to know the school staff.
- Kids are kids, no matter what the color of their skin or ethnicity.

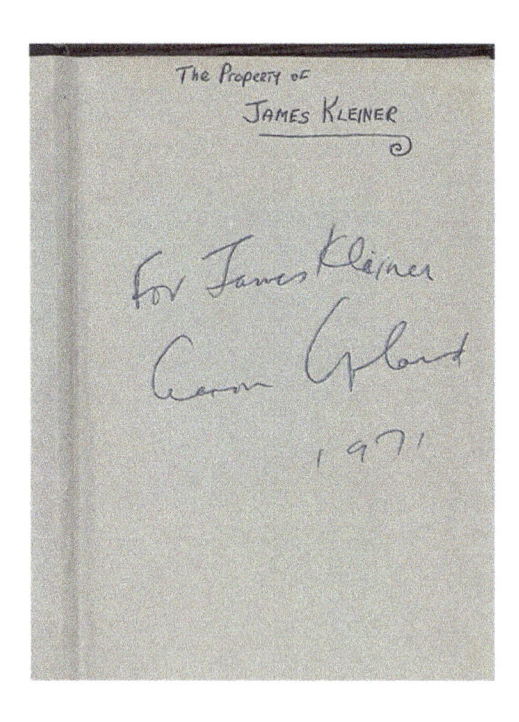

Copland autograph of his book 'What To Listen For In Music' for me at the Hartt School

Bennet Academy, Manchester, Connecticut

ACKNOWLEDGEMENTS

I OWE A TREMENDOUS DEBT to those music educators who shaped my own teaching career while I was a student in the Hicksville Public Schools. My heartfelt gratitude goes to J. David Abt, Charles "Chuck" Arnold, Gerald Burakoff, Thomas Buttice, Henry Gates, Valerien Lagueux, Jr., Gerald Pellerin and Donald Sitterly.

Gratitude also goes to my undergraduate professors at State University College at Fredonia, New York. They include Anthony Barresi, Harry John Brown, Lukas Foss (guest conductor from the Buffalo Philharmonic), Harriet Simons, David Sublette and Dr. Willam Willett.

I feel fortunate to have student taught at Maryvale High School in Cheektowaga, New York, under Stan Bratt, Bill McElroy, Scott Smith, Joseph Riordan, and William Wieckert.

I am grateful to my graduate school professors at the Hartt School of Music, the University of Hartford, Connecticut. They include Aaron Copland, visiting conductor, Edward Diamente, Arnold Franchetti, V. Mariosious, Donald Mattran, Dr. Moshe Paranov, Charles Russo (Principal Clarinet, New York City Opera), Dr. Immanuel Wilheim and Dr. William Willett.

Thanks to all my teaching colleagues, administrators, secretaries, teacher aides, custodians, and cafeteria workers from the multiple schools and towns that made up my career in teaching. I will never forget them.

A special thanks also goes to Dr. Peter L. Boonshaft, who was one of the first people to read my manuscript. His excitement and comments at experiencing my written words filled me with joy.

And, it goes without saying, I am indebted to my students, who were always my main focus. I considered it a privilege to teach them, and learn from them. Without them, this memoir would not exist.

BIBLIOGRAPHY

Cohen, Kerry. *The Truth of Memoir: How to Write about Yourself and Others with Honesty, Emotion, and Integrity*. Ohio: Writer's Digest Books, 2014.

Danza, Tony. *I'd Like to Apologize to Every Teacher I Ever Had*. New York: Three Rivers Press, 2012.

Karr, Mary. *The Art of Memoir*. New York: HarperCollins, 2015.

King, Stephen. *On Writing: A Memoir of the Craft*. New York: Simon & Schuster, 2000.

Lahey, Jessica. *The Gift of Failure: How the Best Parents Learn to Let Go So Their Children Can Succeed*. New York: HarperCollins, 2015.

Van Cleave, Ryan G. *Memoir Writing for Dummies*. Mississauga, ON: John Wiley & Sons Canada. 2013.

Zaia, Mary, ed. *Thank You for Teaching: A Celebration of the Inspiring Teachers in Our Lives*. New York: Castle Point Books, 2021.

James Kleiner

Bennet Middle School Jazz Band, 2004

Bennet Middle School Marching Band wearing Tuxes

Landing On My Feet, Teaching and Learning During a Career in Education

Carmen Arace Middle School, Bloomfield, Connecticut

Cheney Arts Building, Bennet Middle School

James Kleiner

Bennet Middle School at Six Flags New England

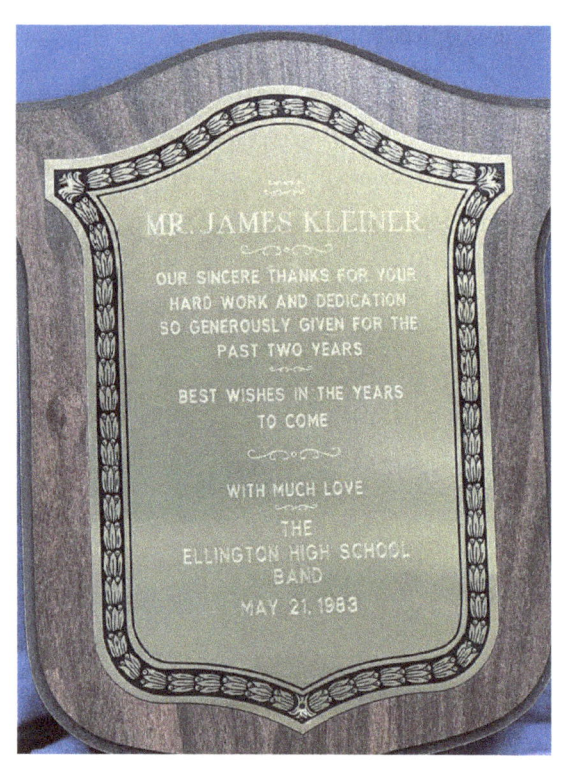

Landing On My Feet, Teaching and Learning During a Career in Education

Plaque given to me by the Ellington High School Band, Ellington, Connecticut

James Kleiner

My 40th birthday celebration. Gerry Burakoff, Bill Willett and myself, 1988

Plaque given to me by the students and staff at Parish Hill High School

T-Shirt given to me by Parish Hill High School students

Landing On My Feet, Teaching and Learning During a Career in Education

Rockville High School Band at the Six Flags, New Jersey Band Adjudication Festival

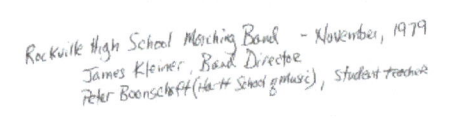

Rockville High School Marching Band - November, 1979
James Kleiner, Band Director
Peter Boonshaft (Hartt School of music), student teacher

Rockville High School Marching Band in the stands at a Saturday football game.
Peter Boonshaft, student teacher and Jim Kleiner, directors

James Kleiner

Rockville High School,
Vernon, Connecticut

Sykes Memorial School,
Rockville, Connecticut

Rockville High School Marching Band on the field

James Kleiner

Vernon Center Middle School Band in concert

Surprise gift by the VCMS Band

Vernon Center Middle School

Landing On My Feet, Teaching and Learning During a Career in Education

Dr. William Willett conducting the Rockville High School Freshman-Sophomore Band

James Kleiner

VCMS students on rehearsal break

Bennet Middle School – Cheney Building Office Desk

Landing On My Feet, Teaching and Learning During a Career in Education

include music as a profession, Janet hopes to continue it on a personal basis for her own enjoyment.

would be like that, but it happened that way. As I placed my right foot firmly on the school seal, suddenly a large
(continued on page 9)

MUSIC TEACHERS of Hicksville High School take time out to get some work done. Cutting up are (from left to right) Mr. J. David Abt, Intermediate Band conductor; Mr. Thomas Buttice, orchestra director; Mr. R. G. Pellerin, Advanced Band conductor; and Mr. Charles Arnold, chorus instructor.

J. David Abt, Tom Buttice, R. G. Pellerin, Chuck Arnold

James Kleiner

1963 NYC St. Patrick's Day Parade, Jim Kleiner marching next to Val Lagueux

Rockville High School Concert Band 1980

J. Kleiner conductor, in background co-conductors Bill Belden and George Sanders, 1980

Rockville High School Wind Ensemble, 1980

James Kleiner

Reunion with Ruth Ann (King) Heller at the International Clarinet Association CLARFEST in Orlando, FL – 2017

Vernon Center Middle School combined bands, 1978